Tilden and Tennis in the Twenties

Bill Tilden at Wimbledon, 1920,
wearing his blue "bearskin" sweater.

Tilden and Tennis in the Twenties

by

Arthur Voss

The Whitston Publishing Company
Troy, New York
1985

For Margaret, Katherine and Art

CONTENTS

There are two great periods in the hundred-year development of modern tennis: the second is the tennis
"explosion" of very recent date which began in 1968 with
the advent of open tennis; the first is the decade of the
1920's, during which the game experienced an almost
equally dramatic transformation, becoming far more
popular than formerly as both a spectator and a participant sport. The Twenties were golden years for tennis because of its superstars: Tilden, Lenglen, and Wills, as well
as for its many other great players.

Tilden's early development and career, culminating in
1919 with the beginning of the championship rivalry between Tilden and Billy Johnston which would make
tennis history during the post-war era.

Suzanne Lenglen wins at Wimbledon for the first time
in 1919, and Wimbledon gains a second star attraction and
its first American champion in 1920 in the person of Bill
Tilden, who also defeats Johnston to win his first national
singles title.

Tilden and Johnston make the long journey "down
under" to win the Davis Cup from the Australians
Brookes and Patterson.

Tilden wins his second Wimbledon title in 1921 and his

second American championship, but Lenglen, after retaining her Wimbledon crown, defaults to Molla Mallory at Forest Hills.

Lenglen wins for the fourth time at Wimbledon in 1922, getting revenge on Mallory with a decisive victory over her in the final. Tilden retains his American championship over Johnston after beating Patterson, the Wimbledon titleholder. An injury to the middle finger of Tilden's right hand, resulting in its partial amputation, happily proves no lasting impediment to his career, and along with Johnston he successfully defends the Davis Cup and wins his fourth straight American championship in 1923.

Tilden's conflict with the USLTA over his tennis writing is finally resolved, and in the 1924 national singles he achives his third final-round victory in succession over Little Bill Johnston, his fourth in five years, and his fifth title in a row. In the opinion of many who saw him in his prime this was the finest year of Tilden's career.

Helen Wills becomes the foremost American woman player, defeating Mrs. Mallory to win the national singles in 1923 and again in 1924, victories achieved in the new West Side Tennis Club stadium at Forest Hills. She also wins the 1924 Olympic title and her third straight American championship in 1925.

Helen Wills invades the Riviera in 1926 and plays a historic match against Lenglen, won by the latter.

An appendicitis operation prevents Helen Wills from competing at Wimbledon and Forest Hills in 1926. Lenglen withdraws from Wimbledon after a scheduling mixup and soon after signs with the promoter C. C. Pyle to make a professional tour of the United States.

       Tilden plays a major role in the development of profes-
sional tennis, which needed him in the Thirties to give it
vitality as much as amateur tennis did in the Twenties.
His homosexual proclivities had unhappy consequences,
but he deserves to be remembered not as a man who came
to the end of his life under a tragic cloud, but as a great
artist-athlete, a tennis immortal.

ACKNOWLEDGEMENTS

I am grateful to Frank Hunter, Watson Washburn, and George Lott, all of whom were Tilden's Davis Cup teammates, for talking to me at length about Bill Tilden as man and player, and also to Jacques Brugnon, the French Davis Cup player, for the same reason.

I am indebted also to others who knew Tilden personally and who provided me with much useful information concerning him and the tennis scene during the 1920's generally: Joseph Bixler, Mrs. Marian Anderson, Ed Faulkner, Norman Bramall, Frank Goeltz, Roy Coffin, John Faunce, and Mary Hardwick Hare.

Arthur C. Nielsen, Sr., James H. Van Alen, William S. Kellogg, Miss Doris Cook of the Southern California Tennis Association, and Mrs. Pat Yeomans were all most helpful in aiding my research, as were the services provided by the New York Public Library, Chicago Public Library, University of Pennsylvania Library and Archives, the International Tennis Hall of Fame and Museum, Newport, Rhode Island, and the William M. Fischer Tennis Library, St. John's University, Long Island, New York.

PROLOGUE

"Of all the changes in the world of sports that took place between the years 1920 and 1930, none was more astonishing or unpredictable than the emergence of lawn tennis as a spectator game and prime box-office attraction."

Paul Gallico, *The Golden People*

"Tilden has rebuilt and dramatized tennis all over the world. He has been the architect and actor in a game that has experienced one of the most remarkable developments in sport."

Herbert Reed, *Outlook* magazine (1928)

In the hundred-year development of modern tennis there have been two great periods, the second of these being the great tennis "explosion" of very recent date. Triggered by the advent in 1968 of open tennis, which, at long last, permitted competition between amateurs and professionals, it continued for almost a decade before the phenomenal boom tennis experienced as both a spectator and a participant sport finally began to show signs of leveling off.

Fewer than ten million Americans played tennis in 1968, perhaps almost three times that number ten years later. During these years tennis became the beneficiary of far more television exposure than previously, and in spectator popularity was outranked by only football, baseball, and basketball. The tennis industry became a billion dollar business, and tournament sponsors provided prize money so generously that champions like Billie Jean King, Jimmy Connors, Bjorn Borg, and Chris Evert became tennis millionaires, and scores of other players not quite of their caliber also profited handsomely, as well as openly, instead of being paid "under the table," as in the old "shamateur" days. Tennis needed badly to rid itself of the hypocrisy that for so long stigmatized the amateur game, and it has benefitted from other changes that have come with the tennis boom. It has also become more highly commercialized than some followers of the game—who deplore what they regard as the loss of some of its former distinctive character and better traditions—would like it to be, but this no doubt was inevitable, being the trend of all modern professional sports.

During the 1920's, the earlier great period in tennis history, tennis experienced an almost equally dramatic transformation, divesting itself largely of an image of being a sissy and snobbish game, and developing into a sport far more popular than formerly with spectators and players alike. This process had its beginning several years earlier when Maurice McLouglin came out of the West to win the national championship at the Newport, Rhode Island Casino in 1912 and again in 1913. McLoughlin had learned his tennis not on the grass courts of an Eastern private club, as had earlier champions, but on the asphalt public courts of San Francisco's Golden Gate Park, and his dynamic hard-serving, net-rushing style of play gave a new aspect of masculinity to the game. When he volleyed and smashed his way to victory over the Australian Norman Brookes in a 1914 Davis Cup match, it was before a record crowd of 12,000 at the West Side Tennis Club at Forest Hills on Long Island.

Also important to the development of tennis as a popular sport was the moving of the national championship tournament in 1915 from the aristocratic and isolated confines of the Newport Casino, where it had been played since its inauguration in 1881, to Forest Hills. There, in a large metropolitan area, it could become one of the major events of the sports calendar. By this time, too, a considerable amount of tennis was being played in almost every part of the country on public park and playground courts—usually with a dirt or clay surface, less often, except in California, asphalt or cement. Much less expensive to build and maintain than a grass court, the clay court was a fitting symbol of the increasing democritization of tennis. Less and less would the game be looked on as an effeminate diversion for the few who had the means to be idle, and more and more as healthful exercise and enjoyable recreation for the many. By 1920, said the *Literary Digest* magazine, with an estimated one million players, tennis had become so popular it could be regarded as the national amateur game.

Tennis thus was in a good position to benefit from a tremendously increased interest in sports during the Roaring

Twenties. For almost any kind of sports contest that might provide it with spectacle and excitement, the general public, with more leisure time and more money to spend than before the war, developed a vast appetite, which was whetted by brilliant performances of super-star athletes with great crowd appeal—Jack Dempsey and Gene Tunney in boxing, Babe Ruth in baseball, Red Grange in football, Bobby Jones and Walter Hagen in golf, and Bill Tilden in tennis, to name only the most outstanding.

Looking back on this period, when for the first time champion athletes were regarded almost as demigods and the promotion of sports contests became big business, sports historians dubbed the Twenties the "Golden Age of Sport." They were golden years for tennis largely because of the superlative tennis skills and the colorful and controversial personality of Tilden, with whose career as an amateur player of international fame they coincided almost exactly, the first of his seven American singles championships having been won in 1920, and the last of his three Wimbledon titles in 1930, after which he turned professional. In championship play he was invincible during the first six years of this period, and only a little less so for the remainder of it. As a box-office attraction no tennis player since has been his equal, with the possible exception of Pancho Gonzales, the game's other great legendary figure.

Women's tennis also had its great player personality— Suzanne Lenglen, perennial champion of France and at Wimbledon, where she drew standing-room only crowds. When she retired from amateur competition in 1926 to make a professional tour of the United States—the first of its kind—she was succeeded by Helen Wills, who, although she lacked the grace and quickness on the court, as well as the colorful personality of Lenglen, dominated her rivals as impressively as Lenglen did, winning a record eight Wimbledon singles titles and seven American championships.

The Golden Twenties not only had these great players— perhaps the three greatest in tennis history—but also a larger number of first-class players to challenge them than at any time until the advent of open tennis in the late 1960's. Among the great American men players were William M. Johnston, twice a national champion before 1920, and during Tilden's amateur heyday his foremost rival; Vincent Richards, a tennis prodigy who, as a fifteen-year-old, was national doubles champion with Tilden; and R. Norris Williams, like Johnston a two-time champion before Tilden began his six-year championship reign in 1920. Among the women there were Molla Mallory, Helen Wills' predecessor as a great American champion, and the only player to boast a victory over Suzanne Lenglen; and the younger Helen Jacobs, who defeated Wills for an American championship and who was also a Wimbledon titleholder. There were also the French Musketeers—René Lacoste, Henri Cochet, Jean Borotra and Jacques Brugnon—who in the latter part of the decade made France the champion tennis nation. Other countries, too, among them Spain, Italy, Japan, Australia, Germany, South Africa, and England, had players of international fame and almost equal talent.

Most of the players mentioned above—Lenglen, Wills, Johnston, Lacoste, Cochet and Borotra, in particular—figure prominently in the account that follows of tennis's first golden age, but Bill Tilden, because he so dominated the tennis scene of the Twenties, is the major character. He, as chief actor, and his brilliant supporting cast played their parts so memorably that tennis became one of the big-time modern sports, and the most international of them all, except for the Olympic Games.

CHAPTER ONE

THE MAKING OF A CHAMPION

In the Catskill Mountains about forty miles south of Albany and a dozen or so miles west of the Hudson is the village of Tannersville, New York. Just outside of Tannersville is Onteora Park, in the late nineteenth century a fashionable summer resort and artists' colony. To Onteora—the word is Indian for "mountain of the sky"—came Mark Twain during the 1880's to occupy a cottage for a season. Here summered the actress Maude Adams, famous for her role as Peter Pan. Here Madame Louise Homer of the Metropolitan Opera and her husband Sidney Homer, the noted composer, spent their summers. Here Hamlin Garland wrote his widely read *Middle Border* books, which graphically described middlewestern farm and village life. And here, around the turn of the century, a little boy by the name of Billy Tilden learned to play tennis with his older brother's cast-off racket.

The Tilden family had a large, comfortable cottage and in addition a tennis court. On one occasion the spacious porch and downstairs rooms provided shelter for nearly two hundred Onteorans when the final match of a tournament they were watching on the Tilden court was interrupted by a sudden thundershower. Billy, or Junior, as he was usually called, when he had no one to play with practiced on the driveway, using the side of the house as a backboard. Once he broke a window pane in his father's den and was forbidden the use of the wall for a month. When he was eight he won the Onteora boys' championship after being down match point to his final-round opponent, thus demonstrating very early what would be a characteristic of his play as world champion in the 1920's, namely, the ability to come from behind to win.

Onteora was a favorite resort of well-to-do citizens of Philadelphia, and it was in the Germantown section of that city that William Tatem Tilden, Jr. was born on February 10, 1893, the son of a prominent businessman and civic leader, who owned a wholesale wool firm. A Republican of some national influence, he was three times elected president of the Union League Club, and his son could remember as a little boy visits to the Tilden home by such political dignitaries as Theodore Roosevelt and William Howard Taft. The mother, from whom her son believed he inherited his love of things artistic, and especially of music, was an accomplished pianist and active in church and social work.

The Tildens, both of whom were of English stock, were not "old" Philadelphia society, but they belonged to the Germantown Cricket Club, described some years later by their son as "the typical conservative club of the elite, and one which takes its social position seriously." Founded in 1854, it was one of the three oldest and largest cricket clubs in the city, the other two being the Philadelphia Cricket Club, founded in the same year, and the Merion Cricket Club, founded in 1865. Tennis was first played at Germantown in 1881, some six or seven years after the game came to America from England, where it was conceived and patented in 1874 by Major Walter Clopton Wingfield, a retired British army officer. Wingfield's game, derived from the venerable game of Court Tennis and the more modern Racquets, but unlike them designed to be played outdoors on a lawn by ladies as well as gentlemen on an hourglass-shaped court, underwent a number of important changes by the time the first All-England Championships were held at Wimbledon in 1877. At the American cricket and croquet clubs where the game was played in the early years, there were variations as to the height of the net, court dimensions and method of scoring, but with the Americans following the lead of the British, the rules and regulations were soon standardized, and there have been relatively few changes in them since.

The Germantown Cricket Club was one of the nineteen original member clubs of the United States National Lawn Tennis Association (the "National" was dropped in 1920 and "Lawn" in 1975), sending two delegates to a meeting held in New York City in May, 1881, for the purpose of forming that body. In 1883, the Germantown, Philadelphia and Merion Clubs jointly held the first tournament to be played in the city, and in 1887, the first women's national championship was played at the Philadelphia Cricket Club, where the tournament remained until 1921, when it was moved to the West Side Tennis Club at Forest

Hills on Long Island. By the turn of the century tennis had become so popular at Germantown and the other two clubs that it supplanted cricket almost entirely. Tournament play and interclub matches developed a number of good players, some of whom competed with considerable success in the national championships, held at the Newport, Rhode Island Casino, beginning in 1881. One of these was William J. Clothier of the Merion Cricket Club, who entered the Newport tournament for the first time in 1896 and whose persistence finally made him Philadelphia's first national champion in 1906. A little more than a decade later Philadelphia had a second national champion in the person of R. Norris Williams of the Philadelphia Cricket Club, who won in 1914 and again in 1916. And finally the Germantown Cricket Club also had its champion when Bill Tilden won the nationals, and Wimbledon as well, in 1920. These Tilden victories caused tennis enthusiasm at Germantown to run high, and the members put on a successful campaign to have the national championships moved from the West Side Tennis Club, which had held them since 1915, to Germantown for 1921, 1922 and 1923. When the tournament went back in 1924 to Forest Hills, which in the meantime had built a new 14,000 seat stadium, Germantown became the site of the Davis Cup Challenge Round matches for that year through 1927. Since Bill ran his string of national championships to four at Germantown, and since he was the mainstay of the American team which won the Cup from Australia and defended it successfully until France defeated the United States in 1927, his home club was the scene of much of his finest play.

His high school and college career, Bill once said, could be described as "hardly notable," either in the classroom or on the tennis court. In his senior year at the Germantown Academy he was captain of the tennis team and played number one, but was no more than a fairly good interscholastic player. At the University of Pennsylvania, which he attended between 1910 and 1914, with interruptions caused by illnesses and deaths in his family and illnesses of his own, but without graduating, he played on the tennis team and won some matches against Ivy League opponents, but as a college player he was considerably overshadowed by his older brother Herbert, who with Alexander D. Thayer won the national intercollegiate doubles for Penn in 1908.

Bill's style of play during his school and college years was influenced by that of Maurice McLoughlin, the "California Comet," who was the national champion in 1912 and 1913. Bill was sixteen when he first saw McLoughlin, who was himself only nineteen at the time and making his first trip East, in an exhibition match at Germantown in 1909. McLoughlin's opponent was Nathaniel W. Niles of Boston, a steady baseliner who was good enough to be ranked number four nationally that year. McLoughlin, with his lightning-fast serve and constant storming of the net, won in love sets and made an instant convert out of Bill. "As a result," said Bill later, "I passed through a five-year period as a leading member of the young 'Pete Swattems'," young Pete being the type of player who "wallops every shot," usually into the net or the backstop. Also as a hard-serving net rusher, Bill, in his eagerness to get to the net, had spells of flagrant footfaulting, once having seven footfaults called on him in one game.

Although his Pete Swattem tactics gave him a reputation for inconsistency and resulted in more than a few early-round tournament losses, causing him to be referred to for a time as "one-round Tilden," Bill did establish himself as one of the better local players as early as 1913. In that year he was runner-up in the Pennsylvania State Championship to Wallace F. Johnson, who had lost in the national singles final the year before to McLoughlin, and with Mary K. Browne of California, the women's national champion, he won the national mixed doubles. In 1914, he won the Philadelphia and District Championship, and the next year he again reached the final of the Pennsylvania State, losing in four close sets to R. Norris Williams, the 1914 national champion. In the national rankings for 1913 (the national association began its annual ranking of players in 1885), Bill was included in Class 3 (31-40), but he was not ranked at all in 1914, and in 1915 he slipped to Class 5 (61-70). This was the year that the twenty-year-old William M. Johnston—Bill's great rival-to-be for championship honors—won his first national championship. Bill, who was two years older, had yet to play in the nationals or, for that matter, in any of the big Eastern tournaments outside his own section, and up to this time it did not seem very likely that he ever would, his father, who died in 1915, having decreed that Bill was not good enough to warrant his doing so, and that he should instead spend most of his time during the summers at Onteora.

From 1916 to 1920, Bill pursued what he called his "graduate studies," endeavoring to master the variety of stroke and develop the tactical knowledge that would make him a champion. As he did so he concerned himself with theory as well as practice, having been first stimulated to do so when he was asked while still in college to help coach the Germantown Academy tennis team. Illustrative of the thought that Bill gave during this time to various theoretical aspects of the game are two articles he wrote in 1919 for *American Lawn Tennis* magazine. In "Variety is the Spice of Life," he argued that one should be able to vary one's game both as to strokes and tactics, and discussed how best to do this, and in "Pace and Speed" he drew a distinction—too fine a one in the opinion of some of the magazine's readers—between these two terms. "Speed" was simply how fast the ball went through the air. "Pace," on the other hand, was the momentum with which the ball came off the court surface after it bounced and was the result of speed plus body weight behind the stroke.

In 1916, good play against several high-ranking players qualified Bill to play at Forest Hills, and although, handicapped by a sprained ankle, he lost in the first round to Harold Throckmorton, the 1916 national junior champion, his season's performance was good enough to earn him a Class 1 (11-20) ranking. In the 1917 "Patriotic" tournament at Forest Hills, which replaced the nationals because of the war, Bill lost in the third round to R. Lindley Murray, but played so well that *American Lawn Tennis* called him "one of the stars of the meeting" and described his service as "the fastest seen on the court this year." With Johnston, who had beaten Murray in the semi-finals of the nationals the year before, not competing, and an out-of-practice Williams, the defending champion, who had become an army officer, upset early, Murray, a handsome blonde left-hander from California, who played a serve-and-volley game like McLoughlin, came through handily.

The war did not, as might have been supposed, bring to a halt Bill's graduate tennis studies, or even slow them down appreciably. Along with some 9,000,000 other American men between the ages of 21 and 31, he became subject to conscription and enlisted in the Radio Signal Corps. Ordered to Pittsburgh for training, he was discovered to have flat feet, which presumably made him unfit for military service, but instead of being discharged, he was assigned, through the influence of Colonel John Brookes, the commanding officer of the Pittsburgh military district and a tennis enthusiast, to a medical corps unit to which he remained attached for the duration as a private. The Colonel and Bill established themselves as doubles champions of the military district, and Bill was given leave to play in Red Cross Ambulance Fund exhibitions and in several tournaments. Early in the summer of 1918 he won the national clay court singles at Chicago, and a few weeks later the national doubles at the Longwood Cricket Club with a fifteen-year-old tennis prodigy named Vincent Richards. National boys champion at fourteen and fifteen and junior champion at sixteen, seventeen and eighteen, a record never equalled, he was such a brilliant volleyer, even before he was out of the boys' division, that he could beat good men players. Vinnie, as he was called, came from a lower middle-class Yonkers, New York family, and Bill had given him some coaching since the time he was thirteen. In the spring of 1918, when he and several other New York junior players visited Philadelphia for an informal team match at the Germantown Cricket Club, he actually defeated Bill in a five-set match.

Bill was the favorite in the national championships, which were resumed in 1918 at Forest Hills, since he had scored a straight-set victory earlier in the season over Murray in addition to having no tournament losses. Murray, however, beat him in straight sets in the final, keeping Bill on the defensive most of the time with his strong serving and volleying. A painful boil on Bill's right ankle also probably helped to determine the outcome, but he did not use this as an excuse, telling his friend, S. Wallis Merrihew, the editor of *American Lawn Tennis*: "It was Murray's day, and I am perfectly satisfied. Only sorry I could not utterly hide the leg." He added that although his season's record might be regarded as better than Murray's he felt Murray as national champion should be ranked first for the year. The USLTA ranking committee subsequently agreed with this view, placing him second after Murray for 1918.

Bill celebrated the end of the war in a hospital bed, having had his appendix removed three days before the Armistice of November 11. It was also the height of the terrible flu epidemic of 1918, but he recovered without any complications and by the end of the year was again a civilian. Anxious to have some competition he conceived and promoted a tournament which was played al fresco in February on two canvas-covered board courts installed on the roof of the Wanamaker department store in Philadelphia. He was also the winner, beating Vincent Richards in the final before 1500 spectators, but only after being down 1-5 and love-30 in the fifth set, with Richards missing a volley by inches to make it love-40 and triple match point. A couple of weeks later, however, Bill lost to this remarkable boy player in the final of the national indoors, after leading two sets to one. The fast board courts of the Seventh Regiment Armory in New York City, where the tournament was held, gave the advantage to a volleyer like Richards, the ball bouncing off the varnished surface so sharply that a baseliner like Bill was often rushed in attempting a passing shot, nor did the slices which he liked to mix with drives to throw off an opponent "take" on such a court. Even so it was an unexpected and embarrassing loss for the now number two ranking player, and for Richards it gave him another record. At sixteen he remains the youngest player ever to have won a men's national singles championship.

Bill and Vinnie also teamed to win the national indoor doubles, but for a time it appeared that Bill might have to find another partner for the 1919 season when Richards was suspended by the USLTA in May for allegedly violating a provision of the amateur rule which permitted a player to be employed by a store carrying sporting goods but not primarily to sell tennis equipment. Richards became suspect in this regard when Alex Taylor, the well-known New York store which had made him a salesman despite his youth, advertised: "Vincent Richards will select your Taylor racket for you."

The apparent corruption of one so young as Richards looked especially bad, and the USLTA was prompted to investigate whether other players might be benefiting improperly from their tennis reputations. Member clubs were sent letters requesting details concerning expense money and railroad fares paid players to compete in tournaments and exhibitions, and firms employing players were asked for information about kinds of sporting goods sold, whether employees received expenses and were paid salaries while away playing in tournaments, and whether names of players were used to advertise or otherwise promote tennis goods. The findings of this "survey," whatever they were, were never made public. Bill Tilden, who worked for a time in 1919 as a salesman for the Mitchell Ness sporting goods store in Philadelphia and who was mentioned prominently in advertisements of the F. J. Bancroft Company as a user and enthusiastic endorser of its "Winner" model racket, appears to have been among those investigated, but no action was taken against him or any other players, and after Richards' name was deleted from Alex Taylor advertising his suspension was lifted. The USLTA inquiry was a tacit admission that tennis was no longer a game whose leading players, as in an earlier day, were all simon-pure amateurs, or even could be expected to be. Yet Association officials would continue for decades their unrealistic and ineffectual efforts to keep tennis an amateur sport and to maintain hypocritically the fiction that it was.

Bill Tilden had come a long way toward establishing himself as one of America's top players, but how would he fare with former champions like Williams and Johnston, both of whom had survived the war, again in competition? A preliminary answer to this question came early in the season when Williams, back only a short time from Europe and short on tournament play, lost to Bill in the Church Cup—an annual intercity competition involving teams from Boston, New York and Philadelphia—and again in the Delaware State final. Bill also beat a somewhat rusty Johnston, only recently discharged from the Navy and not yet match-hardened, in four sets in the East-West matches in Cincinnati in July, but the next week, Johnston turned the tables on him in the final of the national clay courts in Chicago, also in four sets. Then in a rubber match between the two early in August in the final round at Newport, Bill was the victor, 7-5, 8-6, 6-1.

Bill thus came to Forest Hills early in September one up on his foremost rival, and his fine play in gaining the final made him the favorite to win the championship. In the quarter-finals Bill defeated a two-time Wimbledon champion, the Australian Norman Brookes. Although he was now forty-two years old Brookes was still a very dangerous opponent, and Bill had to play at very nearly his best before winning in four sets. In the same round McLoughlin, in what was to be his last championship competition, could win only five games from a brilliant Dick Williams.

Born in 1891 in Geneva, Switzerland, R. Norris Williams, 2nd had a well-to-do expatriate American father, who provided his son from an early age with the best professional coaching, the boy winning his first tournament when he was twelve. The elder Williams' interest in tennis also led to his suggesting to the Swiss Tennis Federation the need for a world-wide body to administer the game, the result being the formation of the International Lawn Tennis Federation in 1913. The father and son were passengers on the ill-fated British luxury liner *Titanic,* which sank on her maiden voyage to the United States in April, 1912, after striking an iceberg. The younger Williams was rescued after spending over an hour in the water, but his father was among the more than 1500 persons who lost their lives.

As a Harvard undergraduate, Williams won the national intercollegiate championship in 1913 and again in 1915, and in his first season of tournament play in the U. S. he was ranked second nationally after McLoughlin. He remained at number two through 1915, and was ranked number one in 1916, after winning the national championship that year. He was also national champion in 1914, but McLoughlin was ranked ahead of him since the former had beaten both Brookes and Wilding in the Davis Cup whereas Williams had lost to both of them. An attractive and dashing player, and capable of dazzling streaks of tennis (he once beat Bill Tilden, who was at the peak of his career at the time and playing his finest, a love set in 6½ minutes, losing five points), Williams could also be erratic and inconsistent, since he insisted on always hitting his ground strokes very hard and so much on the rise that they were virtually half volleys, and he disdained to give himself any margin of safety or to play defensively when he was not at his best. When Bill, who knew him well and greatly admired him personally, once asked him why he would never temporize in his stroking, he replied: "Once in a while I get my great day. I'd rather have one great day than sacrifice it to safety." It was not a "great day" when he and Bill met in the semi-finals, and Bill won without difficulty in straight sets.

Johnston, in the meantime, had beaten in succession the Australian Gerald Patterson, the 1919 Wimbledon champion, but only at 7-5 in the fifth set, R. L. Murray, and Wallace Johnson, to bring about the first of the Tilden-Johnston championship matches that would make tennis history in the post-war era. Bill may have been favored, but Johnston had more experience and the better record in championship play. As a young San Francisco player of only eighteen, he came East for the first time in 1913 and lost a close five-set match to Williams in an early round of the nationals. He lost again to Williams in 1914, in four sets, but in 1915, he beat Williams in four sets in the semi-finals and McLoughlin, also in four, in the final. Of this latter match, the first championship final to be played at Forest Hills, the New York *Times* said that "the 7000 faces in the grandstand wore the tense expression that was so familiar at the Polo Grounds in former years when the Giants had a good chance to pull ahead in the ninth inning," this being evidence "that tennis was rapidly gaining in vogue as a popular sport." Johnston was a finalist again in 1916, losing to Williams after leading two sets to one and 3-0 in the fifth set. The war, as has been noted, kept him out of competition in 1917 and 1918.

Johnston—he was called both Little Bill and Billy—was sandy haired and slight of build, being only about five feet seven and weighing not much more than 120 pounds, but despite his frail and even anemic look he had a tremendously powerful forehand drive which he hit with a Western grip, his palm almost underneath the racket handle and the wrist well behind it. This grip came naturally to players like McLoughlin and Johnston, since it could be used to such good effect in stroking the high bouncing balls that came off the asphalt and cement courts in California. Taking the racket back above his head with almost a roundhouse swing, Johnston put all his weight into the shot as he met the ball well out in front of him at the top of the bound, usually coming up and over it to achieve heavy topspin. The Western grip is not at all suited to grass court play because the ball does not come up nearly as high as on cement or clay, and Johnston was so successful with it because of his short stature which enabled him to get down to low balls on any surface. Another great California player, Don Budge, who was considerably taller, almost six feet two inches, decided after his first season on Eastern grass courts in 1934 that he could not cope adequately with the low and all too frequent bad bounces using a Western grip and switched to the more flexible Eastern, or "shake-hands," grip, which has the palm and wrist up behind the flat part of the racket handle, with the "v" formed by the thumb and forefinger resting on the top surface of the handle. For many years Western grips and heavy topspin were outmoded, but since the advent of open tennis in 1968, with the only major tournaments played on grass being Wimbledon and the U. S. Open (and since 1975 only Wimbledon), heavy topspin has been employed by some of the champions of the present generation, notably Borg, Vilas and Orantes. Jimmy Connors, like Borg, has a Western forehand grip, but hits an almost flat or sliding shot, rather than the exaggerated overspin that Borg's stroke usually generates.

Like most other Western-grip players of the time, Johnston used the same face of the racket for both his forehand and backhand, but instead of hitting his backhand with topspin, as they did, Johnston, since he shifted to almost a Continental grip, which has the palm on top of the handle, hit his backhand with decided backspin. Having to make such a large grip change from forehand to backhand may have handicapped Johnston to some extent, especially in quick exchanges at the net, but it did not prevent him from volleying, as well as driving, with great power and accuracy. As for the Johnston serve, although there was nothing spectacular about it, it was an excellent one for a player of small stature. Its twist and spin and good depth and placement seldom allowed the receiver to take liberties with it, and Johnston almost never double faulted.

Sports-writers were fond of pointing up the physical contrast between the two Bills by comparing them to Mutt and Jeff, or David and Goliath. They might also have likened the bigger Bill to Ichabod Crane, the angular, elongated hero of Washington Irving's famous Sleepy Hollow tale. Six feet one and one half inches in height, although he seemed taller, and weighing only about 165 pounds, he had unusually long legs, slim hips, a narrow waist and somewhat hunched shoulders from which extended long prehensile arms. His face, too, was long, with a lantern jaw, long nose and high forehead. Bill's physique may have been unusual but it was well suited to playing championship tennis and he learned to utilize it to the maximum advantage.

The stroke equipment of Tilden's prime had not yet reached its full development at the time of this first championship encounter with Johnston, nor had he yet hit on the tactics that would subsequently bring him a succession of victories over his rival. He did have the fast flat serve, which later became known as his "cannonball" and was his most highly publicized stroke. It was not made with the racket head brought back slowly and with a full swing and high toss like Poncho Gonzales' serve, for instance, one of the hardest since Tilden's time, but with a rapid motion and a low toss, like that of Roscoe Tanner, one of the fastest servers among today's professionals. Bill's low service toss may have been the reason why he never developed a powerful crunching overhead, hitting the ball as high as he could reach with the racket arm fully extended, but instead dealt with lobs using a stroke more akin to a sharply angled high volley. Nor was Bill more than a fairly competent volleyer at this time. Having eschewed his old McLoughlin style of play, he did not take the net nearly as often as Johnston, usually doing so only when given a short return off which he could hit a strong approach shot that either went for an outright winner or evoked a return he could volley away easily. What made Bill so good was his brilliant and versatile play from the backcourt. With his remarkable control and baffling changes of pace and spin he could be expected to keep an opponent under pressure and on the defensive most of the time, but this turned out not to be the case against Johnston. Exhibiting some of the best tennis of his career, Little Bill beat him decisively, 6-4, 6-4, 6-3, a one-sided victory as popular with many as it was surprising. A little man, who was modest and a fine sportsman, had cut a big man down to his size, and a big man, moreover, who had something less than a winning personality. More than a few fans, himself included, said Al Laney, the tennis writer, were antagonized by Bill's unpleasant mannerisms and seeming arrogance, and wanted to see him beaten.

Bill's loss, paradoxically, proved to be a gain since it taught him what he had to be able to do to successfully counter in the future a Johnston at the top of his form. Ordinarily an excellent lobber, Bill had fallen down very badly in this department against Johnston, but this was not the reason for his defeat. What had hurt him most was the weakness of his backhand drive, which had been so uncertain that he had been constrained to depend most of the time on his heavily undercut backhand slice, which he did control excellently but was primarily a defensive shot. With its low, slow bounce it did not give Johnston much to hit, but it put no pressure on him, and when Johnston hit a forcing approach shot to it and took the net, Bill's return floated up and was easy to volley. What Bill had to do, therefore, was to turn his backhand drive into a consistently strong, forceful shot, similar to his Eastern forehand drive, that he could it flat or with topspin, and enable him both to pass Johnston at the net and to take the offensive away from him in backcourt exchanges.

There was a good chance that Bill would be named to the 1920 Davis Cup team, and this gave him an added incentive to strengthen his game. To this end he went to work for J. D. E. Jones, the general agent in Providence, Rhode Island, for the Equitable Life Assurance Company. A good enough player to have been a semi-finalist in the 1906 national championship, Bill's employer had a son, Arnold, who was the 1919 national boys champion and a protégé of Bill's, and, more important from Bill's point view, a private indoor court. Bill did rustle up

some prospects among friends and acquaintances who were per-
suaded to take out policies with the Jones agency (one was John
McCormack, the famous Irish tenor), but most of his time was
spent on the indoor court, coaching Arnold and working to improve his backhand. Throughout the fall and winter he labored
to achieve the kind of stroke he wanted, and by spring he felt
he had pretty much succeeded, and he found also that hitting
his backhand harder and flatter tended to speed up his entire
game and make him more aggressive.

The experience made Bill a confirmed believer in the value
of intensive practice, and he never got out of the habit of working diligently on a stroke whenever it was not functioning to his
liking. Grantland Rice, the sports-writer, has provided an example of this in his memoirs, telling how he and Ty Cobb of baseball fame, who still holds the record for most base hits, watched
Bill practice one spring day in 1930 in Georgia while he was playing in a tournament at the Augusta Country Club. "Tilden,"
wrote Rice, "had been having trouble with his cut shot and went
out to practice. Cobb watched Big Bill work over that shot for
one solid hour, hitting ball after ball. Cobb admired what he
saw. 'He's quite something,' remarked Cobb. 'He's not afraid
of work'."

Late in March Bill took his new backhand to New York
City to play the national indoors and used it to good advantage
to beat Vinnie Richards in the final, 10-8, 6-3, 6-1. A few weeks
later he learned he would also have a chance to test the backhand in international competition when Johnston, Williams,
Charles S. Garland, a young Yale player who had won the national intercollegiate championship, and Bill were selected to
represent the United States in a first-round Davis Cup match
against France, to be played at Eastbourne, England. Passage
was arranged on a U. S. Army transport through the influence of
Secretary of War Newton D. Baker, who was a tennis enthusiast,
to enable the team to sail in time to play at Wimbledon, an
event which in its more than forty-year history had never been
won by an American, although not for want of trying on the part
of many, several of them national champions, all the way from
Richards Sears, the winner of the first American championship
in 1881 down to Maurice McLoughlin, who had come the closest
when he was runner-up to Anthony Wilding in 1913.

As the ship got underway, Bill could be seen on deck in the
company of his teammates, wearing a dark blue suit and carrying

a large camera. In his luggage below he had twenty "Tilden-Winner" rackets. Brought out a few months before by Bancroft, they were virtually identical to the model Bill had been using for some time, with his name added. The other old-line racket manufacturers, Wright and Ditson, and A. G. Spalding and Brothers, had for a long time named rackets after famous players, but Bancroft had never done so until now. Because players whose names were used on rackets could be considered to be profiting thereby, as Bill probably did, the USLTA banned the practice in 1921. Before this happened, however, Bill Tilden had made it possible for Bancroft to advertise that a racket of their manufacture bore the name of a world champion.

CHAPTER TWO

TWO WORLD CHAMPIONS:
LENGLEN AND TILDEN

Meanwhile, another world-champion-to-be had already taken center stage at Wimbledon in 1919, when Suzanne Lenglen played for the first time in the ladies championship. Born in 1899, in Compiègne, in northern France, young Suzanne began playing tennis at the age of ten on the French Riviera—that playground for the privileged discovered by the English aristocracy in the nineteenth century, glamorized by European royalty early in the twentieth, and later embraced by rich Americans—where the leading players in England and Europe came during the winter months to compete in tournaments at Nice, Cannes, Menton and other Cote d'Azur resorts.

Charles Lenglen, the possessor of a small private income derived from a horse-drawn bus line owned by the Lenglen family, had the leisure to serve as secretary of the tennis club at Nice and to be his daughter's coach. Having been unsuccessful in realizing his ambition as a young man of becoming a champion six-day bicycle racer, Lenglen *père* resolved that he would make a champion out of Suzanne. To this end, he told her she must learn above all to be accurate and consistent. One of his devices to develop accuracy was to place a handkerchief at various spots on the court and reward Suzanne with a five-franc piece each time she hit it. To make her more consistent he had her practice for long periods against a wall. He even had a backboard built with a concave surface so that the return bounce would be irregular and thus more difficult to anticipate, and on rainy days it would be moved into the house so Suzanne would not miss her practice. He emphasized that the worst crime in tennis was to hit into the net because this always gave the point to your opponent. If you hit the ball over the net, even though it might be going out, you still might win the point. The wind could hold the ball in, your opponent might play it, or a linesman might call it good.   To improve her stamina and speed of foot he had her skip rope and run sprints (this kind of conditioning—much in favor with players today—was contrary to the Tilden approach, which was that you got in shape by playing plenty of hard practice sets), and to provide her with strong competition he had her play agianst good men players instead of other girls and women.

Single-minded tennis parents like Charles Lenglen have sometimes succeeded only in eventually turning their offspring against the game, but this did not happen with Suzanne. At thirteen she was playing in women's tournaments and interclub matches, and at fifteen she won the ladies' singles and doubles in the World Hardcourt Championships held in Paris in 1914, just before the outbreak of World War I. Even though the war years limited her opportunities for practice and deprived her of competitive play, her game had reached a high level of development by 1919. Al Laney, a young American solider waiting to be shipped home from France after the Armistice and who was to become a tennis writer for the New York *Herald Tribune,* watched her play against a professional on the Riviera early in 1919 and was greatly impressed. Recalling the scene many years later, he wrote that she had "a natural grace of movement I had never seen equalled on a tennis court and still have not," and "was the equal of a man player in everything but severity, and superior in mobility and accuracy."

That Wimbledon, after a four-year hiatus, should be resumed only a few months after the termination of a long and bloody war that resulted in ten million casualties is testimony both to the resilience of the British and to the fact that the tournament had become an important tradition. The Lawn Tennis Championships—still the official title of the tournament—were inaugurated in 1877 at the All England Croquet and Lawn Tennis Club on Worple Road in the London suburb of Wimbledom. There were twenty-two entrants, and the final match, played before 200 spectators was won by Spencer Gore, a volleyer, over W. C. Marshall, who played from the backcourt. Five years later, in 1882, two thousand people watched Willie Renshaw defeat his twin brother Ernest for the title, and in 1885, a gallery of 3500, seated in permanent stands built that year around the Centre Court, saw the same Willie repel the challenge of H. F. Lawford. (Willie, as defending champion in both these years, "stood out," while the other competitors played through an All Comers tournament to determine who would challenge him.

The U. S. Singles also had a challenge round until 1912. It was discontinued at Wimbledon in 1922). The Renshaws were Wimbledon's first great tennis heroes, dominating the tournament during the 1880's. Willie won the singles seven times and Ernest once, and they were seven times doubles champions. H. F. Lawford won only one championship, but gained fame by giving his name to a much copied stroke of his, a forehand drive made by letting the ball drop quite low and then hitting it with a great deal of force and at the same time pulling up on it sharply to create tremendous overspin. This forerunner of the heavily topped forehands of such present-day players as Bjorn Borg and Guillermo Vilas was still often referred to as a Lawford as late as the 1920's.

Around the turn of the century it was the Doherty (pronounced Do-hért-ee) brothers, R. F. (Reggie) and H. L. (Laurie), who made Wimbledon history and set box-office records. They were handsome young men with wavy black hair who were always immaculately turned out in long-sleeve white shirts open at the throat, long white trousers and white shoes. Former Wimbledon players had worn a variety of clothing—knickerbockers, colored jerseys, brown or black shoes, cricket caps and belts, and even neckties—but after the Dohertys, their all-white attire became de rigueur. (Wearing long trousers, usually tailored of heavy weight white flannel, although sometimes of a not quite so heavy cotton duck, a player who perspired heavily could find himself carrying considerable extra weight during a long hard match, especially on a warm, humid day. It was another Englishman, Henry W. "Bunny" Austin, twice a Wimbledon runner-up, who finally did something about this problem by pioneering in the early 1930's in wearing shorts of the Bermuda variety that had the appearance of flannels cut off just above the knee. However, the premier players of the decade—Vines, Perry, Von Cramm, Budge, and Tilden, who by this time was a professional—continued to wear the more aesthetically pleasing, if not so functional, long trousers, and shorts were not generally worn until after World War II, the first player to win at Wimbledon wearing shorts being Jack Kramer in 1947. Thirty-one years later, variegated and multicolored tennis wear having become the fashion, Bjorn Borg would win his third straight Wimbledon championship wearing box-striped shorts and a baseball-striped shirt, with advertising patches on both garments.) Reggie Doherty, who was also called Big Do, won the Wimbledon singles four years in succession (1897-1900), and Laurie, or Little Do, after his brother's game declined because of ill health, won five singles in a row (1902-1906).   They were doubles champions eight times and won the Davis Cup for the British Isles four times (1903-1906).   Laurie also won the U. S. singles championship in 1903, the only foreigner to do so until René Lacoste in 1926. In British tennis history only Fred Perry, who won English and American championships and Davis Cup victories in the 1930's, compares with them.

Wimbledon also had its heroines beginning with Charlotte (Lottie) Dod, the Maureen Connolly or Chris Evert of her day, who, beginning in 1887 at the age of fourteen, won five ladies' championships.   Blanche Bingley, later Mrs. Hillyard, won six championships over a period of fourteen years, the last one in 1900, and Dorothea Douglas, later Mrs. Lambert Chambers, won seven between 1903 and 1914. She would have done even better had she not lost twice, in 1905 and 1907, to May Sutton, while winning once from her in 1906. May was eighteen the first year she made the long journey to England from Pasadena, California, where her father, a retired English naval officer had settled with his family twelve years earlier. May Sutton was the first American to win a Wimbledon singles title, Suzanne Lenglen, victorious in 1919, was the first European player to do so.

Although new to international competition and playing on a fast grass surface instead of the slow red clay courts she had been brought up on, Suzanne easily won her way through to the challenge round against Mrs. Lambert Chambers, the defending titleholder.   There was a strong contrast between the more experienced Englishwoman, who was almost twenty years older, and her youthful opponent. The former wore the conventional costume of white long-sleeve shirt-waist blouse and voluminous starched petticoat underneath a white skirt which reached almost to her ankles, Susanne a white short-sleeve, calf-length one-piece white dress with pleats, and a white cotton sun hat. The staid English gallery thought Suzanne's attire rather daring, but it had more reason to think so the following year when she appeared in a sleeveless dress with a lower neckline and shorter skirt and with a brightly colored bandeau around her short, glossy black hair.

Suzanne was not pretty. Her nose was acquiline and her complexion was sallow, but she had much Gallic animation and vivacity, and she moved with swiftness and the grace of a ballet dancer about the court. Mrs. Lambert Chambers, a handsome matronly woman, was a steady baseliner who hit the ball hard and with good depth and went about winning her matches in a businesslike manner, whereas Suzanne's play had more variety, if it did not yet fully display the virtuoso quality and near perfection that would mark it later. Suzanne did not have great power on her groundstrokes, mainly because she used the same grip for both forehand and backhand, the Continental, which has the palm and wrist on top of rather than behind the racket handle, but with it she achieved excellent control, and her timing was so good and she got her weight into the shot so well that she had more than enough pace, coupled with her remarkable ability to place the ball where she wanted to, to keep her opponent on the run. Like her groundstrokes, her service was notable for its accurate placement, and she was as much at home at the net as in the backcourt, being a fine volleyer and smasher with unusually quick reflexes.

An overflow crowd of nearly 10,000, including the King and Queen, witnessed the sensational young Suzanne play brilliantly to defeat the redoubtable Mrs. Lambert Chambers, but only after the outcome had been in doubt up to the very end. After losing the first game at love, Suzanne gained a lead of 4-1, lost two games, and then got to 5-3 and set point, but Mrs. Lambert Chambers pulled out the game with the aid of two unretrievable drop shops, and then took the next game, winning the final point with a beautifully placed lob over Suzanne's head. She then broke Suzanne's serve to lead 6-5, but could not hold her own for the set, despite having two set points. Suzanne's service began working better in the next game, and she either served an ace or forced frequent errors off the return to give her leads of 7-6, 8-7, and 9-8. Then she finally managed to break her opponent's service to win the set, 10-8, making a drop volley for a winner on the final point.

In the second set a tired Suzanne lost some of her serving and volleying touch, and Mrs. Lambert Chambers got to 4-1 by virtue of several fine passing shots and lobs. Restored by a liquid stimulant, said to be cognac, thrown to her in a small bottle by her father from the grandstand, Suzanne tied the score at 4-all, but lost the next two games and the set. Suzanne had recourse to more brandy, and when play was resumed gained a commanding lead of 4-1, but Mrs. Lambert Chambers, although "terribly tired, footsore, and weary," as she said in recalling the match some years later, ran four games in a row, breaking Suzanne's serve at love in the last one to lead 5-4. Suzanne then broke back at love, and the excitement and tension mounted as Mrs. Lambert Chambers won a long deuce game to lead 6-5 and then reached forty-fifteen in the next game, giving her two match points. "Was Suzanne now to be in my bag of victories?" she wondered. Alas, no! Suzanne won the first point with a lucky volley off the wood which trickled over the net cord and fell dead in the court, and the second when her opponent netted a fairly easy passing shot after a long rally. After winning this game Suzanne was out of danger, easily holding service twice to lead 7-6 and 8-7, and then breaking Mrs. Lambert Chambers at love in the sixteenth game to win 10-8, 4-6, 9-7.

Both women were so exhausted that they were excused from going to the royal box to receive congratulations. Later, said Mrs. Lambert Chambers, she had a "long chat" with their majesties, one of the King's comments on the match being, "I don't know how you were feeling but I felt quite ill." Suzanne's father's reaction to his daughter's victory was recorded by A. Wallis Myers, the tennis correspondent of the London *Daily Telegraph.* "I have witnessed," Myers remarked wryly, "M. Lenglen's devotion for several years—it is sometimes embarrassing to tournament executives—but his joy on this occasion was ecstatic. The deliverance of France's lost provinces did not produce stronger emotion than the deliverance of Suzanne from what looked like certain defeat." Suzanne was indeed fortunate to win. So, too, was tennis in having her dramatic victory to usher in the game's golden era of the twenties.

Besides being blessed with Suzanne, who returned to defend her title, the Wimbledon of 1920 acquired a second star attraction and an even more striking personality in the person of Bill Tilden, who won over the galleries not only with his fine play but also with his showmanship. Bill's trademark was a fuzzy wool blue pullover sweater, and when he came out on the court wearing this "bearskin," as the British dubbed it, and carrying an armful of rackets he made a striking figure. Since it was little used by English players, some spectators regarded Bill's frequent, as well as effective, use of the drop shot as unsporting, but they were awed by his miraculous returns of an opponent's apparent winners. When he slipped and sprawled at full length on a damp court trying for an impossible get, simultaneously crying "Peach," his favorite expression of praise for an opponent's good shot, the gallery loved it. After one such exclamation, a spectator also got a laugh when he cried out, "A little bit crushed, that Peach!" Bill deliberately tried to amuse galleries—that was part of the show he put on—but he also believed his performance ought to include the best tennis he was capable of. A tennis star, he said, had the same obligation to his public that an actor owed his audience.

Suzanne, too, entertained the galleries with her consummate grace and skill, but her matches were so one-sided that there was little drama or excitement attendant on them. She had no trouble retaining her singles championship, losing only three games to Mrs. Lambert Chambers in the challenge round, and easily won the doubles with Elizabeth Ryan and the mixed doubles with Gerald Patterson. Bill Tilden, on the other hand, was not quite so dominating in his progress to the men's title. Prior to Wimbledon, in the London Queen's Club tournament, he beat two strong opponents decisively, the South African Brian I. C. Norton and Japanese Zenzo Shimizu, but lost to Johnston in the final, 4-6, 6-2, 6-4. They did not meet again at Wimbledon, as expected, Johnston losing in four sets in the second round to J. Cecil Parke, a British Davis Cup player, who had pre-war victories over McLoughlin and Williams to his credit. Bill then beat Parke, for whom he had been a ball boy in a 1909 Davis Cup match at Germantown in 1909, decisively, but needed five sets to beat another British Davis Cupper, Algernon R. F. Kingscote, Bill losing the fourth set after having a match point. Then Bill again beat Shimizu, 6-4, 6-4, 13-11, after trailing 1-4 in the first set, 2-4 in the second and 2-5 in the third, which qualified him to meet the standing-out title holder, Gerald Patterson.

Bill already held a victory over Patterson, having beaten him in four sets in an Australian-American team match following the 1919 American national championships, and was confident he could gain another. However, in the third set of his match against Shimizu, he had twisted his knee chasing one of Shimizu's deep lobs, and some thought was given to having him default the challenge round so that American chances in the Davis Cup play following Wimbledon would not be jeopardized. But Bill had a whole day to rest before playing, and the knee mended sufficiently so that he was less handicapped by it than Patterson seems to have been by a lack of match-play competition, or, as one British commentator put it, he "had made the fatal error of playing no public single" before meeting "a challenger exalted by the ecstasy of successive triumphs." Bill did lose the first set, but once warmed up had little trouble with his opponent, who, although strong at the net, did not have good enough ground strokes to enable him to cope with Bill's varied pace and spin. A big, handsome man with a magnificent physique, Patterson hit his service and overhead with terrific power and great accuracy, and he had a fine match temperament, but his awkwardly produced, undependable backhand was an Achilles heel that Bill took full advantage of, winning by a score of 2-6, 6-3, 6-2, 6-4.

Instead of taking some time off to rest and relax after his victory, Bill, restless and energetic as always, immediately went to work writing a book on tennis, commissioned by the London publishing house of Methuen and Company. With the aid of Sam Hardy, the non-playing American Davis Cup captain, and his other temmates, and with the help also of Mrs. Hardy, who advised on matters of organization and style, and by dictating to an amanuensis, Bill was able to finish *The Art of Lawn Tennis* in the short span of ten days. The publisher's motive, no doubt, in bringing out the book was to capitalize on Bill's newly-won fame as Wimbledon champion (the frontispiece, a photograph of Bill hitting a high backhand volley, had the caption "William T. Tilden. Champion of the world in action," and as author he was similarly identified on the title page). But in no sense was it a hurry-up, slip-shod job. Bill's keen tennis intelligence and a natural gift for expressing himself in a clear, lively style, already reflected in articles he had written for *American Lawn Tennis,* enabled him to produce a comprehensive and readable exposition of stroke techniques and of match-play strategy and tactics, liberally spiced with references to his own experience on the courts and analytical commentary on the styles of other leading players.

An American edition of *The Art of Lawn Tennis* came out in 1921, and the next year the American publisher brought out a second edition, revised and enlarged by Bill. The book went through eight editions by 1927 and ten all told by 1935, undoubtedly an all-time record for a tennis instruction book. Nowadays, such books seem almost to rival cookbooks in the frequency with which a new one comes off the presses, but before 1920 only a few were in print, and only one had been written by a recent champion, Maurice McLoughlin's *Tennis As I Play It,* published in 1915. Today, also, a large percentage of the tennis-playing population can have the benefits of instruction from teaching professionals, whose numbers are almost legion, but who were almost a non-existent species in the 1920's, to be found at a relatively few private clubs such as the Newport Casino and the West Side Tennis Club. A beginner might have the help of a relative or friend in learning the rudiments of the game—how to score, where to stand to serve and receive, and so forth—but after that he was usually pretty much on his own. To become a good player with a game that was technically sound, instead of remaining more or less a novice, as a good many players at the time seemed content to do, he had of necessity to be self-taught, and *The Art of Lawn Tennis,* as this writer can testify, provided much assistance and inspiration in this endeavor.

Bill emphasized such fundamentals as keeping your eye on the ball, and he told you in detail how to make all the shots correctly, but he also insisted tht you must be a "thinking" player with a knowledge of the "laws of tennis psychology," a good psychologist being one who mixes up his attack with the intention of breaking up his opponent's game. You do not change a winning game but should always change a losing one. You play to the score, and you don't take unnecessary chances on important points (this is now called percentage tennis). But, above all, your strategy and tactics must always be compatible with high standards of sportsmanship, the most important law in this regard being that you must be a good loser as well as a good winner. "Lose cheerfully, generously and like a sportsman," Bill admonished you. "This is the first great law of tennis, and the second is like unto it—to win modestly, cheerfully, and like a sportsman."

Bill also made good sportsmanship a prominent theme in several of the fifteen short stories he wrote during 1921 and 1922 and collected in *It's All in the Game and Other Tennis Tales,* published by Doubleday, Page and Company in the latter year. The book is dedicated to "Buddie," the hero of the title story, as well as several of the others, whose inspiration, wrote Bill, was "largely responsible for these stories, although he doesn't know it." Of Bill's early protégés, Buddie, who is described as well-built, of medium height and with light curly hair, most nearly resembles Arnold Jones, the 1922 national junior champion.

In the title story the fifteenth-year-old Buddie comes to the attention of the national champion, Dick Thomas, a kind of composite of R. Norris Williams and Bill himself, who "played tennis for the love of the game and held a keen interest in young players." Thomas works with Buddie to make him a better tennis player (Bill thereby getting considerable tennis instruction into the story), but he stresses above all that Buddie must not lose his temper, as he had when Thomas had first seen him play. The next year Buddie reaches the finals of the national junior championship, and Thomas the men's championship, the two tournaments being held concurrently (as they actually were at Forest Hills in the early 1920's). Upset by a bad line call against him, Buddie loses his temper and the match. In the men's final which follows, Thomas has what appears to be a winning shot called out, but, in contrast to Buddie, takes the decision "without turning a hair," and goes on to win the match. Afterward the admiring Buddie asks him: "How did you do it? How did you keep your temper in that fourth set?" Thomas replies with a smile: "All tennis players take what comes in a match, boy. It's all in the game."

Other stories are similarly edifying, Bill extolling such virtues as honesty, generosity and clean living. Faced with a moral dilemma, a character can be counted on to do the right thing. Frank, the intercollegiate champion in "The Hole in the Pinch," wonders "whether if it came to a question of keeping my title through a point I knew was illegal but which no one had seen but me, or telling of it and losing, I'd be sportsman enough to tell it. I always say to myself I would, but I wonder what I'd do in the pinch." The plot gives Frank and the reader an opportunity to find out, and of course Frank measures up when put to the test. Likewise, David Morton in "On a Line with the Net," after reaching match point by failing to reveal he had touched the net while the ball was still in play, makes up for his deceit by throwing two points and eventually loses the match, but his father, who is aware of what his son has done, is proud of him for having gained a moral victory.

Bill said that he fashioned his story situations out of his own tennis experiences or those of his friends, but most of his plots seem highly contrived and his characters and their actions none too plausible. Even so the stories display considerable talent in employing the conventions and cliches of the juvenile fiction of the day, enough certainly to give them considerable appeal for the boy readers for whom they were designed. Bill had the facility also of turning them out in quantity, publishing another collection, *The Phantom Drive and Other Tennis Stories* in 1924.

The Art of Lawn Tennis was the first of a whole shelf of books that Bill would write, and which would, along with scores of syndicated newspaper articles, numerous magazine pieces, several stage plays and minor miscellaneous writings, make him far and away the most prolific of tennis-champion authors or of writer-champions in any sport. Besides his tennis stories, Bill published a tennis novel, *Glory's Net,* in 1930, and also wrote three volumes of autobiography and reminiscence, the latest and fullest of these being *My Story* (1948). Outstanding among his several books on how to play tennis is the classic *Match Play and the Spin of the Ball* (1925), a penetrating theoretical and practical analysis of stroke production and of strategy and tactics, addressed primarily to the advanced player. It was reissued in a modern edition in 1969. Also happily still in print, in a paperback edition, is *How to Play Better Tennis* (1950). Written during his last years, when teaching tennis was Bill's chief means of support, its lucid style makes it a pleasure to read, and its content makes it one of the very best books of its kind, of value for every type of player from beginner to advanced, a superb distillation of all that Bill had learned about the game during his long career.

After his accomplishments at Wimbledon and as author, Bill still had the main business for which he had come to England to take care of, namely to play Davis Cup matches. He and Billy Johnston won two singles and a doubles quite easily from the French team of André Gobert and William Laurentz, both being leading European players. The match was played at Eastbourne two weeks after Wimbledon, and the two final singles were canceled because of rain. The next weekend the two Bills won over Parke and Kingscote representing the British Isles, taking all five matches. Johnston was carried to five sets in both his singles, and the doubles also went to five sets. Bill, demonstrating, that his Wimbledon triumph was no fluke, on the same Centre Court, again defeated Parke in straight sets and Kingscote in four.

Despite Bill's fine play abroad there were some who thought he had been lucky to win at Wimbledon, and they were quick to point out that he had not yet beaten Johnston in a major tournament. Johnston was also decidedly more popular with many who were willing to concede that Tilden might possibly now be his superior. Having a feeling, said Al Laney, for the modest and unassuming Little Bill that was almost akin to love and turned off by what they regarded as unpleasant personality traits in Big

Bill—it must be admitted that his manner and behavior did appear at times to warrant such epithets bestowed on him as supercilious, arrogant, disputatious, quarrelsome, opinionated, dogmatic—these Johnston partisans would have taken great pleasure in seeing their hero repeat his 1919 national championship victory over Bill. They were to be denied this satisfaction, but only after one of the most suspenseful and dramatic final-round matches ever played at Forest Hills.

On his way to the final Bill beat Vincent Richards 6-3, 3-6, 6-3, 6-0, his victory disabusing Richards' supporters of the notion, apparently held also by Richards, that the younger player's great self-confidence and his intimate knowledge of Tilden's tactics gave him an advantage and that Bill's realization of this would make him fearful of losing. Johnston's strongest opponent before the final was R. Norris Williams. Each player had two legs on the championship trophy, and a third victory would give him permanent possession of it. Johnston won 6-3, 6-4, 7-5, but the match was hard fought until Williams had the misfortune to twist his ankle when leading 5-2 in the third set.

Played before a record crowd of over 12,000 that jammed the West Side grandstands, the Tilden-Johnston final produced super tennis on the part of both players. Bill won the first set at 6-1 in less than ten minutes with the same kind of magnificent play he had exhibited in the final set of his match with Richards. Johnston, who had not played at all badly and was getting better all the time, came back to win the second set, also at 6-1. In the third set, with Bill serving at 3-1 in his favor, a small plane circled low over the court several times and then crashed only a few hundred feet behind the crowded grandstand. Bill could feel the shock of the impact through the earth, but, though momentarily unnerved, he and Johnston, who was similarly affected, continued play on order of the umpire, an action which perhaps avoided a panic, only a few spectators leaving the stands to see the wreck of the plane which carried to their deaths the pilot and an army staff photographer who was taking pictures of the match for recruiting purposes. Bill finally won the set 7-5, but lost the fourth by the same score after being within two points of the match at 5-4. It had been theatening rain, and at 5-all an intermittent drizzle turned into steady rain which became increasingly harder. The crowd in the stands began to move to the exits seeking shelter, and after hitting back a Johnston serve, Bill appealed to the umpire to stop play, who responded by calling "Let," and Bill therefore made no attempt to return Johnston's volley made almost simultaneously with the call, even though it was within easy reach. As the players started to leave the court, George T. Adee, a former USLTA president and the tournament referee, cried out from his box: "I over-rule the umpire and declare that the point is Johnston's." This was highly irregular, since it was the referee's function to interpret rules and settle disputed points and not to usurp the prerogatives of the umpire, who, in this case, happened to be Edward C. Conlon, the head of the 600-member Tennis Umpires Association, and an official of long experience and unquestioned ability in handling big matches. Conlon protested vigorously, but Adee stubbornly refused to change his decision, and when play was resumed a few minutes later and the point given to Johnston, who did not want to take it, Bill was so upset that he served three double faults to lose the game, and Johnston held serve to win the set. In the final set Bill dropped his serve twice to fall behind 2-3, with Johnston's service to come, but having recovered his composure, he hit out powerfully, especially off the forcing backhand that he had lacked in the 1919 final, to run four straight games for the set and the first of his seven American championships.

Besides his backhand, and in spite of the breaks he suffered in the fifth set, Bill could thank his service in great measure for his victory. Whereas Johnston did not serve a single ace in the entire match, Bill had twenty aces or near aces to his credit in addition to numerous overwhelming serves which evoked weak returns that Bill could put away for the point, usually with a winning ground stroke. Bill's forehand drive, hit almost flat with an Eastern grip, along with his backhand, both of which he liked to make on the run with his weight moving into the shot, was an important factor in countering Johnston's strong volleying attack with low, hard-hit passing shots. Johnston, who went to the net much more than Bill, was the superior volleyer and smasher, but Bill, mixing up his drives with vicious chops and slices was stronger and more consistent off the ground. Following the philosophy of playing "to win" rather than playing "not to lose," instead of hitting a defensive shot when he could just barely get to the ball, he daringly went for an outright winner which often came off, a tactic which would be a distinguishing feature of his game during his long championship reign, as it would also later mark the games of such great champions as Budge, Laver, and Jimmy Connors.

The fierceness of Bill's serving throughout the match, because it appeared to make for the margin of difference between him and Johnston, prompted talk that it gave him more of an advantage than was good for the game and that perhaps some handicap should be put on the server, thus renewing an issue which had been raised serveral years earlier after Maurice McLoughlin had become a dominant figure in American tennis largely because of his powerful serving. In 1915, J. Parmly Paret, a tennis historian and analyst, reported that of thirty-five leading American and two British players he had questioned, twenty-five were opposed to countering any possible advantage a player such as McLoughlin might have by limiting the server to one ball, since this would require making the serve too safe and put the server too much at the mercy of a receiver with a strong service return. Paret reported even less support for other suggestions for handicapping the server, hardly any of the players being in favor of shortening the service court or having a special service line some distance behind the baseline.

Bill Tilden's alleged advantage on service was different from that of McLoughlin, who regularly followed his high bounding serve to the net to cut off the weak return it often evoked. No net rusher, Bill, on the other hand, whenever he needed a crucial point, seemed to be able almost invariably to win it by delivering a cannonball serve that traveled "like a shell," in the words of one commentator, who, probably not intending to pun, wondered if it might not be a "disservice" to the game if rising young players should be successful in copying this service.

As was the case back when Paret made his survey, there was not enough sentiment to do anything about curbing the supposed advantage of the ultra-strong server, and any limitation placed on him would certainly have affected Bill, with his all-around game, much less adversely than a player like McLoughlin whose chief weapon was his serve. Years later when "Big-Game" tennis became the fashion, beginning with Jack Kramer, and matches often seemed monotonous because they were all serve and volley with almost no rallies, Kramer himself conducted some experiments with his touring professionals involving the server in order to give more variety to the play. These included giving him only one ball instead of two, stationing him a foot or more behind the baseline, and employing a three-bounce rule which prevented the server from volleying the service return and also required the receiver to hit his next shot after returning service as a ground stroke. But instead of any of these ideas being adopted officially, the trend since Bill Tilden's day has been to give the server even more of an advantage by liberalizing the footfault rule, the server now being able to swing his back foot over the line, and also to jump off the ground with both feet, before hitting the ball, neither of which he could do in the 1920's.

The two Bills enacted a virtual duplicate of their championship final match less than a week later in the East-West matches at the Germantown Cricket Club. There before a home-town gallery, Big Bill was again the winner, 6-2, 7-5, 5-7, 6-4, both players making the same number of earned points and Big Bill only eight fewer errors. Although not as significant as his Forest Hills victory, it was a happy one under the circumstances for his supporters, since it meant they need have no reservations whatsoever in toasting him as world champion at the big testimonial dinner held at the Club in his honor.

CHAPTER THREE

BRINGING BACK THE CUP

The Davis Cup victories in the summer of 1920 over France and the British Isles qualified the United States to play Australasia (Australia and New Zealand in combination), the current holder of the Cup, and for this purpose Bill Tilden and Billy Johnston, along with Sam Hardy as their non-playing captain and Watson Washburn as a reserve member of the team, sailed in mid-November for the Antipodes. It was just twenty years earlier that a competition for what was officially called the International Lawn Tennis Challenge Trophy, but popularly known as the Davis Cup, had been inaugurated, a British team having crossed the Atlantic to play for a handsome foot-high silver bowl donated by Dwight F. Davis of St. Louis, a young Harvard graduate who was the number two ranking American singles player as well as national doubles champion with Holcombe Ward. This small beginning gave no hint that one day over fifty countries would compete for the Davis Cup, thereby making tennis the most truly international of sports.

The American team in the inaugural match consisted of Malcolm Whitman, the current national champion, Davis and Ward; the British of A. W. Gore, Wimbledon singles champion in 1901, 1908, and 1909, H. Roper Barrett, later a three-time Wimbledon doubles champion, and E. D. Black, the Scottish champion. Four singles and a doubles were scheduled, with two singles players of one team playing each of the two on the other, a format which has been followed ever since. The British found the grass on the courts of the Longwood Cricket Club outside of Boston, where the matches were played, twice as long as at home, sagging nets which had to be adjusted every few games, and "soft and mothery" balls which the American players with their twist serves were able to make swerve disconcertingly in the air and break four or five feet after hitting the ground. Even more confusing, the Americans served different kinds of twists.

The doubles team had the right-handed Ward, whose American twist service swerved to the forehand and broke to the backhand. His partner, Davis, being left-handed, had a twist serve that did just the opposite, while Whitman, who, along with Davis, played the singles, employed a reverse twist service that swerved to the backhand and broke to the forehand. The British players could win only one set in three matches, the final two singles not being played because of rain. Even so, the international friendship and good will Davis hoped the competition would achieve was apparently realized, the British finding nothing to complain about as to American sportsmanship and hospitality. The galleries were most impartial, they said, and "the female portion thereof not at all unpleasant to gaze upon."

In 1903, on their third attempt—there was no match in 1901—the British won the Cup and kept it for four years before losing it to Australasia, which withstood challenges by the British and the Americans until 1912, when the British regained the Cup. During this time Australasia had two players regarded by many as the best in the world: Norman Brookes, a small, wiry left-hander from Melbourne, who won at Wimbledon in 1907 when he was twenty-nine years old, and after an absence of seven years returned to win again in 1914; and Anthony Wilding, a big blonde handsome New Zealander, who, beginning in 1910, won four Wimbledons in a row before Brookes took the title away from him.

Nicknamed the Wizard because of his uncanny ability to almost always be in position to return his opponent's best shots, Brookes also had what was probably one of the best left-handed serves in tennis history. Like Neale Fraser, another great Australian left-handed server of a later day. Brookes could serve a baffling variety of serves from the same stance and with the same motion—flat, slice, or high-bounding twist—which kept the receiver off-balance and uncertain as to what to expect. "No matter how I disguised my intention of receiving his service," Bill Tilden said of Brookes, "he always twisted the ball so it was bounding into my body when I made my return. . . . Forehand or backhand, he made me play my return of service stepping away from the ball. This was done by a supreme command of spin." At the net, which he sought at every opportunity, Brookes was a deadly volleyer. Wilding, on the other hand, who was seven years younger, was primarily a baseliner with powerful groundstrokes. After going to England to study at Trinity College, Cambridge, he remained abroad, spending much of his time playing tournament tennis in England and on the Continent, although he did return home for long enough in 1908 and again in 1909, after he and Brookes took the Cup from the British in 1907, to aid Brookes in resisting challenges from the United States.

The 1908 Davis Cup challenge round, played at Melbourne, was closely contested, Beals Wright, the American champion in 1905, beating both Brookes and Wilding, and Wright and Fred B. Alexander, the current American doubles champions, losing the doubles at 6-4 in the fifth set, after leading 3-love. The next year Brooke and Wilding had no trouble winning all five matches from an inexperienced American team of two twenty-year-old Californians, Maurice McLoughlin and Melville Long. In 1911, at Christchurch, New Zealand, a much stronger American team made up of Wright and William A. Larned, the national champion of that year, also lost 5-0, but in 1912, with Wilding not playing, Australasia lost the Cup, three matches to two, to the British Isles. In 1913, with the British holding the Cup, which made for much less travel than during the Australasian tenure for a team coming through to the challenge round, there were seven challenging nations instead of two as in most previous years. The United States defeated Australasia, with neither Brookes nor Wilding playing, Germany and Canada, and became once again, after a ten-year interval, the champion nation with a 3-2 victory over the British Isles. J. Cecil Parke beat both McLoughlin, the American champion of 1912 and 1913, and R. Norris Williams, the 1914 champion, but his teammate, Charles P. Dixon lost both his singles, and the Americans won a close five-set doubles match. In 1914, Australasia, one again represented by Brookes and Wilding, qualified to challenge the United States by defeating Canada, Germany and the British Isles. On the first day of challenge-round play, a gallery of almost 12,000 saw Wilding beat Williams in straight sets, and McLoughlin defeat Brookes, also in three sets, the first going to a record 17-15, with McLoughlin serving twelve aces in it. McLoughlin also beat Wilding, but Williams lost to Brookes, and the Americans lost the doubles. Thus the Cup went back "down under," where it remained during the war years. In 1919, when competition was resumed, the United States, giving as a reason that it would be unfair to countries that had suffered much more from the war, did not compete, and Australasia retained the Cup by beating the British in the challenge round.

The pre-war American Davis Cuppers who had made the long sea voyage to Australia were motivated by the honor of playing in what had become an important international sporting event and by the glory that would accrue to them and their country if they brought back the Cup. This was true of Tilden and Johnston also, but in their case the trip, if successful, could result in another important benefit. Tennis was now a popular spectator sport, as dramatically attested to by the stands being jammed to capacity for the 1920 Tilden-Johnston final at Forest Hills, and most certainly to regain the Cup would be financially very profitable for the USLTA. It had been expensive to send a team across the Atlantic in order to gain the challenge round against Australasia, and it would cost even more to send it to the South Pacific. The total might come to as much as $50,000, but if the Cup were won, as there was every reason to believe it would be, and the next year's challenge round held at Forest Hills the deficit could be made up and no doubt a handsome profit turned in addition. Also, some of the countries challenging for the Cup would be playing their preliminary matches in the United States, and this would provide important tennis events for clubs other than the West Side Tennis Club, as well as additional revenue from gate receipts for the USLTA.

These commercial considerations were touched on in a New York *Times* editorial on American prospects for regaining the Cup, and in an article in the magazine *American Lawn Tennis,* written in response to the "frequent questions" of readers who wanted to know how players who were amateurs could afford to take all the time required to play on the team and who paid their expenses. Tilden, the magazine explained, was unmarried and "the fortunate possessor of an independent income—not a large one but an income nevertheless." Since he was in the insurance business with J. D. E. Jones, an enthusiastic veteran player, it was possible for Tilden, although to be sure not easy, to arrange for such absences as the trip he had made to England and the one he would be making to play against Australasia. Readers could be assured, however, that he was exceedingly anxious to get back to Providence and to his work. As for the other members of the team, Johnston was also in the insurance business, Washburn was a lawyer, and Samuel Hardy, the team's captain was able to devote so much time to tennis affairs because he worked in a promotional capacity for A. G. Spalding and

Brothers, the sporting goods manufacturers. And as far as the player's expenses were concerned, they, of course, were paid by the USLTA. The article's purpose clearly was to persuade the reader that the quest for the Cup was being undertaken in the spirit of true amateurism, but since it seemed to protest over-much in attempting to do so he could be pardoned if he remained somewhat skeptical.

In memory of Anthony Wilding, who was killed in action in Flanders early in the war, the 1920 challenge round was played in New Zealand, the specific site being Auckland, where Bill Tilden and his teammates arrived on December 8. This early arrival—the matches were not scheduled to begin until December 28—was intended to provide ample time for the team to practice and to become fully acclimated, since it was the season when the weather was likely to be quite hot. The two Bills brought their games to a peak with long, hard daily practice sessions and swept all five matches against their Australasian opponents, who were Norman Brookes and Gerald Patterson.

The forty-three-year-old Brookes, who as the Australasian captain had been expected to name a younger player for the singles and play only the doubles, gave all he had in trying to justify selecting himself, pushing Big Bill to 10-8, 6-4, 1-6, 6-4, and Little Bill to 5-7, 7-5, 6-3, 6-3. Patterson, although he took the first set from Bill, was never in the running in the next three, and against Johnston he was so badly off form that he could win only five games. The doubles went to the Americans in four sets.

Brookes and Johnston were the stars of the challenge round, the former for playing so well against both Tilden and Johnston. Had he been younger the results might have been different, since he led Johnston 5-2 in the second set after winning the first, and also led Tilden 5-3 in the first set before losing it. Johnston played his usual unrelentingly aggressive tennis and was the best man on the court in the doubles. Bill Tilden's great variety of stroke and cannonball service impressed the spectators, and the distinctive Tilden personality did not escape notice. R. M. Kidston, a Sydney tennis writer, described him as "a perpetual chaffer and a big globule of quicksilver, never at rest and keen to express his point of view," this last being a nice way, it would seem, of calling Bill at least somewhat opinionated and dogmatic. Kidston also spoke of Bill's "highly strung temperament," and thought that what appeared to be conceit was really confidence in himself.

The American and Australasian teams remained in New Zealand for another week to play in that country's championships. Bill won the singles from Watson Washburn and the doubles with Johnston, gaining another victory over Brookes and Patterson. Before returning to the United States, the Americans also played exhibition matches in Melbourne and Sydney against Brookes and Patterson and other leading Australian players. Bill was the only participant undefeated in singles, winning all five of his matches.

Arriving back in San Francisco on February 17, the victorious American team was welcomed at the pier by the mayor, a band, and three hundred fans. After losing an exhibition match the next day to Johnston, Bill boarded the Overland Limited for Philadelphia, arriving there three days later to receive another mayoral welcome at the City Hall and to be honored at a reception at the Manufacturers' Club. There was also a testimonial dinner at the Bellevue Stratford Hotel a few days later in honor of the local boy who had made good. Four hundred attended, including the Governor and other dignitaries, and Bill was presented with an engraved silver platter. The Davis Cup team was also honored officially by the USLTA, this being done at a dinner in New York City on April 22. A congratulatory telegram from President Harding was read, which also expressed his pleasure that the team would be playing exhibition matches on the White House lawn the following month, these having been arranged by a Presidential Aide who also happened to be a USLTA official. Bill and the other guests heard the dinner speaker, British Ambassador Sir Auckland Geddes, declare tennis to be the greatest of games, as well as deliver himself of humorous sallies like the following: "Tennis is a game that can be safely trusted to develop qualities of companionship, character and truth, for you can't lie about tennis as you can golf."

For the USLTA to be paying public tribute to Bill was rather ironic, since shortly before the Davis Cup dinner he had had his first serious dispute with that body. The Association wanted Bill to defend his Wimbledon title and also to go over early enough to play in the French Championships, and Bill had said no, for reasons he explained as follows: "Figuring that I had an income of my own, the Association decided not to take care of my living and traveling expenses completely on this trip. When they extended the invitation to lead an American group abroad, they informed me that I would be graciously allowed one

thousand dollars. Out of that enormous sum I was supposed to
pay my boat fare over and back, live three weeks in Paris—and
then four weeks in London. Anyone who has ever made such a
trip has a pretty good idea of how far the amount would go. Besides I felt it beneath the dignity of the United States to have its
champion travel in any way except first class. I so notified the
Association, and told them that unless they were willing to pay
my complete expenses, both traveling and living, I had no intention of going abroad."

This was the state of affairs early in May when the Davis
Cup team (Wallace Johnson substituting for Bill Johnston)
played its exhibition at the White House. Five days of rain had
turned the court into a sea of mud, but Bill especially didn't
want to be deprived of the honor of performing for the President, and at his urging the court was dried out by burning two
hundred gallons of gasoline on it. Before the matches President
Harding received the team in his office, and, as they were leaving,
told Bill he would like to speak to him for a moment. Having
heard that Bill would not be defending his Wimbledon title, the
President wondered if Bill could see his way to changing his
mind, since international sports did so much to promote good
will and understanding among nations. Bill was so flattered that
he assented on the spot. Bill explained why he had previously
refused to go, and, according to Bill's account, the President
agreed that the USLTA was being ungenerous. Commenting on
the incident later, Bill said, "I do not know whether Mr. Harding's views reached the Association or not, but I do know that
forty-eight hours later I received word that they would pay my
complete expenses." Bill probably relished this triumph over
the USLTA almost as much as any he had achieved on the tennis
court. He had been magnanimous but it had cost him nothing.
Our international sports ambassador would now travel and live
abroad in a style befitting a champion, with the Association
rightfully, if reluctantly, picking up the tab.

For the rest of his amateur career, it might be added, Bill
continued to hold to the philosophy that he was entitled to go
first class at the expense of the USLTA and tournament com-
mittees, and, powerful gate attraction that he was, he almost
always had their full cooperation in this regard. As Al Laney
put it, Bill "traveled like a goddamm Indian prince." Usually
at a tournament, out of town players would be put up at private
houses, but Bill would stay in a hotel suite. On his numerous

transcontinental railroad journeys to play on the Pacific Coast he would travel in a compartment. Sometimes he even required local transportation during the week of a tournament in the form of a chauffeur-driven car with the driver on call any hour of the day or night. Tournament players who came after Bill Tilden, according to George Lott, a younger compatriot of Bill's on the tournament circuit and a Davis Cup teammate, owed Bill eternal gratitude, for "Tilden," observed Lott, "was the man who set the precedent for tennis players to live in a style to which they were not accustomed."

CHAPTER FOUR

BIG BILL, SUZANNE AND MOLLA

His conflict with the USLTA resolved, Bill Tilden went abroad in mid-May, early enough to play in the World's Hard-court Championships in Paris before defending his Wimbledon title. He arrived in time to get in several days of practice on the slow red clay courts of the Stade Francais in St. Cloud, the site of the tournament, and one afternoon, after finishing a work-out with Molla Mallory, his mixed doubles partner, he was approached by none other than Suzanne Lenglen, who asked him if he would like to play her a set. Bill readily acquiesced and proceeded to beat her 6-0 before a sizable crowd of spectators, including several newspaper reporters who made sure that the en-counter was fully publicized. Suzanne tried her hardest during the first three games, but getting nowhere pretty much gave up after that, and declined Bill's cordial invitation to play another set. When he recounted the incident years later in his auto-biography, *My Story*, Bill confessed that he was not very proud of what he had done, since he had intentionally played poorly against Mrs. Mallory hoping to inveigle Suzanne into playing, his idea being to beat her decisively to demonstrate that it was ridiculous to believe, as had been suggested in the French press, that Suzanne might be as good as, and perhaps even better than, the top men players. The French Tennis Federation had actually considered nominating her to play Davis Cup but decided not to do so on the grounds that best of five set matches (women's were always three sets) were too strenuous for a woman. Suzanne, who had recently been awarded a French Academy gold medal for excellence in women's sports, had been quoted to the effect that she had no desire to play Tilden or William Laurentz, the French champion, but she apparently could not resist the temptation to see how she might do in a practice match. More than a little piqued at the result, she told the re-porters that whether Bill or she had won six games she really didn't know.

Suzanne got revenge on Bill, in a sense, a few days later when she met Mrs. Mallory in the women's final. Bill, not averse to employing a little gamesmanship, but also convinced of what he said, remarked to Suzanne before the match, "No woman in the world can beat Mrs. Mallory today." Replied Suzanne, "America had its day yesterday," referring to Bill's victory in the men's final over Jean Washer of Belgium, "this is France's day."

Mrs. Mallory was indeed a formidable opponent. As Molla Bjurstedt she was several times champion of her native Norway, and after emigrating to the United States in 1914, she won the American championship five times. Another acquisition was a wealthy New York stockbroker husband, Franklin I. Mallory, whom she married in 1919. Born in 1892 of Lapp heritage, she had high cheekbones, almond eyes, a nut-brown complexion and a sturdy physique. She lacked the grace of the more glamorous Suzanne but was noted for her fine court covering, and with her great endurance, fiercely competitive spirit and powerful ground strokes was capable of putting the French girl on the defensive. The slow court and the softer ball used abroad, however, favored Suzanne's steadiness and finesse, and she won 6-2, 6-3, although she had to come from behind when she was down 2-3 and 30-40 on her service in the second set. At this point she said her feet were paining her and wanted to default, but her father insisted she continue, and when Mrs. Mallory, seeking to press her advantage, hit out in trying for a clean winner off a weak Lenglen serve, and then through over-anxiety lost two more points and the game, Suzanne regained her confidence and ran out the set.

Bill had won as easily as Lenglen even though he had been handicapped by a bad case of boils and had spent most of the time in bed when not on the court. He was scheduled to play in two minor English grass-court tournaments before Wimbledon, but instead entered a London nursing home, remaining there for rest and treatment until only a week before defending his title against Brian I. C. Norton of South Africa, the winner of the Wimbledon All Comers. Before leaving the United States Bill announced that he had asked the Wimbledon officials to allow him to play through the tournament because he felt he should be on an equal basis with the other contenders. It was lucky for him that the request was not granted—the challenge round not being abandoned until the next year—since he was in no condition to play a succession of tournament matches. He had, observed A. Wallis Myers, the British tennis writer, a "decidedly convalescent look" when he played Norton and needed a good deal of cooperation from his opponent in order to eke out a victory.

Norton, a handsome blonde youth of twenty-one was a brilliant player with excellent strokes, but he was also a happy-go-lucky person who believed tennis should be played more for enjoyment than as a serious business. He had achieved good victories over two leading internationalists, Zenzo Shimizu of Japan and Manuel Alonso of Spain, and against Bill he won the first two sets without difficulty, 6-4, 6-2, but Bill then took the third set, 6-1, when Norton became over-confident and careless. In the fourth set Bill dropshotted often and effectively, but this aroused the indignation of some of the gallery, who regarded Bill's insidious little chopped shots which barely cleared the net and often caught Norton flatfooted as unfair and greeted them with whistles and boos and expressions of sympathy for Norton, who became so upset over this discourtesy to his opponent that he threw the set. In the final set, Bill, finding himself down 4-5 and 30-40, match point against him, hit a shot during a long rally that he was sure would go out. But as he ran to the net to congratulate Norton, the ball fell on the line, and the latter, thinking Bill was coming in to volley, hurried his passing shot and hit it out, whereas any kind of good return would have found Bill unprepared to deal with it. Thus reprieved, Bill drew on his last bit of reserve and ran out the set 7-5. Afterward in the clubhouse he fainted dead away.

Bill continued to feel the effects of his illness after his return to the United States in mid-July. He skipped the big Eastern grass-court tournaments but played in the National Doubles at Longwood in late August, which he won with Vincent Richards over R. Norris Williams and Watson Washburn, the doubles winners at both Newport and Seabright. Next came the defense of the Davis Cup against the Japanese team of Ichiya Kumagae and Zenzo Shimizu, who had upset Australasia to reach the Challenge Round. Kumagae, a left-hander, was well-known in this country, having been in business in New York City since 1917 and having achieved tournament victories over most of the leading American players, including Tilden and Johnston, although he was more at home on hard courts than on grasss. Both he and Shimizu, who was making his first visit to the

United States, employed the heavily looped ground strokes needed to control the lighter ball used in their country at the time their games were being developed. Kumagae was the harder hitter, Shimizu the more subtle, and both were indefatigable court coverers.

An Oriental team being a novelty in international tennis, there was an unusual interest in the matches, the gate for the three days of play exceeding $80,000. On the opening day, a crowd of more than 14,000 saw Johnston dispatch Kumagae with methodical precision, 6-2, 6-4, 6-2, and then, by contrast, Bill come within two points of defeat against Shimizu before winning, 5-7, 4-6, 7-5, 6-2, 6-1.

This was one of Bill's numerous "cliffhanger" victories that over the years gave him a reputation for deliberately putting himself in an apparently hopeless position in order to thrill the gallery by snatching victory from his opponent's grasp. But commenting on the match some years later, Bill said that to beat Shimizu he felt he had to constantly rush the net and that the intense heat and Shimizu's superb lobbing had almost been his undoing. Calling on all his reserves he had somehow managed to save the third set. A cold shower during the ten-minute rest period which followed had revived him, and Shimizu had succumbed to weariness in the last two sets. Bill also revealed to Al Laney, the New York *Herald Tribune* tennis writer, that he had been bothered by a boil on his right foot, but had not mentioned it at the time because he feared to do so would detract from Shimizu's fine play. The Americans won the remaining three matches, and when Bill and Shimizu met again in an early round of the National Championships, Bill won easily in straight sets.

Grantland Rice, the widely-read sports columnist, said that he long subscribed to the Tilden dramatic-comeback theory, until Vincent Richards "straightened me out about the Shimizu match some thirty years later." Bill had been in agonizing pain from the boil during the first three sets, said Richards, and after it had been lanced had insisted on resuming play against the doctor's advice. "That Granny," said Richards, "took guts." Against a lesser opponent Bill might play at less than his best to encourage him or to put on a better show for the gallery, but that he ever consciously did so against a player of his own class in an important match is hard to believe. Bill could play poorly when he lost concentration or wasn't feeling well, but stimulated by the imminence of defeat he could play super tennis. Supremely confident that he could win, he was not affected by fear of losing as another player might be. Sometimes Bill might risk defeat to stubbornly prove a point, to show, for example, that he could beat Borotra, a great overhead smasher, by constantly lobbing him, or that he could beat Billy Johnston without using his cannonball service. But this was not deliberately letting up against such great players just to tantalize and then beat them, as some people liked to believe he did.

The Cup matches having been played at Forest Hills, the Nationals were held for the first time at the Germantown Cricket Club in Philadelphia. Immensely proud of Bill's achievements, his home club had declared its determination to become the greatest tennis club in the world and went to great lengths in its preparations for the event. The entry was a strong one, but unfortunately Tilden, Johnston and Richards were all bunched together in the customary "blind" draw, this leading the USLTA the next year to adopt a "seeded" draw in which the better players were so placed that they would not meet until later rounds. Johnston and Richards met in the third round with the former coming from behind to win after losing the first two sets. The two Bills met the next day in what should have been the final, Big Bill winning 4-6, 7-5, 6-4, 6-3. Not as dramatic as the previous year's final, the match was nevertheless very close for three sets. Little Bill came within two points of winning the second set and led 4-3 in the third with his service to come. But he had begun to tire, feeling the effects of a combined attack of tonsilitis and ptomaine poisoning suffered the week before and of his hard match with Richards. Also at this point Bill made a couple of lucky shots—a net cord and winning volley off the wood of a Johnston passing shot—from which Little Bill was unable to recover.

In the final, Bill played another Philadelphian, the veteran Wallace Johnson, who had almost beaten McLoughlin years before in the 1912 final. Bill had beaten Johnson something like 22 out of 24 times, but playing on a soft, damp court well suited to Johnson's chop strokes, the two battled to 8-8 in the first set, Bill fighting off two match points, before the match was halted by rain. Two days later when the match was started over on a dry court, Bill ran through his opponent, 6-1, 6-3, 6-1, in forty-five minutes, a most unfraternal way to conclude this first national championship to be held in the city of brotherly love.

So it was that in 1921, Bill continued to be invincible on the court, leaving no question as to his title as world champion. Not so his female counterpart, Suzanne Lenglen, whose default to Mrs. Mallory, after losing the first set of their match in the National Women's Championship at Forest Hills, was the sensation of the tennis season. Suzanne, who had easily retained her Wimbledon title, trouncing Elizabeth Ryan, a Californian who made her home in England and was Suzanne's doubles partner, in the final, 6-2, 6-0, agreed to come to America in mid-August to play a series of exhibition matches to raise money for the American Committee to Aid Devastated France, and it was expected that she would play in the nationals as well. The visit of this "athletic Jeanne D'Arc of our time," as she was described by one of the several French newspapermen who accompanied her to the United States, had created, he declared even more interest in Paris than that of Georges Carpentier, the French boxer, who had been knocked out by Jack Dempsey in a heavyweight title bout in Jersey City in July. When, followed by her mother, her tour manager, Captain A. R. de Joannis, the vice-president of the French Tennis Federation, and Mme. de Joannis, she came ashore wearing a big red hat and pumps with red heels to be greeted by a crowd of reporters at the New York pier, there was no hint that she would come to grief as had Carpentier and the Maid of Orleans. The New York *Times* announce her arrival in a long front-page story and also carried an article on the same page with Suzanne's byline entitled "Mlle. Lenglen Writes Her Own Story of Her Trip and Her Tennis Hopes," the first of a series, the *Times* said, that Suzanne would write during her stay.

Suzanne's father's health did not permit an ocean voyage, and the resulting decision as to whether she should go without him and two attacks of bronchitis she suffered delayed her arrival until Saturday, August 13, only two days before her first tournament match was scheduled. Not having played any "real tennis" for more than a month—a court had been rigged up for her on the deck of the liner *Paris,* but it was reported that her principal exercise had been dancing nightly in the ship's ballroom—she announced that if a practice session the next day should reveal she was not completely fit she would not compete. Her first match being postponed until Tuesday, she did not have her practice workout until Monday, a scant half-hour session with Sam Hardy before a large and curious crowd of spectators, players, and cameramen, after which she said she felt satisfied with her condition and ready to give a good account of herself. Along with this paucity of practice, it turned out that Suzanne was to have no match at all before playing Mrs. Mallory. The unseeded draw resulted in an even more unfortunate situation than that in the men's championship several weeks later when, as has already been noted, Tilden and Johnston, who should have been the finalists, met in the fourth round: Mlle. Lenglen and Mrs. Mallory were drawn to meet in the second round! Furthermore, Suzanne's first-round opponent, Eleanor Goss, who would probably have given her a good match since she was the number five ranking American woman, defaulted. Mrs. Mallory, on the other hand, may well have benefited from being pushed to a 7-5 first set in defeating a strong first-round opponent, Mrs. Marion Zinderstein Jessup, the country's number two ranking player.

There was no indication that Suzanne was disturbed by any of the foregoing. As she sat in a box waiting for the end of a long drawn out match full of interminable rallies between two very steady women that preceded hers with Mrs. Mallory, she appeared composed and confident. Wearing a white fur-trimmed cape over a sleeveless silk dress with a pleated skirt, a gold bracelet on her left arm which flashed in the sun, and a crimson headband around her glossy black hair—a tennis costume not seen before at Forest Hills, and which Bill Tilden said struck him "as a cross between that of a prima donna and a streetwalker"—she was the cynosure of all eyes, including those of a young girl in pigtails from California named Helen Wills, who was the winner of the National Girls Championship held concurrently with the women's tournament, and who would be Suzanne's opponent five years later in another historic match of the era.

When Mrs. Mallory walked off the court after losing to Suzanne in Paris, she said to Bill Tilden: "I can beat her! The next time I play her I'll beat her!" Now, Bill, who was Molla's self-appointed coach as well as loyal supporter, got her away from the crowd to a secluded corner of the clubhouse where he could keep her calm and relaxed and counsel her on how to play Suzanne. Bill conceded that Suzanne was a very great player, but he also felt sure that some of her mannerisms, such as her acrobatic jumping, which he believed caused her to lose speed and power, especially on her forehand drive, fooled people into thinking she was greater than she really was. What he told Molla to do was to give Suzanne no time for her acrobatics by hitting every ball hard and for a placement. Following his advice Molla ran Suzanne relentlessly from corner to corner with deep paceful drives and won the first set 6-2. But good as her play was, it became obvious that something was the matter with her opponent, who, from the third game on, had several coughing spells and played at times in a weakly defensive way altogether uncharacteristic of her. In the second set Suzanne served first, losing the first point after a long rally and the second when she doubled-faulted. She then walked with uncertain steps to the umpire's chair, coughing and crying, and told him she was too ill to go on and would have to default.

Suzanne was put to bed in her suite at the Forest Hills Inn and examined by a physician who found her to be suffering from the after-effects of bronchitis and advised her to take a complete rest for a week. In a statement to the New York *Times,* Suzanne said she had had a sleepless night before the match because of a hacking cough, and though she had not felt up to playing she had done so because she did not want to disappoint the spectators. The *Times* expressed no criticism of her for defaulting, but did say that Mrs. Mallory had played so well that it was doubtful that Suzanne even at her best could have beaten her. A. Wallis Myers, the British tennis writer, who had come to American to report on Suzanne and on the tennis scene generally, wrote in the New York *Herald* that when he talked to the French girl at her bedside he found her physically and mentally worn out, "genuinely hors de combat." He also said that he felt sure Mrs. Mallory would have won in straight sets had the match been completed.

Despite the apparently extenuating circumstances, Suzanne's default did appear to have deprived Mrs. Mallory of a well-deserved victory, and a good many people, among them Molla herself, believed she had quit because she could not face the possibility of defeat. And it did not help Suzanne's cause with her critics when she appeared at the West Side Club the next afternoon, less than twenty-four hours after her default. After expressing her regret to the tournament officials and to Mrs. Mallory both for her default and for her inability to partner Mrs. Mallory in the doubles, in which the two were entered, she stayed on to watch some of the matches.

During the next two weeks there were numerous and sometimes conflicting reports as to Suzanne's condition and possible future activities. She was entered in the National Mixed Doubles with Billy Johnston as her partner but then withdrew, a return match with Mrs. Mallory was talked of, out-of-town exhibition matches were scheduled and then canceled. She visited West Point and went to the Polo Grouds to see the Giants baseball team play, and every three or four days one of her signed articles appeared in the *Times.* Ghostwritten, of course, they dealt mostly with subjects pertaining to tennis and with Suzanne's re-actions to things American, and they kept the reader informed as to the state of Suzanne's health and her hopes for resuming play.

Scheduled to play a mixed doubles exhibition with Vincent Richards as her partner after the Davis Cup Challenge Round match on September 3, she fainted on her way to the Forest Hills and the match was canceled. Two days later, on the concluding day of the Davis Cup matches, she and Dean Mathey, a leading Eastern player, defeated the strong California team of Mrs. May Sutton Bundy and Willis Davis, 6-2, 6-1. Suzanne was in good form, and the gallery enthusiastically applauded her brilliant stroking. During the following week she played two more ex-hibitions but these brought on coughing spells and shortness of breath. Another medical examination, the third of her visit, found her unfit to play for two or three months, and a week later she sailed for home.

At a hearing in late November the French Tennis Federation determined that Suzanne should not be blamed for her default or for not carrying out her American tour, and it also condemend the USLTA and the American press for unjustly criticizing her. This verdict was arrived at even though Captain de Joannis, who had stoutly defended Suzanne in Amerca, now testified that it was his belief she had been well enough to play Mrs. Mallory and had defaulted because of her fear that she would lose. His resignation of his office of vice president was tendered soon afterward and accepted by the Federation.

In an article published in a French magazine about this same time which gave Suzanne's version of her "disastrous American trip," she said she vividly remembered that Bill Tilden put on a "triumphant air" after her default. This he may well have done, but she and the Committee to Aid Devastated France owed him their gratitude for volunteering his services in her place. He recruited a group of leading players, along with him-self, who played a series of twelve matches during October at clubs in metropolitan New York and nearby New Jersey and

Connecticut. Bill was the star performer, usually playing Vincent Richards in the feature match and invariably winning, although the score was usually close. Afterward Bill would auction off the balls and rackets used by the players, his rackets going for $60 to $75 apiece. The matches drew overflow crowds, and the tour was a decided financial success, the Committee benefiting to the extent of more than $10,000. Always the showman, Bill found the experience of playing for a worthy cause immensely gratifying, as he would again years later when he played many Red Cross and other benefit matches during World War II.

CHAPTER FIVE

STILL WORLD CHAMPIONS

It was characteristic of Bill Tilden that he had not bothered to ask the USLTA for its approval of the exhibition matches he had organized to aid the French, and at the Association's annual meeting the following February, the delegates voted by a large majority to condemn any such exhibitions it had not officially sanctioned. Bill attended the meeting, held in New York City, and argued in his defense that he should be free to play for charity, but the argument prevailed that without USLTA control unscrupulous promoters might profit, and, it was implied, also the players. Bill also argued unsuccessfully in favor of a proposal to rescind the rule which forbade players from writing newspaper reports on tournaments in which they were currently playing, a rule which was to make for much subsequent conflict between him and the Association. And, mindful of the premature meeting between him and Johnston in the 1921 Championships, the delegates made sure a possible 1922 final between the two would not be precluded by voting to adopt a seeded draw.

The year 1921 was an exceedingly good one financially for the Association, a $17,000 profit being realized from the Davis Cup matches and another $14,000 from the National Singles. It came as somewhat of a surprise, therefore, when the Association announced a few weeks later that it could not afford to send Bill, or anyone else, as an official representative to Wimbledon, adding that a trip abroad for Bill might take too much out of him physically, as had appeared to be the case the year before, and leave him in less than top condition to defend the Davis Cup. Whether or not Bill agreed altogether with this reasoning, he was quoted as concurring in the Association's decision, although he had said earlier he expected to defend his title. That the USLTA should take a solicitous attitude toward Bill was understandable. Retaining the Cup was more important than

Bill's winning another Wimbledon, since there was considerable profit as well as prestige in being the champion nation.

Yet it would have been especially fitting for Bill to have defended his title in the first championship to be played at the "new" Wimbledon on Church Road, which would open this year, since he, along with Lenglen, had been largely responsible for drawing the large post-war crowds it was needed to accomodate. Much more spacious than the old premises on Worple Road, the new layout was mainly the creation of Commander G. M. Hillyard, the secretary of the All England Club for eighteen years, beginning in 1907. Like the American tennis official, Julian Myrick, who was the force behind the new stadium built by the West Side Tennis Club in 1923, Hillyard realized that tennis had a tremendous potential as a spectator sport and had the determination and drive to do something about it.

Much thought went into the planning of the new grounds. So that there would be less likelihood of a player having his concentration disturbed by play on an adjacent court, the outside courts were laid out separately with hedges and paths between them, and staggered rather than arranged in rows. The stadium court, still called the Centre Court, although not centrally located like its Worple Road namesake, could seat about 11,000 and had standing room for another 3,000. Court 1, a smaller stadium court adjacent to the Centre Court held about 7,000. The stands of both of these courts were so designed that wherever one sat he felt in close contact with the players and almost as if he were part of the match. This could also make a player feel something like a goldfish in a bowl, but though it needed some getting used to, more than a few champion players through the years have testified that they were stimulated to play their best tennis on the Centre Court.

Hillyard imported a turf from Cumberland of the sort used for the best bowling greens, believing it would make the best surface for the Centre Court, but it turned out to be too soft and velvety for hard play. As a result Hillyard instituted the practice of reseeding the Centre and No. 1 Courts each year with a hardy seed which could be cut very short, making for a fast, true surface which held up well throughout the fortnight over which the tournament was played. Ever since, these two courts have been considered the finest grass courts in the world. With the U. S. Championships having been switched from grass to clay and then to a hard synthetic surface, Wimbledon is the only major tournament still played on grass unless one counts the Australian Championship, which since the coming of open tennis has lost some of the prestige it formerly had. Grass courts have become an anachronism, even in England, but tradition being what it is at Wimbledon and the courts so good, it seems inconceivable that "The Championships" will ever be contested on any other surface.

The Wimbledon of 1922 did not have Bill Tilden to grace its Centre Court, but it got along quite well without him from the standpoint of spectator interest, since it not only had its star performer of the three previous years, La Belle Suzanne, but also Molla Mallory to whom she had defaulted in the first game of the second set after losing the first, at Forest Hills in 1921. This had left them tied at a match apiece, Suzanne having beaten Molla earlier in the Hardcourt Championships at Paris. Thus if they met at Wimbledon, it would be the rubber match that had been proposed the preceding summer in the United States but never played.

The great interest that developed in a possible match between the two was first generated early in April when Mrs. Mallory announced she would sail in mid-May to play at Wimbledon. In two previous tries she had not done well there, losing to players whom Suzanne then beat with ease in the challenge round—Mrs. Lambert Chambers, who could win only three games from Suzanne in 1920, and Elizabeth Ryan, who lost 6-2, 6-0 in 1921. As was the case with Mrs. Lambert Chambers, it was no mean feat for Suzanne to have beaten Elizabeth Ryan so decisively, even though the latter's forte during a more than twenty-year career of tournament tennis was clearly doubles. (During that period she won nineteen Wimbledon championships in women's and mixed doubles, six of them with Lenglen—a record number not surpassed until 1979 when Billie Jean King won her twentieth—but she never succeeded in winning a major singles championship). The same age as Mrs. Mallory, to whom she lost in the 1926 U. S. women's final after being at match point, she was born in Anaheim, California, but from 1912 on lived in England where she played in the first of her many Wimbledons that year. The next year on the Riviera she began her long-standing doubles partnership with Suzanne Lenglen, who was then only fourteen. Famous for her chop stroke, which had such vicious spin that opponents had great difficulty handling its bounce, especially on a damp grass or slow clay court, she could also with the same motion drop the ball softly just over the net, making the stroke "a disguised drop and chop," as she called it. Noted also for her great aggressiveness at the net, her sturdy build enabled her to kill overheads with all the power of a man.

Undiscouraged by her setbacks at Wimbledon and encouraged by her success at Forest Hills, Molla Mallory was now eager in 1922 to demonstrate that given the opportunity to play Suzanne she could repeat her victorious performance over the Frenchwoman. Late in April, after making her first tournament singles appearance at Monte Carlo since losing to Mrs. Mallory, Suzanne confirmed reports that she was returning to major competition and would play at Wimbledon, where she hoped, she said, to meet not only Mrs. Mallory but also Miss Ryan and such leading British players as Miss McKane and Mrs. Beamish. She added that she regarded Elizabeth Ryan rather than Mrs. Mallory as her most dangerous rival. More determined than ever to do well at Wimbledon after this remark of Suzanne's was called to her attention, Mrs. Mallory, who was something of a party girl and not ordinarily given to doing much training, underwent an intensive 10-day period of hard practice before she sailed against the strongest men players at the West Side Tennis Club.

Passing through Paris on her way to Brussels for the Hardcourt Championships, Suzanne told reporters that she too had been training and that her health was again very good. She was especially pleased, she said, to have beaten the strong American player, Eleanor Goss, in the Monte Carlo tournament in love sets with the loss of only ten points, and she added ironically, "I am so afraid of Mrs. Mallory that I am going especially to Wimbledon to meet her." During the month before Wimbldeon, however, it looked as if the only contest between the two might be a war of words. In Brussels, Suzanne played Kitty McKane in the semifinals and although she won 10-8, 6-2, she complained of pains about her heart. Her father tried to persuade her to retire at 8-all in the first set, but she refused, saying, "I will play till I drop." After pulling out the first set, she regained her confidence, the lack of which when Miss McKane led her 5-4, 6-5, 7-6, and 8-7, may have had something to do with the pains, and the next day she easily defeated Miss Ryan, 6-3, 6-2. The next week a Paris heart specialist found her to be in satisfactory condition and only in need of a short rest after her strenuous play in Brussels. But she had more heart pains while defeating Mme. Golding, who led 3-1 in the first set in the French Championship final but then succumbed 6-4, 6-0, and her father and French Tennis Federation officials insisted she should not enter the Wimbledon singles but only the doubles and mixed doubles. Molla Mallory, having been informed of all this, was quoted as saying she believed Suzanne was not prepared to face her again, and she told the press for the first time how she had accomplished her Forest Hills defeat of Lenglen: "I went to the courts determined to hit my hardest. I was convinced that Mlle. Lenglen could not stand up under big speed so I slugged everything and everything came off. Mlle. Lenglen cannot stand up to the big stuff. She is wonderfully safe, but there is nothing else to her game. She must be played from the back of the court since she is clever with her slow passing shots. I concentrated on every ball at Forest Hills and left the court without even knowing what Suzanne was wearing."

Suzanne's response was to announce that she would definitely defend her Wimbledon title, even if she had to be carried from the court. She insisted that she had never spoken disparagingly about Mrs. Mallory, having said only that she felt she had more to fear from Miss Ryan whom she considered the better player. She did not want to fight her tennis battles in the newspapers, and her racket would speak for her at Wimbledon. She did wonder, however, if Mrs. Mallory would ever make it to the final, having lost in pre-Wimbledon tournaments since coming to England to Mrs. Beamish and Miss McKane, both of whom *she* had always beaten.

Despite these assurances of Suzanne's, it was not until June 26, the opening day of the tournament, that the Wimbledon officials got a definite promise from her that she would play in the singles. This was at least some consolation to them for having to hold the opening day's ceremonies in the rain, during which the crowd of 7000, including the King and Queen, was given a look at the new Centre Court when the tarpaulin protecting it was raised briefly and then lowered again. Later, with the rain holding off most of the time, a men's singles and doubles were played. Suzanne and Molla were among those present and exchanged brief greetings. The definite prospect of their meeting gave the tournament tremendous interest, and although the weather throughout much of the two-week meeting was rainy and windy, spectators by the thousands turned out regularly, equipped with mackintoshes, overcoats, umbrellas and other such gear.

Mrs. Mallory had a very lucky draw, Lenglen, McKane and Ryan all being in the opposite half. Suzanne beat McKane in the second round after a close second set, 6-1, and 7-6, and Ryan in the quarter-finals, who came even closer to winning a set before going down 6-1, 8-6. Mrs. Mallory had a much easier passage up through the quarter-finals, winning in straight sets from four lesser English players. In the semi-finals both women were in top form, Mrs. Mallory losing only four games to Mrs. Beamish and Suzanne five to Mrs. Peacock, and the many who queued up from 7 A.M. the day of the final match, hoping to get standing room, along with the thousands who long before had reserved all the Centre Court seats, had every reason to expect that it would be close and exciting. Instead the Centre Court gallery, whose numbers dwindled to 5000 when rain delayed the beginning of the match for almost four hours, saw an off-form Mallory almost completely outclassed by a player who was far too steady and accurate for her. Molla, who lost 6-2, 6-0, said afterward that even though she had not played one third as well as at Forest Hills and Suzanne had played better than Molla had ever seen her play before, she still believed the result would have been different if she had only been able to win the first two games, which had been close, and thereby put Suzanne under pressure. She also complained about being expected to play after such a long wait and then to have had to begin the match at the late hour of 7 P.M. when the light was bad and there were shadows on the court. Suzanne, on the other hand, had no grounds for complaint, admitting that she had played much better than she had against McKane and Ryan, hitting harder and not being at all nervous. And to a reporter she added, "I think they are better players, don't you?"

The triumph of their sports heroine appealed tremendously to French national pride. *Tennis and Golf,* the official publication of the French Tennis Federation printed an article by one of its prominent members who signed himself "Daninos," in which Mrs. Mallory's defeat was referred to as "an exemplary chastisement, an effective spanking." There were other strong Lenglen partisans in the Federation, and its president, Henry Wallet, brought down their wrath on his head when he officially disowned these remarks as insulting to the tennis association of a friendly country. And one French tennis writer took the view that Suzanne's victory was something less than world shaking, saying, "A triumph at tennis does not quite console us for the spectacle of the unfavorable exchange rate of twelve francs to the dollar, and it is not worth so much as a good international loan." On her return home Mrs. Mallory, still smarting from her defeat, delivered an angry tirade against the press for distorting her rivalry against Lenglen, making it appear, she said, to be a personal feud when it wasn't at all. Presumably she found some consolation in the following weeks by being supreme in the major American women's tournaments and retaining her national title with an easy victory over Helen Wills, the promising young girls' champion from California.

Since 1913, when the International Lawn Tennis Federation was founded, Wimbledon had been designated by that body as the World Grass Court Championship. (Believing that its championship should be considered just as important as Wimbledon, the USLTA refused to join the ILTF until 1923 when the designation, which the Wimbledon officials felt somewhat uncomfortable about anyway, was withdrawn). Suzanne was certainly entitled to be recognized as world champion, but Gerald Patterson, who became a second-time Wimbledon winner in 1922, did so in the absence of Bill Tilden and other strong international competitors, defeating in the final the Englishman Randolph Lycett, who was twice a Wimbledon doubles champion but not especially distinguished for his singles play. In recognition of this, Patterson said he would not regard himself as world champion unless he won the American Championship also. If he did not, he would be willing to challenge the winner to a five-set match for the title. Bill Tilden, when asked his reaction to this, said that if he retained his American title he would be happy to play Patterson, and he added that he was most interested in seeing Patterson's backhand since he had heard a great deal about how Patterson had been working to correct his weakness on that side. This probably sounded snide to some ears, but Bill seems merely to have been expressing a natural curiosity as to what Patterson had been able to do about the stroke. Later, Patterson decided that a special championship match would be superfluous since it was only logical that whoever won the American Championship should automatically become the number one world player. Bill made such a match seem altogether uncalled for by beating Patterson in both the Davis Cup Challenge Round and in the National Singles, and in which, incidentally, Patterson's backhand showed no noticeable signs of improvement.

In their first match, played in the Challenge Round at

Forest Hills before a crowd of 15,000, Bill, his game somewhat below par except for his serve, had to struggle to win the first two sets, being down 4-5 and 15-40 on service in the second, but after that, Patterson's resistance collapsed and Bill took the third 6-0. In contrast, Johnston, giving one of his characteristically businesslike performances, defeated James O. Anderson, a tall, rangy man with a powerful flat forehand drive who played very aggressively from the baseline. Anderson, who was the 1922 Australian champion and had a victory the previous year over Bill Tilden to his credit, had lost a very close five-set match to Patterson at Wimbledon and by some was thought to be the better player.

In the doubles, the Australian team of Patterson and Pat O'Hara Wood, who had lost in the National Doubles final at Longwood to Tilden and Richards in four sets, turned the tables on their conquerors with surprising ease, 6-3, 6-0, 6-4. Bill's inexplicably poor play—he missed many easy set ups and made many other unforced errors—was not involuntary, at least so said Richards many years afterward. Bill was not trying to win but getting back at his young partner for angrily denouncing him during the Longwood match after Bill had carried his poaching to such an extreme that he was virtually pushing Vinnie off the court so he could make the return. Bill may have really meant to throw the match, as Richards supposed—there wasn't much risk involved since he and Johnston were odds on favorites to win the two remaining singles—but one would like to think it was the friction which continued between the two after Longwood that had made for his poor play, as well as affecting Richards who also played at less than his best.

In the two final singles matches, Bill had to go five sets to overcome Anderson, and Johnston, his game more efficient and lethal than ever, beat Patterson 6-2, 6-2, 6-1, indicating that he would be a most dangerous threat to Bill in the National Singles. Each being already a two-time champion, the winner would gain his third leg on and permanent possession of the handsome championship trophy which had been in competition since 1911, and had engraved on it in addition to their names those of Larned, McLoughlin, Williams and Murray. Johnston dearly wanted to win the cup and retire, and when he led two sets to one and 3-0 in the fourth, there seemed little doubt that he would achieve his goal. But Bill wanted the cup just as badly, and through courage, tactical skill, and some good luck snatched victory from an almost certain defeat.

Neither Johnston nor Bill experienced any real difficulty in getting to the final, the former beating Richards in one semi-final in straight sets, and Bill beating Patterson in four sets in the other. Johnston was the more impressive throughout the tournament and he continued to be in winning the first two sets from Bill, 6-4, 6-3. Bill's service was erratic, and Johnston, although he played somewhat more cautiously than usual, was the more aggressive and steadier during the many long rallies. Finally abandoning his defensive play, Bill broke through Johnston's serve at the beginning of the third set by hard, accurate driving, and continuing to be aggressive and making some marvelous gets of apparent winners by Johnston won the third set 6-2, Johnston came back to win the first three games of the fourth set, all hard fought, but Bill pulled out the fourth game after it went to deuce and then ran five more for the set. He then got to 4-1 in the final set, but Johnston, giving a demonstration of his famous fighting spirit, held his serve and broke Bill for 4-3, and, although he lost his next serve, again broke Bill to make the score 5-4. But Bill, his confidence seemingly not in the least shaken, hit out boldly to break Johnston once again for the set and match. Johnston throughout almost all of the match played his finest tennis, and he lost only because his opponent played a brainy, resourceful game calculated to wear him down both physically and mentally.

Bill Tilden was now unquestionably world champion, and among the memorabilia in the Tennis Hall of Fame at Newport is the racket with which he achieved this honor. After inscribing on it the scores of his quarter-final, semi-final and final matches against Shimizu, Patterson and Johnston, he gave it to his young protégé, Alexander "Sandy" Wiener, who, in 1959, donated it to mark the occasion of Bill's posthumous induction into the Hall. It is heavier (14 1/2 ounces) and has a larger handle (5 3/8 inches) than today's typical rackets. (Handles back in the 1920's were commonly as large as 5 1/2 inches, and an article in the British medical journal *The Lancet* attributed cases of tennis elbow—"a common form of disability suffered by tennis players," remarked the physician author, "it being most frequently observed in late summer"—to players using rackets with handles too large for their hands, thereby forcing them to put too much strain on arm muscles in gripping, although it was also acknowledged that faulty methods of stroking such as "flicking from the elbow" in hitting one's backhand could be responsible as well). The handle of Bill's racket is of bare wood, leather grips not having come in until the 1930's. Some players like Billy Johnston and René Lacoste wrapped their handles with adhesive tape, but Bill preferred the feel of the wood. He also used a very thin seventeen gauge gut (a not quite so thin light sixteen gauge is now the thinnest generally available) and liked it strung very tight, believing this gave him added power by moving the ball off the racket faster.

Anyone else would probably have taken a week's rest after such an exhausting match as his final-round victory over Billy Johnston, but not Bill Tilden. The next day saw him back out on the same Germantown court playing an exhibition against four opponents all at once, two in the back court and two at the net. The quartet, all good friends of Bill and fellow German-town Club members, were quite good players but couldn't win even one of the five sets played, although the last one went to 8-6 when Bill began to tire. It was not reported if the friends got to hit into the whole doubles court and not just the singles, but one would guess that he almost surely gave them this added advantage. A week later in very different surroundings, Bill and Vincent Richards played an exhibition in New York City's Central Park as part of a campaign to promote interest in munici-pal tennis and to persuade the authorities of the need for more courts, there being only twenty-nine for some 6,000 persons who applied annually to use them. More than a half a century later, the situation seems not to be greatly improved, the courts in the public parks still leaving something to be desired both as to their number and their condition.

Still another exhibition match appeared to have serious con-sequences for Bill. While playing Wallace Johnson at the Bridge-ton, New Jersey Tennis Club early in October, he ran into the backstop trying to return a deep high bounding shot and scratched the middle finger of his racket hand. What seemed at first merely a trivial abrasion turned out to be a serious infection. The swelling and pain became increasingly worse, with poultices and heat applications being of no help, and early in November, with a real possibility of the infection spreading to the whole arm, the end of the finger above the second joint was amputated.

Bill's injury and operation received considerable publicity in the sports pages, and the tennis world was naturally much con-cerned as to whether or not his game might be seriously affected.

Sam Hardy, Bill's old Davis Cup captain, visited him in the Germantown Hospital soon after the operation and reported that it had been successful, that there was no possibility of further infection, and that Bill should be out of the hospital in another two weeks. The finger was stiff and would need much manipulation to loosen it up, but there was every likelihood that the stiffness would disappear, and it was Hardy's opinion that Bill would not be permanently handicapped. Bill himself believed his groundstrokes would not be affected but that his touch on his volleys might be, since he played his shots more off the ends of his fingers than many other players. He hoped to resume playing in a month or so, and though he felt he might drop down to the second half of the first ten in the national rankings as a result of his injury, he would not mind since match play and his love of the game would keep him as keen as ever.

But the finger did not improve and when interviewed early in December, Bill said pessimistically that he did not expect to be able to play before February and that he was sure his middle finger would be useless in gripping the racket. This might not affect his drives but would otherwise seriously inhibit his style of play. "All my volley shots," he lamented, "and all those delicate little cut shots on which I always depended so much are lost to me. Then there are all those little shots I have made from out of position, pickups, flick shots and the like. I know I cannot make them again." The supremely confident Tilden was a man of the past. "The psychology of the thing is this. In the last five years I have never really lost confidence in my ability to return any ball I could reach. When I missed I was surprised. In the future I know this is going to be reversed."

A week later, on December 14, Bill had another inch removed from his finger, and it healed so rapidly that only two weeks later he got back on a tennis court for a workout at a Philadelphia armory. He was able to grip the racket firmly and hit with quite good control, and to watch his backhand drive zoom over the net, said a spectator, one would have thought Bill had never had anything the matter with his finger. The following week Bill, Vincent Richards and Frank Hunter travelled to Chicago to play exhibition matches at the Drake Hotel, held under the auspices of the Chicago and Western Tennis Associations. On the first day Bill beat Hunter in a close match, and the next day taking on both Hunter and Richards again nosed out Hunter in the afternoon and lost to Richards, 4-6, 6-0, 6-3, in the evening.   Although the soreness and inflammation in his finger had not altogether disappeared, Bill felt happy he had done so well.   Hunter was certainly no pushover since this year he would be a semi-finalist in the National Singles and runner-up to Johnston at Wimbledon, and the fast board court gave a definite advantage to a volleyer like Richards.   Further evidence that his game would not be adversely affected by his injury was forthcoming in February when he won an indoor invitation tournament at the Buffalo Tennis and Squash Club.   In the semi-finals he beat R. Lindley Murray 6-0, 6-4, playing the best tennis that Bill Larned, the former national champion, who umpired, had ever seen Bill play, and in the finals defeated Richards (who had recently won the National Indoors, in which Bill did not play) in five sets after being down two sets to one.

Bill also had a chance to test his finger against Billy Johnston who, on his way abroad to play at Wimbledon and other tournaments, stopped off in New York for a few days early in May.   In Central Park he, Bill and Richards played one-set exhibitions before a crowd estimated at 15,000, Bill winning from both the others.   The next day Bill took Little Bill back with him to Philadelphia to give a talk on tennis to the boys at Germantown Academy and to play an exhibition on the school's new courts, which Bill won 5-7, 6-4, 6-3.

Bill gave the finger a good workout in other exhibitions in May and early June, including one at the White House before President Harding (Harding himself didn't play on the White House court as Teddy Roosevelt did or, much later, Jimmy Carter, but the public interest he showed in tennis helped to make the game more popular).   He also won the Philadelphia and District Championship over his old rival, Wallace Johnson, and at Forest Hills in the Church Cup matches, an inter-city team competition, beat Vincent Richards, and with Johnson beat Richards and Hunter.   Late in June, after he won the New England Championship at Hartford and the Great Lakes Championship at Buffalo, both over Manuel Alonso, the former Spanish Davis Cup player who had settled in Philadelphia and had become Bill's touring partner, Bill and Alonso journeyed westward to play in two tournaments Bill had won the year before.   He lost to Alonso in a four-set final in the Illinois State at the Skokie Country Club outside Chicago, but beat him the next week in the National Clay Court final in Indianapolis, and again late in July in the Southern California final in Los Angeles.

Alonso had the grace, attractive personality, impeccable court manners, and fine all-round game also possessed by two famous later Spanish players, Manuel Santana and Manuel Orantes. He was definitely a world class player, and the competition he afforded Bill, who wanted to be tested strongly in match play, undoubtedly helped greatly to strengthen the latter's game.

Having been assured he would play Davis Cup, Bill took a rest from tournament competition, passing up Newport and the other grass court events held during August, but toward the end of the month he won the National Doubles with B. I. C. Norton over the former Davis Cup pair of Williams and Washburn, and with Molla Mallory he won the Mixed Doubles over Kathleen McKane and J. B. Hawkes, the Australian Davis Cupper. The next week he again faced Hawkes across the net in the Davis Cup Challenge Round at Forest Hills, winning easily 6-4, 6-2, 6-1. However, Billy Johnston, who had won the Wimbledon singles earlier in the Summer, and who had not lost a singles match in three years of Davis Cup play, unexpectedly lost to James O. Anderson, 4-6, 6-2, 2-6, 7-5, 6-2. Little Bill's confidence was shaken when he uncharacteristically blew an easy shot in the fourth set, which would have given him a commanding lead, the only time, said Big Bill afterward, he had ever seen this happen to Johnston. The U. S. won the remaining three matches, Bill and Dick Williams defeating Anderson and Hawkes in the longest doubles match in Davis Cup history, 17-15, 11-13, 3-6, 6-3, 6-2, Johnston having no trouble with Hawkes, losing only three games, and Bill beating Anderson in four sets.

Playing perhaps a little too defensively in the doubles, in an effort to compensate for Williams' unsteadiness, Bill was told during the rest period after the third set by Harold Hackett, a member of the Davis Cup Committee, that he should be more aggressive and go to the net more often. No matter that Hackett was qualified to give such advice, being a former national doubles champion and McLoughlin's doubles partner in 1913 when the U. S. won the Cup from the British Isles, for anyone to tell Bill that he should change his game bordered on lese majesty. In writing about the incident in a "Passing Shots" column he contributed to *American Lawn Tennis,* Bill denounced Hackett for his temerity, and Hackett, in an angry reply in the same magazine that was also printed in the New York *Times,* asserted that the Davis Cup Committee had the same responsibility as a baseball manager or football coach and that the advice given Bill was called for "because he chose to park his intelligence outside the stadium and failed to play his position properly." Just because Bill was a fine singles player did not mean that he understood the fundamentals of doubles. Bill was so incensed that he announced he would bring the matter before the next USLTA meeting and that he might quit Davis Cup play. He added that he and Williams had been under a handicap since they had never played together before and because they were both left-court players. With Bill playing the unfamiliar right court, it took the first three sets before he began to feel natural and confident on that side. After that he and Williams did take the net more often, but because they had decided they should play "desperately" and not because of Hackett's advice. Having had his say Bill did not pursue the matter further as he had threatened, and Hackett no doubt felt vindicated since the match appeared to have been won by the kind of tactics he had suggested, although what he had done was to interfere in what really was the business of the Davis Cup captain, in this case Williams, from whom the players naturally expected such advice. What he and his fellow committee members could also be faulted for was picking Bill to play doubles at all when it would have been more logical to pair Williams with his regular partner, Watson Washburn, with whom he had won the Cup doubles against Japan in 1921.

There was no criticism of Bill's play in the National Singles Championship at Germantown. He lost only one set in the tournament—to Washburn in the first round—and won his fourth straight title by beating Johnston in the final before 12,000 spectators in fifty-seven minutes, 6-4, 6-1, 6-4. Bill was in top form, and when Little Bill advanced to the net behind his forcing forehand drive he was thwarted time and again by marvelous passing shots hit on the run. Bill's volleying was also unusually good, this being the result of his having worked diligently to strenthen his net game, since he found, as he had anticipated, that after his finger injury he could no longer hit the soft drop and other touch volleys which often had won him points. Commenting on this a couple of years later in his newly published *Match Play and the Spin of the Ball,* he wrote: "Gradually my incessant punching of volleys and overheads began to pay dividends. I actually reached a point when I was reasonably certain of winning at the net. I gained confidence and with my confidence grew my effectiveness. I have always felt that the keynote of success against Johnston in the finals of 1923—and partially so in 1924—was the fact that on crucial points when I advanced to the net, I could win the point outright by volley or smash if I could place my racquet on the ball at all." Thus, happily, Bill's finger injury turned out to be something of a blessing in disguise. Within a year after its occcurrence he was hitting his shots as hard as ever and with every bit as good control, and he was a champion who, in the words of the New York *Times,* "towers above all opposition on the courts, the one player who can do everything he wants with a ball, and who can defeat any other player in the world any time he wants to defeat him."

CHAPTER SIX

AMATEUR OR "EVIL INFLUENCE"?

Anyone who made the playing of tournament tennis his chief occupation, as Bill Tilden did, could hardly be expected to hold down a regular job or follow a career. As previously noted, he did work for brief periods on a newspaper and for a sporting goods store in Philadelphia and in the insurance business in Providence. This was before he became a Wimbledon and American champion, and after that he had no further such employment. For a time Bill had no need to support himself, being the recipient of a fairly substantial inheritance—though not as large as some people supposed—amounting to about $60,000, according to Frank Deford, his biographer.

Like other leading players, Bill got his rackets and other equipment furnished gratis, and when he played in a tournament his traveling and living expenses were usually taken care of by its sponsors. In golf the rule that an amateur player had to buy his own clubs and balls and pay his expenses was strictly enforced, but in tennis, although lip service was still paid to amateur ideals, the standards they called for were badly eroded during the Twenties. In golf the situation was far healthier since a great player could be a professional like Walter Hagen, the first golfer to make a million dollars, or he could be an amateur, if he could afford to be, like Bobby Jones. Hagen had the best of both worlds; he could play in professional tournaments and he could play against amateurs like Jones in open tournaments and exhibitions, but a champion tennis player had no such option.

Getting expenses, even the extremely generous ones he was able to demand, was not enough for Bill after his inheritance dwindled away, as it soon did, for Bill liked to live well and early exhibited a faculty for never holding on to money for long. The problem was to find some means of support that would still leave him plenty of time to practice and play tennis, and it was solved after he became champion by his getting a contract to write articles on tennis for a newspaper syndicate. Other star athletes had newspaper bylines, especially baseball players, with sportswriters usually serving as ghost writers for them. Paul Gallico, in *The Golden People,* his lively account of the great sports heroes of the Twenties, tells of a sportswriter who, on entering the press box at the conclusion of a World's Series game and seeing a number of his colleagues pounding out stories under the names of players who had just left the field, cried out: "My God, it looks like a haunted house!"

Since they were professional athletes, no one saw anything wrong in these ball players capitalizing on their reputations in this way, but Bill, although his articles were written by him and very well written too, as an amateur was supposed to be content to play for the fame and not for any fortune that his superlative tennis skills and showmanship might incidentally bring him. At least this was the attitude of the Amateur Rule Committee of the USLTA, which early in 1924 presented a resolution to the Executive Committee of the Association recommending that a player who wrote for a newspaper or magazine be deprived of his amateur status. In a lengthy statement accompanying the resolution the Committee made clear its thinking about amateurism and how it should be preserved. When tennis was played only by the leisure class, said the Committee, there was no problem, but now tennis had become a game of the people. Competition had become so keen that some players were devoting too much time to the game, and although they did not actually teach or play tennis for money were profiting financially on the side. This was wrong. "The ideals of true sportsmanship are not being upheld when a man plays the game with any interest in it whatsoever other than the interest to play the game as a game untrammeled by thoughts of business, to play the game for the game's sake, and to play it merely as a recreation and for pleasure." A younger player should take up "some kind of business or profession at or about the same age as his fellows" and play tennis "not in the least because of or by means of writing tennis articles for money." One such young player the Committee no doubt had in mind was Vincent Richards, some of whose newspaper articles were ghosted by Ed Sullivan, a sportswriter who covered tennis for the New York *Mail* and who would later become a famous television personality.

The new rule was adopted at the Association's annual meeting in February of 1924, but with the proviso that it would not go into effect until January 1, 1925, so that player-writers could fulfill their current contracts. Bill, who had expressed strong opposition when the rule was first proposed, said that he might have to give up tournament tennis if he were forced to give up his writing, and he contended that he could be regarded as a journalist as well as a tennis champion because he had been a sports writer and a drama and music critic for a Philadelphia paper as early as 1913, three years before he played in his first national singles championship. He said he would be willing to play in 1924 on the Davis Cup team and in the national championships, but changed his mind when Holcombe Ward, the chairman of the Amateur Rule Committee, who had been national champion twenty years earlier and who was not one of Bill's admirers, made public a Committee report which charged Bill with acting contrary to the spirit of true amateurism by making a business of his tennis writing and in so doing being a bad example for younger players, who would be influenced to do likewise. That Bill's tennis writing could, with some justification, be regarded as a "business" was indicated by the details in the report concerning his newspaper contract, supplied by Bill himself to the Committee. It called for a weekly story from January to May and October to December, two articles a week the other months of the year, and daily reports during the Davis Cup matches and national tournaments—over 100 stories in all, to be sold to about 110 newspapers. Bill's remuneration was not specified, but, according to Vincent Richards, his contract with the Philadelphia *Ledger* syndicate at this time paid him $12,000 a year (He later made as much as $25,000), Richards having one with another syndicate good for $8,000. "It was by doing this writing," Richards explained some years later, "that Bill and I were able to play tennis the year round—to be first-class tennis bums."

The Amateur Rule Committee report, hardly remarkable for tact in making its case against Bill, evoked a response from him in the form of a letter to Julian Myrick, the chairman of the Davis Cup Committee, expressing astonishment at his being regarded as not only "no longer an amateur but also as an 'evil influence' in the game." Since his amateur status had been questioned, it followed that the USLTA would not want him to represent it in international competition, and, therefore, in order not to cause the Committee embarrassment he was resigning as a member of both Davis Cup and Olympic teams. Only if his amateur status was clearly recognized would he be able to play. It was also for him a matter of self respect.

A prompt reply from Myrick, which expressed surprise at Bill's resignation and assured him he was eligible to play on the Davis Cup team, but which made no reference to his standing as an amateur, was not enough to satisfy Bill, and he replied that his resignation would have to stand. This put the Committee in a predicament. To rob the Challenge Round of its main box-office attraction would undoubtedly result in lessened receipts for the USLTA. But since the player-writer rule had been passed, even though it had not yet gone into effect, there was really no way Bill could be given a clean bill of health as an amateur. A lengthy session of the Committee, attended also by Dwight F. Davis, who, besides being the donor of the Cup and a past president of the USLTA, was at this time the Assistant Secretary of War, and by several other former presidents of the Association, concluded with Bill's resignation being accepted, "one of the most momentous decisions," said the New York *Times,* "in the forty years' history of the United States Lawn Tennis Association."

Bill's only comment after learning the Committee's decision was, "This closes the incident so far as I am concerned." But instead of staying closed it engendered considerable controversy. The Germantown Cricket Club and numerous other clubs and organizations in Philadelphia came to Bill's support, urging that the rule be amended. It was brought out that some of the prominent clubs which had supported the rule had done so with only a small majority of their membership, the West Side Tennis Club, for example, favoring it by only a 181-155 vote. A group of twenty-eight New York metropolitan area tournament players called for a reinterpretation of the rule, and another player group, calling itself "The Bill Tilden Fair Play Society," which included Sam Hardy, Frank Hunter and other friends of Bill's, addressed a letter to George Wightman, the USLTA president, Julian Myrick and Holcombe Ward asking to what extent tennis officials benefitted in a business way through their connection with the game and how such benefits compared with those alleged to have accrued to Tilden, who was "no less a writer than they are business men." This was a good question which never got an answer. The letter also implied that personal dislike of Tilden might have influenced those who had impugned his amateur status, and it concluded: "We want peace. We want to play the game. But we will not have peace at any price. We propose to be loyal to Tilden, one of the finest characters the game ever knew, to the bitter end, come what may. And we hope it will not be necessary to go through with the organization of a new national association of players, rather than executives, who are in sympathy with Bill."

All these manifestations of strong support for Bill moved President Wightman to announce that a special meeting of the Association would be called in the near future "to settle the matter," and he followed this with a letter to member clubs throughout the country obviously designed to influence delegate voting in favor of the player-writer rule. Bill in a lengthy statement written for *American Lawn Tennis* and reprinted in the New York *Times* said he welcomed the calling of a special meeting because it would let the tennis players of America decide the question. He also said that the USLTA's definition of an amateur as "one who plays tennis only for amusement and physical benefits derived therefrom and merely as a pastime" was unrealistic, and that the USLTA, and not the players, was responsible for commercializing tennis and for acting contrary to the amateur spirit, as it had when it sent him thousands of miles in 1920 and 1921 to bring home trophies. Furthermore, no champion or prominent athlete could avoid capitalizing on his fame if he engaged in some kind of business, which he surely had a right to do in order to support himself. "Frankly," said Bill, "I cannot see why he should not do so provided he does not do it by a direct return from his sport. The reward is no more than his due, a just return for the effort he has expended on his game and the pleasure he has given the world by his skill." In his own case he believed that he was being less commercial than if he sold bonds, at which he could probably make as much or more money, because "I am giving expert opinion in my tennis articles, thus providing value received."

The special meeting was never held, the Association's Executive Committee, early in June, agreeing to defer action on the rule until after the current playing season at the request of a player group headed by Maurice McLoughlin. At about the same time, Bill was quoted as saying that a compromise reached with the USLTA clearly recognized his amateur status, thus making it possible for him to rejoin the Davis Cup team. A player would be permitted to write articles but not signed daily reports of a tournament in which he was competing. This was really not a compromise but only a proposal which might or might not be approved later, but it enabled Bill and the Davis Cup Committee without loss of face to get together again, and early in August came the announcement that Tilden and Johnston would be the nucleus of the Davis Cup team.

The conflict between Bill and the USLTA was finally resolved when the report of a "Special Committee of Seven," appointed the preceding November to consider the player-writer rule, was adopted at the Association's annual meeting early in 1925. The committee had two members opposed to the rule, Bill and his good friend *American Lawn Tennis* editor S. Wallis Merrihew, two who favored it, Jones Mersereau and Arthur Hellen, both members of the Amateur Rule Committee, and three well-known "neutral" members, Senator George Wharton Pepper of Pennsylvania, Devereux Milburn, the polo star, and Grantland Rice, the sportswriter.

Milburn, who was wealthy enough to be a simon-pure amateur, may have already taken a position on the issue, however, since he had turned down an offer of $5,000 to write up the International Polo matches the preceding year. Rice quotes him as saying, "I would like to have accepted that money to write about my sport, but I simply felt that as an amateur, I couldn't accept it." To which Bill had replied, "It's a matter of taste, not amateurism." In the main, the committee's recommendations constituted a victory for Bill, since they incorporated a compromise suggested by him permitting a player to use his name as author of newspaper and magazine articles and books, but not his titles or any statement concerning his reputation. Nor, as proposed earlier, could a player report currently on a tournament in which he was entered. Nothing was really changed by the new rule so far as Bill was concerned. To continue to negotiate lucrative contracts with the newspaper syndicate all he needed was to be able to use his name as a byline, and for another three years he continued his merry way as a player-writer. Then, as we shall see later, USLTA officialdom, never fully reconciled to Bill's getting the better of them in this matter, seized on a technicality to find him in violation of the rule and had the satisfaction of temporarily suspending him.

While the player-writer controversy was going on, and before he was named to the Davis Cup team, Bill played in a succession of tournaments, all of which he won: the South Atlantic Championships, Middle States Clay Court, Orange Lawn Tennis Club Invitation, Rhode Island State (where he played five semi-final and final singles and doubles matches totaling 157 games in one day from 10 A.M. to 6 P.M., and then spent the evening playing bridge. Bridge, along with listening to classical music, was a great passion of Bill's, and he spent almost as much time at the bridge table as he did on the tennis court), Great Lakes Championships, New England Championships, Western Championships, National Clay Court, Illinois State, and Southern California Championships.

Traveling all over the country to play in these tournaments, and in a good many exhibition matches as well, Bill found himself at times feeling somewhat surfeited with tennis, something that almost never happened to him, but some rest during August served to dispel this staleness, if that's what it was; and the player-writer controversy, more or less on his mind for some months, now being settled, he felt ready and eager to defend his national singles title against one of the strongest fields in the history of the tournament. Entered were the Davis Cup teams of Australia, France, Japan, Mexico, and Canada, B. I. C. Norton of South Africa, Manuel Alonso of Spain, and all the leading American players. Billy Johnston was expected to come through to the final against Bill, but Vincent Richards, who was in the same half with Bill, was thought to be an equally dangerous threat, his game being much improved since returning from Europe where he had won the Olympic Games singles championshp over Henri Cochet, a rising young French player, and the doubles with Frank Hunter over Cochet and Jacques Brugnon. Richards' relatively weak groundstrokes, which in the past had made him vulnerable to the pressure Tilden put on him with powerful deep drives and skidding slices, now had more pace and depth, and his volleying, always his strong point, was never better.

Playing Richards in the semi-finals on a very hot and humid day, Bill came close to succumbing to exhaustion and his opponent's brilliant play before winning 4-6, 6-3, 8-6, 4-6, 6-4. Most of the gallery was clearly for the underdog Richards, but Bill cleverly evoked admiration from it in the third set with a grandstand gesture that was characteristic of him. In making a volley for which he had to stretch very wide, Richards slipped and fell, and Bill, who had only to make an easy return to win the point, threw up a high, short lob instead, giving Richards time to regain his feet. Jumping up and seeing the ball still in play, Richards instinctively smashed it away for the point. To the gallery, Bill's return appeared to be a fine act of sportsmanship, which he pointed up by putting his hands on his hips and giving Richards a look that said in effect, "How could you take advantage of me like that?" The gallery's applause for Bill was prolonged, and a little later when the players changed courts he got another ovation. Apparently stimulated by being transformed for the time being at least into the gallery's favorite, and benefitting from a slight falling off in the play of a temporarily disconcerted Richards, Bill managed to pull out the close third set. After winning the fourth set to even the score, Richards had a game point on Bill's serve for a 3-1 lead in the fifth, but then Bill, as he had so often before in pulling out close matches with Richards, was able to produce the strong serving and driving he needed to triumph.

In the other semi-final, Johnston overwhelmed Patterson, the two-time Wimbledon champion, 6-2, 6-0, 6-0. Patterson won the first two games but was helpless thereafter in the face of the barrage Johnston laid down with his powerful forehand and forceful volleys. This was a Johnston who appeared even greater than the player who had beaten Bill in the 1919 final or the one who had forced him to the limit in 1922. In defeating Richards, Tilden had demonstrated once again his ability to rise to the heights when he had to, but a Johnston who could make Patterson look like a novice would surely extend Bill to the limit and quite possibly beat him.

But once again Little Bill's many supporters, among them most of USLTA officialdom, were destined to be disappointed when he was beaten 6-1, 9-7, 6-2, the match lasting only a little more than an hour. It was Big Bill's third final-round victory in succession over his rival, his fourth in five years, and his fifth title in a row. Many said that Bill played the finest tennis they had ever seen in the first set, which took only twelve minutes. Usually Bill began a match in a relaxed, easy fashion, but impressed by Johnston's play of the day before he started off in deadly earnest. He said afterward that no thought of losing ever entered his mind, and that he had not hit more than two balls before he knew he had his touch and would be able to play his best. Johnston had been able to hit outright winners off Patterson's cannonball serves, but not off Bill's which were often aces or near aces. Bill's high-bounding, wide-breaking twist second serve to Little Bill's backhand also forced errors or weak returns. And to keep Johnston from getting the shoulder-high balls he could pound on his forehand and keep Bill on the defensive, Bill hit drives and slices of low trajectory deep to the baseline.

Bill continued his superlative play in the long second set and was matched by an almost equally brilliant Johnston, but at 7-all Bill broke his opponent's serve with three magnificent passing shots and then easily held serve for the set. In the third set Johnston could not keep up the pace under Bill's sustained pressure, and in the last three games he could get only three points, Bill speeding up the play with rain imminent and ending the match with a service ace. Wrote the veteran tennis writer, A. Wallis Myers, of Bill's performance: "Never in a quarter of a century of first-class tennis have I seen such amazing hitting and phenomenal control."

Bill kept his tennis at the same high level the following week in the Davis Cup matches, the Australians, who had beaten China, Mexico, Japan, and France, again reaching the Challenge Round. He and Vincent Richards, who was making his debut as a Davis Cup singles player as a reward for having beaten Johnston in the East-West matches and for forcing Bill to the limit in the National Championships, easily won all four singles from Patterson and Pat O'Hara Wood, and Tilden and Johnston, playing together for the first time since 1920, when they brought the Cup back from Australia, won the doubles in four sets. It was the most decisive of the United States' five straight Cup victories, and it culminated a year that many of those who saw him in his prime believed was the finest of Bill's career.

CHAPTER SEVEN

MISS POKER FACE

Almost as dominating a figure as Bill Tilden at Forest Hills in 1924 was a young girl from Northern California named Helen Wills. Still a month away from her nineteenth birthday, she won her second women's singles title in a row, defeating the thirty-two-year-old Molla Mallory in the final, 6-1, 6-2. This was her third national championship of the year, she having earlier won the women's doubles with Hazel Hotchkiss Wightman and the mixed doubles with Vincent Richards, the latter with a final-round victory over Tilden and Mrs. Mallory, the champions in 1922 and 1923. (Tilden was the first player to win all three championships in one year, in 1922, for which the USLTA awarded him a special medal. He did so again in 1923.)

Earlier in the season in England, however, young Helen lost twice to Kathleen McKane, once in a Wightman Cup match, and again to the British girl in the Wimbledon final after leading by a set and 4-1 and four times having game point for 5-1, only to have her rival, a fine match player who never gave up, rally to win five games in a row and the set, and then go on to take the third, 6-4. (Suzanne Lenglen, who had lost only three games to McKane in the 1923 final, was not fully recovered from an attack of jaundice, and after winning an exhausting three-set match from Elizabeth Ryan defaulted to McKane.) Shortly afterward in the Olympic Games in Paris, with Lenglen not competing, Helen gained a measure of revenge by easily winning the women's title from Didi Vlasto of France, who had put out Miss McKane in the semi-finals.

Helen cried after her loss at Wimbledon, which was hardly unusual under the circumstances, but it was the only time she ever did after losing a match, although it should be added that subsequently she seldom had reason to do so. Even as a young schoolgirl in pigtails wearing a white middy dress and the white eyeshade which would become her trademark, just as a bandeau was Lenglen's, Helen was not given to showing emotion on the court, and the sportswriters—Ed Sullivan appears to have been the first to do so—took to calling her "Little Miss Poker Face." Later, after she matured and was well on the way toward acquiring her total of seven United States singles championships and her eight Wimbledon titles, with her classically beautiful features, her almost regal and, some thought, haughty bearing, and her near-invincibility on the court after Suzanne Lenglen turned professional, she was known as "Queen Helen." She did not have Lenglen's speed of foot and stroke variety, but she could win matches just as decisively, with groundstrokes which had more mechanical power, said Bill Tilden, than those of any other woman he had ever seen, and with a service so strong, said Elizabeth Ryan, that when she played doubles with Helen, she could count on her almost always to serve two aces, or near-aces that evoked weak returns, per game. No woman player since, with the exception of Maureen Connolly in the early 1950's and Chris Evert Lloyd today, has had the ability to keep so much pressure on an opponent from the baseline.

Born in Berkeley, California in October, 1905, Helen Wills began playing tennis at the age of thirteen with a racket belonging to her father, a doctor away at war in France. A model used by Maurice McLoughlin, it weighed fifteen ounces and had a 5½ inch handle. Later on, in the 1920's when many players, especially women, turned to lighter, more easily managed rackets with smaller handles, Helen continued to use a fairly heavy frame with a five-inch grip, finding it best suited to her hard driving style. At fourteen Helen became a junior member of the Berkeley Tennis Club where she was coached by William C. "Pop" Fuller, whose avocation for more than a quarter of a century was to seek out and train promising junior players in Northern California, most of them girls because he considered them more teachable. Helen Jacobs, three years younger than Helen Wills, who became one of her chief rivals, and winner of a Wimbledon title and four American championships, was another Fuller pupil.

Fuller wasn't much of a player himself, not having had a racket in his hand until he was over forty. He threw balls at his pupils instead of hitting to them with a racket because he didn't want them to copy his faulty strokes. But he was an effective and painstaking teacher who stressed the fundamentals of good stroking and footwork, and in Helen he had an apt pupil who, from the beginning, exhibited the poise and concentration on the court for which she became famous, and she worked like a Trojan, said Fuller, to improve her game. Fuller provided her with strong competition by having her play with good junior boy players, one of whom was Edward G. Chandler, who later won the National Intercollegiate Championship in 1925 and 1926 playing for the University of California. Chandler, who was valedictorian of a senior class of 2200 students and a Phi Beta Kappa, was ranked number five nationally in 1926, and with a physique and a strong all around game resembling Bill Tilden's he might have become a champion had he not chosen to give up big-time tournament tennis to attend the Harvard Law School and pursue a law career (years later he did become a national champion, winning the 45 and over senior doubles three times in the 1950's with Gerald Stratford, his old college teammate, and also the 65 and over senior singles in 1970).

Helen Wills was definitely an overachiever. She worked diligently on the court to improve her strokes, and she studied very hard so she would be sure to make her preparatory school honor roll every month. At the University of California her goal was to be elected to Phi Beta Kappa. This she achieved as a junior, a very high honor, since the great majority of members are not chosen for this honoary scholastic fraternity until they are seniors. She did acknowledge later that she had been overly concerned with gaining this honor for its own sake and not suf-ficiently with learning for the sake of really knowing something.

Helen's early progress in tennis was rapid. At fourteen, in her first tournament, she extended a leading woman player in the San Francisco Bay area to a close three-set match. The fol-lowing year, 1921, she won the Pacific Coast Junior Girls Cham-pionship and was sent by the California Tennis Association to Forest Hills where she beat a girl three years her senior in straight sets to win the National Junior Girls Championship. In 1922, now sixteen, she retained her girls' title and gained valuable experience playing in nine women's grass-court tournaments, meeting Mrs. Mallory in four of them. She won a set in each of three of these matches, but in the fourth, and most important, the final of the National Women's Singles, Mrs. Mallory won easily, 6-3, 6-1, with hard, deep driving superior to Helen's. With a strategic sense that did credit to her tender years, Helen tried to vary her game by drawing Mrs. Mallory to the net, and by herself going up to volley, but she did not yet have sufficient control and match-play experience for this to be successful. The losses to Mrs. Mallory did much to impress on Helen the value of strong accurate and steady driving as the basis for a winning game. Through rigorous practice sessions against men opponents during the off season she improved so much in this regard that in 1923, a month or so short of her eighteenth birthday, she won two singles and a doubles match in the first Wightman Cup matches to be played between the United States and Great Britain, beating the number one British player, Kathleen McKane, in straight sets. Two weeks later, she won her first National Singles Championship, trouncing Mrs. Mallory in the final, 6-2, 6-1.

These victories were accomplished in the new 14,000-seat concrete horseshoe-shaped stadium of the West Side Tennis Club. Completed in a little more than six months at a cost of $150,000, it was built with the understanding that the Club would be awarded by the USLTA one of the principal tennis events each year for the next ten years—the Davis Cup Challenge Round in 1923, the National Singles from 1924 through 1928, and either the Singles or the Davis Cup from 1929 through 1932. The structure could have been called "The stadium that Bill Tilden built," just as the Yankee Stadium, which also opened in 1923, was called "The house that Babe Ruth built," since both were needed to hold the crowds these superstars attracted.

The new West Side stadium, a dramatic symbol that tennis had become a major spectator sport, was in sharp contrast to the grandstand of the Newport, Rhode Island Casino, where the National Championships had been held from their beginning in 1881 until they were moved to Forest Hills in 1915. The Casino grandstand was acquired from the Barnum and Bailey Circus, and, according to a Newport historian, "with its round hinged seats of solid wood painted a bright vermilion, it looked rather like a great gaudy typewriter, with people scrambling about over it and finally perching on the keys." Situated on the shady side of the championship court, it was not intended for the hoi polloi, its reserved seats being occupied by Vanderbilts, Astors, Belmonts, Goelets and other privileged summer residents of the resort's palatial "cottages," for whom the annual tennis week was more of a social than a sporting event.

These personages gave the tournament a kind of ritualistic aspect, as is suggested by the following descriptive account in a 1907 issue of the *American Lawn Tennis* magazine penned by its editor, S. Wallis Merrihew, whose prose, as here, sometimes tended toward the flowery and orotund:

At Newport tradition and rule count for much. The match for the championship court is decided upon the day previous and posted upon the Casino bulletin board. Eleven is the hour set and at eleven or a little before the audience begins to assemble. Automobiles by the dozen and a few carriages roll up to the Casino entrance on Bellevue Avenue and discharge their loads of fashionable-gowned and well-groomed spectators-to-be. Through the outer green-sworded enclosure they leisurely wend their way to where the play takes place. The plain every-day courts are on either side, but the championship one is down in the far corner; the way is therefore long and the dames and damsels with their squires parade thither, stopping to chat and to exchange salutations with friends and acquaintances prior to taking their positions in the grandstand. On the other courts the play begins a little earlier. A little before eleven the players emerge, usually in pairs, from the dressing rooms and make their way to the courts. Groups of friends and admirers gather around to watch the play and to criticise and comment. By one o'clock the matches on the championship, as well as on the other courts, are usually over and the spectators disperse even more leisurely than they assembled.

But within a few years after this was written, the championships had clearly outgrown the Casino's social atmosphere and limited facilities. McLoughlin and the other young players from California, in particular, never felt at home performing before the Casino socialites, the number of entries increased so greatly—there were over two hundred in 1911—that it was difficult to get all the early-round matches run off, and worst of all, were the conditions which existed after Newport's tennis week became so popular that it attracted thousands of visitors daily. On the day of a big match many who tried to get to Newport on one of the overloaded hourly ferry trips never made it, and those who did found a paucity of seating once they got inside the Casino's sacred precincts. Even worse than trying to reach Newport or trying to get within sight of the court was getting out of the Casino. A narrow hall was the only means of egress as well as ingress, and the congestion as the exiting spectators tried to force their way through this bottleneck was almost suffocating. No such problems with tennis galleries existed at the

West Side Tennis Club. Having moved in 1913 from upper Manhattan to the site it still occupies alongside the Long Island Railroad in Forest Hills, it could accommodate without difficulty the record crowd of 12,000 that came out to see the first day's play in the 1914 Davis Cup Challenge Round, featuring Maurice McLoughlin against Norman Brookes and R. Norris Williams versus Anthony Wilding. It was also easily accessible to a large population area. Under the circumstances it was hardly surprising that the USLTA transferred the championships to the West Side Club in spite of the Newporters' strong protests.

Newport did keep its tennis week alive by instituting an invitation tournament which became one of the prime events in the grass-court circuit of tournaments leading up to the Nationals at Forest Hills. Much later in the mid 1950's through the efforts of a fourth-generation Newporter, James H. Van Alen (who later became famous for devising the Van Alen Simplified Scoring System, or VASS, in which 31 points comprise a set, and for the idea of the tie-breaker, now generally used in various forms to obviate long-drawn-out deuce sets), the Casino, whose buildings and grounds had deteriorated over the years, was refurbished and made the site of the National (later International) Lawn Tennis Hall of Fame and Tennis Museum. Now that the U. S. Open is no longer played on grass, or at Forest Hills, having been moved in 1978 to a new USLTA facility at Flushing Meadow, New York, the Casino endeavors to carry on tradition, albeit with commercial sponsorship, by holding the Hall of Fame Championships, the only American grass-court professional tournament.

Newport might never have lost the Nationals, and West Side might never have built its stadium had it not been for the persistence and untiring efforts of Julian S. Myrick, whose ambition was to make the club at Forest Hills the premier tennis center in the country, if not the world. Probably the most active and influential American tennis official of the twenties, he served a three-year term as USLTA president, and afterward in numerous other capacities, including the important chairmanship of the Davis Cup Committee and as non-playing captain of the American team that won all five Olympic Games tennis titles at Paris in 1924.

Myrick took up the game to which he became so devoted at the age of 30 in 1910 when he joined the West Side Club, at that time still located at 238th Street and Broadway. He played an important part in the Club's move to Forest Hills in 1913, and in the staging there of the 1914 United States-Australasia Davis Cup match referred to earlier. In 1914, as president of the West Side Club he led the movement which brought the National Championships to Forest Hills from Newport. After the 1920's, as a kind of elder statesman, Myrick continued to exert considerable influence on USLTA policies and programs. In his seventies, still active in tennis affairs, he accompanied the Davis Cup team captained by Billy Talbert which went to Australia in 1954 and brought back the Cup after Tony Trabert and Vic Seixas gained a 3-2 victory over the formidable team of Lew Hoad and Ken Rosewall. Talbert gave Myrick, who had provided members of the team with copies of Norman Vincent Peale's *The Power of Positive Thinking,* the credit for giving players the motivation they needed to win. Wrote Talbert in his official report of the match: "On behalf of the team I would like to thank Julian S. Myrick (Uncle Myke), USLTA representative, for his great help, fine leadership, and his positive 'will to win' which rubbed off on the team."

Myrick, whose dynamism and drive also made him highly successful in the life insurance field, regarded tennis as a commercial enterprise which could be profitable to the USLTA (he got the National Singles for the West Side Club, he said, by promising that Forest Hills would make more money than any tournament ever held at Newport, which turned out to be the case), but he was also in complete agreement with the Association's policy that tennis should remain a strictly amateur game, one which, in theory at least, if not entirely in practice, players like Bill Tilden, even though they brought big crowds to the Davis Cup and National Championships should not be allowed to benefit from financially. For this reason, and also because each regarded the other as headstrong, stubborn and opinionated, there was little love lost between Myrick and Tilden. Their mutual dislike, according to Bill, contributed to his great comeback victory over Johnston in the 1922 National Championships. When the two players changed courts with Johnston leading two sets to one and three-love in the fourth set, Myrick, who was seated in a chair alongside the umpire's stand, although even as the USLTA president there was some question as to his right to be there, smiled coldly at Bill, and said, emphasizing the word "been": "Well, Bill, it's been a great match." Bill said that he saw red, and after answering, "Yes, Mike, so far," he walked out on the court to serve, determined that he would win the match or die in the attempt, and, as has already been noted, he did the former.

To Myrick must also go a good deal of the credit for the inauguration of the Wightman Cup matches, although the idea was conceived by that grand old lady of tennis, Hazel Hotchkiss Wightman (1886-1974), the first of the women volleyers, holder of more American national championships than any other player, devoted and indefatigable teacher of tennis to many generations of boys and girls, and contributor to the development of a long line of great American women players from Helen Wills and Helen Jacobs down to almost the present.

A native Californian who grew up in Berkeley, Hazel Hotchkiss was U. S. women's champion three years in a row, in 1909, 1910, and 1911. In 1919, she married George Wightman, a proper Bostonian who later became a president of the USLTA. Her tournament tennis was somewhat restricted for several years while she became the mother of three children, but in 1919, in her thirty-third year, she won a fourth National Singles title with a 6-1, 6-2 final-round victory over Marion Zinderstein, who had eliminated Molla Mallory, the defending champion.

It was not long after this that the thought occurred to Mrs. Wightman that since men's tennis had the Davis Cup the women's game ought to have something similar. What she had in mind was an international competition on a smaller scale involving the United States, England and France, since these three countries, with the emergence of Suzanne Lenglen as the 1919 Wimbledon champion, all had strong women players. As the Davis Cup had done for the men, so the new women's competition would promote friendly rivalry and international good will as well as raise the standard of women's tennis, thus adding to its appeal.

Encouraged by Julian Myrick, who had recently become USLTA president, Mrs. Wightman went out and bought a silver cup for $300 from a Boston jewelry store on which she had engraved *Challenge Cup—Ladies Team Match,* although the cup has always been called by the name of its donor. After the USLTA received the cup, it developed that the British and French tennis associations had little or no enthusiasm for an international women's match, the principal reason being the expense involved in sending a team across the Atlantic. The Wightman Cup competition might never have come into being had it not been for the visit in the Summer of 1923 of four of England's leading players, led by Kathleen McKane, to play in the National Championships and other tournaments. Myrick and his fellow USLTA officials wanted to stage some memorable tennis event to dedicate the new Forest Hills stadium and also serve as a curtain raiser for the women's singles and the Davis Cup Challenge Round to follow. Mrs. Wightman's cup was remembered and arrangements were made pretty much on the spur of the moment with the English women to play a two-day team match against an American team consisting of Mrs. Wightman, as captain, Helen Wills, Molla Mallory and Eleanor Goss. Five singles and two doubles were to be played, which would give the English team an opportunity for more play than would be the case if the Davis Cup format of four singles and one doubles were followed. Three players would take part in the singles, the first and second on each team playing two matches against the other two, as in the Davis Cup, and the number three players playing the fifth match.

On the opening day, the matches drew 5000 spectators who were treated to a good deal in the way of pomp, fanfare and speeches, but not much in the way of a contest. The Americans won all three matches played, two singles and a doubles, and on the next day captured the three remaining singles and the second doubles, only two of the seven matches going to three sets. Although the makeup of the two teams remained almost identical, this result was almost completely reversed the following year at Wimbledon, when Great Britain won six matches to one, Mrs. Wightman and Helen Wills scoring the only American point when they won the second doubles. This home-court advantage, if that's what it was, continued to exist up through 1930, each team winning four times but only once away from home. From that time on the United States dominated the series, compiling through 1970 a lead of 35 matches to 7. With the launching by the International Lawn Tennis Federation in 1963 of the Federation Cup, a world-wide women's team competition and with the advent of open tennis a few years later, which turned all the best women players into professionals, the prestige of the Wightman Cup, like that of the Davis Cup, has been somewhat diminished, but it remains an important tennis tradition. Associated with it have been all the great names in American women's tennis from Mallory and Wills to King and Evert, and over the decades there have been many fine players among their English opponents.

The inaugural Wightman Cup match was a turning point in

Helen Wills's career. Mrs. Wightman chose her to play the number two singles instead of Eleanor Goss, who had beaten her a few days earlier in the Seabright tournament, and the fact of her selection gave her the confidence she needed to offset her youth and relative inexperience. Her confidence was also bolstered during her two singles matches by the presence of Mrs. Wightman, the two team captains being authorized to sit by the sidelines and coach their players when they changed courts. Following Mrs. Wightman's advice to "Use your head and be patient," Helen achieved her first big win in triumphing over Miss McKane, and followed the advice again two weeks later to beat Mrs. Mallory, with the loss of only three games, to win her first U. S. title.

Her one-sided defeat by a player whom she had beaten decisively the year before was so unexpected that Mrs. Mallory was convinced it was due almost entirely to Mrs. Wightman's coaching, but Mrs. Wightman would admit to no more than perhaps having accelerated Helen's development somewhat, thereby enabling her to win the championship a year or two sooner than she otherwise would have. Helen, as Mrs. Wightman had perceived, had the qualities not only to become a champion but a great one as well. She had considerable physical strength and a natural inclination to play aggressively. She had developed soundly produced strokes and the energy and determination to work hard to improve them. Her footwork and volleying, her two weakest points in the beginning, she had already greatly strengthened under Mrs. Wightman's tutelage. Best of all, she was blessed with an ideal match-play temperament. "Before a final tennis match," she once said, "I could always sleep very well and show a genuine interest in food. So I imagine my nerves must have been fairly good." She did not feel nervous during a match because she believed if she kept trying her hardest she would win. Even if she didn't win she would win another match eventually, and to think this way gave her confidence. She had phenomenal concentration because her habit was never to remember past errors but to think only of the immediate point to be played. And never was there a more disciplined athlete. She did not have to train for a tournament because she was always physically and mentally ready. Unlike Mrs. Mallory who never took training too seriously, being known to smoke and stay up late dancing during a tournament, Helen went to the other extreme, rigorously eschewing any activity, no matter how interesting or enjoyable, if she thought it might in any way keep her from playing her best tennis. For example, she did little or no reading during a tournament, believing it would weaken her eyes, a far cry from the players on the women's professional tour today, at least some of whom, we are told, pass a good deal of their time when not on the court watching television in their hotel rooms. Sometimes Helen seemed to carry her discipline to unnecessarily extreme lengths, as when on a visit to Brussels she declined an invitation to tour the battlefield of Waterloo one morning for fear it might be a little tiring and affect her play in an informal and not at all important exhibition match that afternoon.

What Helen Wills learned from Mrs. Wightman that was perhaps of greatest value to her was the importance of playing what is now called percentage tennis. During her early development she had to be reminded again and again by Mrs. Wightman to be content during a baseline driving exchange with keeping the ball in play and deep in her opponent's court instead of prematurely trying to end the point with a risky put-away shot, and, when off balance and out of position, to play a safe shot—a high deep lob, for instance, if her opponent had hit a forcing shot and taken the net—instead of going for a winner.

A capable doubles player, although never a great one, which seems to be true of most great singles players, Helen got a full sense of the importance of strategy and tactics by playing doubles with Mrs. Wightman, who was the team tactician, crying out when necessary such commands as "Yours!" and "Run, Helen!" During the years they played together, Mrs. Wightman, despite her age, was probably the best volleyer in women's tennis, with the possible exception of Suzanne Lenglen. She could half-volley, volley, and smash from so-called "no-man's land" in mid-court as well as from close to the net, a skill she had developed because she could not rely on her relatively weak chopped groundstrokes to win for her and thus sought to get to the net at every opportunity. With other doubles partners, some of them very good and all of them younger than Mrs. Wightman, Helen lost Wightman Cup and other matches, but never did she lose with the redoubtable Hazel. Together they won two Wightman Cup matches, in 1924 and 1927, the Olympic and Wimbledon Championships, in 1924, and two U. S. Championships, in 1924 and 1928, the second when Mrs. Wightman was forty-two years old.

Besides profiting from Mrs. Wightman's coaching, Helen was always alert to make experience her teacher. Her loss to Miss McKane in the 1924 Wimbledon final, for example, impressed on her the importance of not losing one's concentration in a match, not to allow oneself to be confused and distracted, as she was, by the excitement and enthusiasm of the gallery as Miss McKane rallied to win the second set after being on the brink of defeat. Helen had her powers of concentration tested again soon after Wimbledon when she played in the Olympic Games in Paris. Held in Colombes, an unattractive manufacturing district on the edge of Paris, the conditions, for the tennis players at least, left much to be desired. The courts, which were not laid down until the last minute and were dry and dusty as a result, were close by the big stadium where the track and field events were held, and often from it as players were contesting an important point would come the crack of a starter's pistol or a roar from the crowd. From most of the courts there was an uninterrupted view of the surrounding field, on which could be seen wrestlers, gymnasts and other athletes either competing or practicing, and in the tennis stands a little old woman vendor hawked oranges, bananas and ice cream. The officiating, said R. Norris Williams, who won the mixed doubles with Mrs. Wightman, was the worst he had ever seen. He confessed to feeling on edge all the time he was playing, but none of this, he said, bothered his partner, nor did it appear to bother Helen, who may have taken Mrs. Wightman as her model. Or she may have already begun to employ a device she said later she found helpful in maintaining her concentration. It was to say over and over again to herself, "Every shot," which meant she would try to make each shot her best, to think only of what she needed to do to make it so, such as watching the ball, using the right footwork and being sure to follow through on her drives.

In the final of the singles against Didi Vlasto, a strong young French player who had put out Miss McKane (Lenglen, who was still ill, did not enter), Helen had to play against a much more demonstrative and vociferous gallery than at Wimbledon. Her strategy, since she had an opponent who had a very strong forehand and tried to run around her backhand, was to hit a succession of looping, high-bounding shots wide to the backhand side to open up the court for a faster and usually winning shot wide to the forehand. Because these tactics slowed down the play considerably, they evoked much booing, whistling and foot-stamping, but Helen, unperturbed, persisted in employing them to win 6-2, 6-2.

To win Olympic championships in singles and in doubles with Mrs. Wightman was an exhilarating experience for Helen. So was sightseeing in Paris after the Olympics were over, so much so that on her last day there happening to pass a shop on the boulevard with a window display of beautiful shoes, on impulse she went in and bought fifteen pairs. The purchase was made with some college scholarship prize money she had brought with her and which she originally intended to buy some books with as a souvenir of her visit. And perhaps still under the influence of Paris on the boat coming back to America she was sure she had fallen in love with a college professor who was a fellow passenger. There was no time for romance, however, while she was performing the "hat trick" of winning three U. S. championships in singles, doubles and mixed doubles, or after she returned to California to begin her sophomore year in college. The extra-curricular activities enjoyed by most students were not for Helen, her days being taken up almost entirely with classes and tennis practice and her evenings with study. Before she settled down to this routine, Helen's California friends and admirers honored her with a "Helen Wills Day" and presented her with a handsome Buick automobile, the California Tennis Association approving the gift even though she was an amateur. Helen thus made history of sorts by being the only woman player to receive such an award until the days of open tennis and women's professional play a half century later, when it became possible for a Billie Jean King or a Chris Evert Lloyd now and then to pick up a car along with her prize money for winning a major tournament.

Although Helen did not go abroad again in 1925, she faced as strong opposition as the year before. The British Wightman Cup team, led by Kathleen McKane, played in the National Championships, and other entrants included Molla Mallory, Mary K. Browne, and May Sutton Bundy, all former champions, and the formidable Elizabeth Ryan, the Californian who lived mostly in England, the winner of six Wimbledon doubles championships and runner-up in singles to Lenglen in 1922. Helen avenged her two losses in England the previous year by winning both her Wightman Cup matches, defeating Joan Fry, who earlier in the Summer had been runner-up to Lenglen at Wimbledon, 6-0, 7-5, and pulling out a long, hard-fought match against

McKane, 6-1, 1-6, 9-7. In the Championship she repeated her victories over both these opponents, defeating Fry in the quarter-final round and McKane in the final to win her third title in a row. It was Helen's fourth win over Miss McKane in the six times they had met, and it pretty well established her superiority over the player who had given Suzanne Lenglen her closest opposition, but who nevertheless had always been beaten quite decisively. Helen did lose the first set of the final to Miss McKane, but she had looked as devastating as a Lenglen in winning the second and third sets in only twenty-four minutes, 6-0, 6-2. How would she be able to do, it was natural for Helen to wonder, and many tennis fans wondered too, against the great Frenchwoman, who had lost only five games in five matches this same year at Wimbledon? The answer would come the next year when the two would play a match which remained unrivalled in tennis history in the amount of publicity it received until the famous, or infamous, as some have called it, battle of the sexes in Houston's Astrodome in 1973 when Bobby Riggs suffered an ignominious defeat at the hands of Billie Jean King.

CHAPTER EIGHT

THE MATCH OF THE DECADE

After her all-victorious tennis season of 1925, Helen Wills did not enroll for her senior year at the University of California. Having realized her ambition of making Phi Beta Kappa, and being still only twenty, she felt she could afford to postpone her graduation for a year. What she wanted to do, she told her parents, was to play during the winter and spring on the French Riviera, where she would be able to compete against the best women players of England and Europe and especially against Suzanne Lenglen. It took considerable persuading, but Helen's mother, who always accompanied her on tennis tours, was at last prevailed on to make the trip, it being agreed that besides playing tennis, Helen, being a serious student of drawing and painting, would be able to further her education in this respect by visiting art galleries and museums in France and Italy.

A news story from Berkeley late in November announcing that Helen and her mother would leave for France early in January evoked the comment from Allison Danzig, the New York *Times* tennis writer, that "the long awaited battle of the century of the tennis courts at last threatens to take place now that Helen Wills is going to France to pursue the elusive muse of art and the still more elusive artistic queen of the courts." Tennis fans, he added, had been demanding such a meeting, and this was the only way for it to come about, since Suzanne had vowed after her unhappy visit in 1921 never to return to America.

A precedent for Helen's trip had been set by Molla Mallory three years earlier when she had gone abroad in March of 1923 to beard Lenglen in her Riviera lair. Despite the 6-2, 6-0 defeat Suzanne had dealt her in their 1922 Wimbledon final, Molla persisted in believing she could once again bludgeon Suzanne into submission with powerful driving, as she had done at Forest Hills in 1921. Because Suzanne, as was her custom, confined her

Riviera play mostly to doubles, they met only once in singles, at Nice, but that was enough to leave no doubt as to Suzanne's complete superiority. Poor Molla lost 6-0, 6-0, winning only eight points in the first set and eleven in the second. She could get to deuce in only two games, and in neither of these could she get to advantage, thus going the whole match without having a single game point. Suzanne was just too accurate and steady, running Molla all over the court, getting back almost all of her best shots, keeping the ball on Molla's backhand much of the time, and waiting for the error that rarely failed to come. A victory for Suzanne could have been predicted, the slow court and heavier balls than Molla was used to, being in her favor, but not such an utter disaster. No wonder that Molla refused to talk to reporters about the match on her return home.

Resisting the challenge of a Helen Wills would surely be a far different matter for Suzanne, and her reactions to the news of Helen's proposed "invasion," as the press termed it, were of course sought out. Interviewed in Nice early in December, she said she was "greatly pleased" to learn that Helen would be playing on the Riviera since it would give a great boost to the interest in tennis, and, she might have added, to the revenue the clubs holding the tournaments would take in. As for herself, her tournament schedule had been arranged before she knew Helen was coming, and it would be the same one she had followed in the past. She expected to play singles in only two tournaments, one at Nice and the other at Cannes. In the other Riviera tournaments she would play only women's and mixed doubles. And apparently anticipating that her very limited singles play might evoke unfavorable criticism, as indeed it did later, she added to the reporter: "Please tell your American journalist friends not to say I quit or that I am afraid to meet her if I should not be entered in some tournament in which Miss Wills takes part."

Meanwhile, back in California, Helen was engaging in daily practice sessions, working hard to make her backhand as strong an offensive weapon as her forehand. A few days after Christmas she and her mother departed Berkeley for New York City, where during a brief stay she picked up eighteen rackets and three eyeshades at the A. G. Spalding and Brothers store and had a practice session at the Brooklyn Heights Casino Club indoor court, the first time she had ever played indoors, there being no indoor courts in California. Arriving in Paris after a stormy Atlantic crossing, Helen was greeted by a crowd of more than a thousand

French tennis fans, a small army of reporters, and an official welcoming committee headed by Pierre Gillou, the secretary of the French Tennis Federation, whose speech of welcome was interrupted by Jean Borotra, who came hurtling through the crowd to grasp Helen's hand with Gallic fervor. Borotra, the Wimbledon and French champion in 1924 and runner-up for these titles to his countryman, René Lacoste in 1925, had a penchant for flamboyant actions of this sort, both off and on the court.

It was scarcely more than a day after Helen's arrival in Cannes, where she planned to stay while playing in several tournaments there and at other resorts within motoring distance, that reporters following her activities were able to describe the initial meeting—though only an off-court one, to be sure—between her and Suzanne. Helen had gone to a club run by one Frank Gould thinking she might be able to see Suzanne playing in a tournament there, and as she was on the point of leaving after watching Henri Cochet, the French Davis Cup player, win a match, Suzanne came sweeping out of the clubhouse, vivacious as always, and greeted her effusively. Suzanne, it was reported, wore a Parisian coutourier's dress in pastel blue under a fur coat, three ropes of pearls, beige stockings, suede shoes and white kid gloves. Helen had on a simple cloth coat, a little green cloche hat, and black patent leather shoes.

When the two would meet on the court was another matter. Both were entered in the Hotel Metropole tournament, beginning the next day, but Helen only in singles and Suzanne only in women's and mixed doubles. Helen's entry came as a surprise since she had told reporters in Paris that she planned to practice for two weeks before playing her first tournament so that she would be fully accustomed to the slow clay courts and to the softer, heavier balls than she was used to at home. Her matches in the Metropole tournament drew packed galleries, as large as any ever to watch tennis at Cannes. She needed more play clearly to reach her best form, her service and groundstrokes being erratic at times, and she appeared a little self-conscious under the gaze of Suzanne and her parents who were among the spectators, but she was able to win a hard-fought final match, 6-4, 7-5, from Didi Vlasto, whom she had defeated for the Olympic Games title two years earlier. "She has made much progress," was Suzanne's verdict after the match.

Mlle. Vlasto, after losing to Helen, declared herself too

exhausted to partner Suzanne in the women's doubles final to follow, and Jacques Brugnon, with whom Suzanne had reached the mixed-doubles final, having had to play a hard five-set match in winning the men's final, also felt incapable of playing another match. Deprived of seeing the great Lenglen play and of comparing her performance with Helen's, the crowd staged a miniature riot and demanded its money back. The incident was a demonstration of what a tremendous gate attraction Suzanne was. She had become so much of a Riviera institution that, as John Tunis, an American sports writer who knew both tennis and the Riviera well, put it, to make a visit to the Riviera without seeing Suzanne play would be like a visit to Rome without seeing St. Peter's.

The next week Helen won the Gallia tournament, also in Cannes, in which Suzanne did not even play doubles, her explanation being that she had to say home in Nice to take care of her convalescent father who was recovering from a serious illness. Helen beat Helene Contoslavos, an attractive and graceful young Greek girl living in France, who had carried her to two 6-4 sets in the Metropole tournament, fairly easily in the final, but her play was adversely affected by the inordinate amount of publicity her activities were receiving, and she was disturbed by reports from New York that she might be violating the player-writer rule and thereby jeopardizing her amateur standing. Helen did have a contract with a news syndicate, the proceeds of which were being used to defray the expenses of her European trip, but she was not writing news stories reporting her current tournament play, which would have been in violation of the rule, but instead a series of articles on playing the game, including one on the style of Suzanne Lenglen.

During the Gallia tournament it was reported that Helen was not sure whether she would play singles the following week in the tournament at Suzanne's home club in Nice, the reason being that instead of the quite lively ball being used in the Gallia tournament, which was well suited to Helen's hard-driving game, a comparatively "dead" English ball favored by Suzanne would be used. Suzanne also was vague as to whether she would play at Nice, and there was, in addition, a report that Helen had said she might not play in the Carlton Club tournament at Cannes, which followed Nice, if the English ball were used there also. All this gave cause for wondering if a Lenglen-Wills match would ever really come about. "Suzanne and Helen," commented one reporter cynically, "probably will meet in the Olympic Games in Amsterdam in 1928." (Events gave this remark an added irony, tennis being dropped from the 1928 Olympics, and thereafter, when the Olympic Committee and the International Lawn Tennis Federation could not agree on which body should have the authority to define amateur standards, and on certain other issues.)

Suzanne entered the singles at Nice, withdrew after being criticized for appearing to wait until she was sure Helen would be playing only in the doubles, and then, after much frantic pleading on the part of the tournament officials, was prevailed on to reenter. Originally, there seemed every likelihood that the Nice club, of which Suzanne's father was the secretary, would have the honor, as well as reaping the considerable financial benefit, of staging the much-anticipated Lenglen-Wills match. Why this now would not come about was attributed in the press to shady Riviera tennis politics. The Riviera syndicate of club and hotel operators, it was alleged, believing that Lenglen would have a walk-over, didn't want the match to take place so early in the season and possibly destroy a good deal of Helen's box-office value. This they wanted her to retain for at least several more of the tournaments in which she would be playing, and thus the adoption of the English ball for the Nice tournament to discourage her from playing in the singles. Tournaments on the Riviera were not sporting events, but crassly commercial operations, and Helen Wills, a naive young girl, was being exploited as a resort attraction to draw crowds and enrich tournament promoters. *L'Auto,* France's leading sports magazine, called on the French Tennis Federation to take the matter in hand and arrange for a Lenglen-Wills match to be played at a club which would apply the gate receipts to supporting the development of promising young French tennis players.

Suzanne and Helen did finally face each other across the net in the Nice mixed doubles final, Suzanne and Count Umberto de Morpurgo of Italy defeating Helen and Charles Aeschlimann, the Swiss champion, 6-1, 6-2. Suzanne was a much better doubles player than Helen, and she and her partner, with whom she often played, also had much the better teamwork. Helen won a serve at love to give her team a 2-1 lead in the second set, aceing Suzanne twice in the process, but instead of keeping up the pressure, she and Aeschlimann resorted to defensive play and their opponents ran out the match with their strong net play.

Playing only mixed doubles at Nice gave Helen time for other activities besides tennis. She and her mother moved from the Hotel Gallia to an ocean-front suite at the more fashionable Hotel Carlton which had been occupied not long before by French Premier Briand while attending an international conference. She had fittings for a wardrobe designed for her by a famous Paris dressmaker who had a branch in Cannes, one of the garments being a rose-colored coat trimmed with fur which was quite as spectacular as anything Suzanne was in the habit of wearing. She went tea dancing one afternoon with a young man from San Francisco visiting the Riviera with his mother. His name was Frederick Moody, and he would become Helen's husband four years later. At dancing, however, Helen proved no rival for Suzanne, who had danced the previous night away until 2 A.M. at the Restaurant Ambassadeur. Because Helen had an agreement not to pose for cameramen or give interviews to reporters other than those connected with the International News Service, for whom she had contracted to write her articles, she spent a good deal of time dodging the other representatives of the press who were overrunning Cannes. In her efforts to avoid them she was assisted by Fred Moody and several other young male American admirers, whom the newsmen called Helen's Boy Scouts.

If most of the reporters found Helen less than cooperative, they all had something to write about when it was announced that both she and Suzanne had entered the singles in the Carlton Club tournament at Cannes the following week. The Carlton Club was run by Albert Burke, the French professional champion, and his two brothers, Edmund and Tom. Their father, Tom, senior, had come to the Riviera from Dublin in the eighteen nineties and was the first tennis professional in France. Suzanne may have decided to play singles at Cannes, whether the powers said to be managing Riviera tennis wanted her to or not, because it was now being said repeatedly that she was afraid of Helen and would never play her. Also the surroundings at Cannes would be almost as familiar and the conditions as favorable to her as at her home club in Nice, the Burkes being good friends with whom she frequently practiced.

The atmosphere in which the now almost certain Lenglen-Wills match was awaited became much like that surrounding a heavyweight championship prize fight. There was heavy betting, a Greek syndicate operating the baccarat tables in the Cannes and Deauville casinos announcing it had 5,000,000 francs to wager on Lenglen against 1,000,000 on Wills.   The odds ran as high as 7-1 against Helen, and the most frequent bet was that she would not win five games in two sets.   Tickets for the match, which normally would have been fifty francs, were priced at three hundred francs, the equivalent of almost $12.00, and some were scalped for as much as fifty dollars each.   In comparison, the highest priced ticket to see Tilden and Johnston in a Forest Hills final or playing in the Davis Cup Challenge Round cost three dollars.

The gate receipts promised to be the largest ever for a Riviera tournament, with the Burkes expanding the seating around the center court or, what the French called, *le court d'honneur,* to accommodate a thousand more spectators than the two thousand Suzanne usually drew when she played a singles final.   The Burkes were also dickering to sell the exclusive rights to film the match for a reported $100,000. This was protested by both Helen and Suzanne and by four big American newsreel companies who would be discriminated against thereby. When Suzanne threated not to play unless all the newsreel people were treated equally, the Burkes tried to extract from them a combined bid amounting to that offered for the exclusive rights.   Failing in this, they then tried to negotiate individual fees without success, and at last gave up altogether, their representative saying: "We were just desirous that the Burke family make a little money, but we desist in the interest of sport." The Burkes may have desisted also because the matter had come under investigation by the French Tennis Association.

Amidst all this sideline furor, the tournament got underway, Helen and Suzanne each winning three matches without the loss of a game.   Helen's third opponent was Mlle. St. Omer Roy, a promising young player who usually managed to win two or three games from Lenglen. After her match with Helen, she said: "No player in the world can hit balls so hard in the corner of the court.   I have played Suzanne many times but have never felt the manifest inferiority I experienced today before Miss Wills."   Helen then lost two games to Eileen Bennett, a very good young English player, to reach the semi-finals, while Suzanne won for a fourth time in two love sets, saying afterward: "If I am going to lose a game in this tournament, they will have to get it out of me at the point of a gun."

There was additional time for suspense and tension to

mount when the tournament had to be carried over into a second week because of three days of rain. The delay was regarded as advantageous to Suzanne, who was said to need the rest, but not to Helen, who needed the practice and who instead was forced to keep to her hotel room where she did some sketching from a window overlooking rain-soaked palm trees and the foggy Mediterranean. At long last, however, it was determined that the big match would come off when, in the semi-finals, Helen defeated Didi Vlasto, 6-1, 6-4, and Suzanne beat Helene Contoslavos, 6-0, 6-2. Both the losers played under some strain because, as they told reporters, they couldn't help thinking that should either pull an upset there would be few people who would appreciate it. Actually, neither match was won as decisively as the scores would suggest. Helen was down love-four in the second set, and Suzanne, who had never before lost a game to Contoslavos, fell behind love-two. Helen showed no sign of being nervous when Vlasto got her big lead, but Suzanne appeared agitated in the second set, and after the match complained of a linesman's decisions and of having a pain in her side.

That evening, her match with Suzanne being scheduled for the next morning at eleven, Helen declined an invitation to a dinner party and dined alone, her mother having a cold that Helen was taking every precaution not to catch. After consuming a substantial meal of soup, filet mignon, potatoes, peas, and ice cream and cake, she retired early and slept soundly through the night. In the meantime, Suzanne, it was reported later, had what was described as "a tearful dispute" with her parents at their villa in Nice. Her ailing father, perhaps recalling her unhappy visit to America without him, had ordered her not to play because he was not well enough to go with her to Cannes and coach her from the sidelines. Suzanne, saying if she did so she would be called a quitter, refused to obey. The dispute was said to have been so intense that Suzanne, when her father had told her in the morning as she was getting ready to leave for the match that she would lose, had stormed out of the villa saying she would never return.

Tuesday, February 17, 1926, the day of the match, dawned bright and fair, a perfect one for tennis. "Heaven," said Helen, "looked after the weather, and the Burkes after the arrangements, which were partly good and partly bad." This was a more charitable view than that taken by most of the writers who covered the match, John Tunis, for example, calling the conditions under which the match was staged "atrocious." For these the Burkes were not altogether at fault, their club and its environs leaving a great deal to be desired as the setting for a match which more appropriately should have taken place at Wimbledon or Forest Hills. Situated on a narrow back street behind the towering Carlton Hotel, the club covered just enough ground to accommodate a small one-room clubhouse and six courts, alongside one of which, the center court, was a small wooden grandstand. Bordering the club on the opposite side was an even narrower alley, and on the other two sides were the backs of several buildings, including a garage, a small factory from which came the sound of buzzing machinery, and several small villas.

By nine o'clock, two hours before the match was scheduled to begin, the street outside the club was jammed with people waiting to buy tickets. When they learned there would be no seats for most of them because of the large advance ticket sale, many, along with others who presumably did not have the price of a ticket, found various vantage points from which to view the match. The more agile climbed tall eucalyptus trees overlooking the court, from which the police, on orders from the tournament committee tried unsuccessfully to dislodge them. Others paid a fee to an enterprising householder for a place at one of his second-story windows which provided a view of the court. When his windows were filled he sold space in his attic from which one could look out through an opening in the roof, the tiles of the roof being removable. His neighbors whose windows and roofs also overlooked the court, or some part of it, followed his example, and the roof of the garage provided space for additional spectators. Perhaps a thousand persons, a third as many as were seated inside, looked down on the match from these positions, and several hundred more crowded together in the narrow alley, pressing against a fence which barred their view of the court but where they could hear and noisily cheer the proceedings.

Inside there was much noise and confusion as the stands, on which some carpenters were still hammering, filled early. The most distinguished spectators had seats down in front reserved for them, and included an ex-king of Portugal, princes, dukes, counts, maharajas, and various other persons with and without titles. Much like at a Hollywood premier in the golden days of the movies, they were hailed and commented on by the crowd as they proceeded to their seats. No thought was given to providing a press section for the sports writers and the other writers commissioned to do special pieces on the match, such as Blasco Ibanez, the popular novelist. They sat crowded in with the other spectators with no room for note pads or typewriters except on their knees. When the players made their appearance shortly after eleven they were given a noisy demonstration. While they posed for the photographers, Suzanne smiled and blew kisses to the crowd. Helen was her usual undemonstrative self, "as emotional," wrote John Tunis, "as a Methodist minister at a funeral." There was also a marked contrast in attire. The bandeau Suzanne always wore was a bright pink, and over her white silk dress with its short skirt that "barely kissed the knee from above," as one journalist poetically put it, she wore a white coat with a white fur collar. Helen had on her eyeshade, as always, and wore her customary middy blouse and calf-length pleated skirt and a blue cardigan sweater. Along with all the other publicity accorded the match there had even been a minor controversy as to whether Helen's longer skirt length might not give Lenglen some advantage. Asked to give his opinion on the matter, former U. S. Ambassador to Belgium Brand Whitlock opined that Helen's skirt was "decently long."

Because their impartiality might be questioned, no Americans or Frenchmen were asked to serve as officials for the match. Commander George Hillyard, R. N. of the All England Club, who had for several years called the final of the ladies' singles at Wimbledon, was the umpire, and most of the linesmen were his countrymen, one being Cyril Tolley, a former British Open golf champion. These gentlemen, even though Helen appeared to be the victim of two or three bad calls during the match, no doubt endeavored to be fair to Helen, but since Suzanne, the perennial Wimbledon champion, was as much a heroine to most of the British spectators as she was to the French, they could perhaps be regarded as something less than truly neutral judges. This and the fact that probably something like nine-tenths of the crowd, both within and without, favored Suzanne didn't particularly bother Helen. She had experienced this sort of situation before while playing abroad, although not in such extreme form, and was able to look on it philosophically as something to be expected.

Even after the officials had taken their places and the players had begun their warm-up rallying, the crowd, both inside and outsdie, continued to be noisy and unruly. Suzanne was

on the side of the court against whose backstop the crowd of
people in the alley was pressing, and she shouted angry orders
for them to desist lest they push it over.   The crowd inside gave
little heed to a request for less noise addressed to them in English
by Commander Hillyard, who also called the score in English instead of French.   Charles Aeschlimann, the Swiss champion,
stood up to ask in both French and English for quiet and order,
but with no more success.   This was obviously not the usual
more or less decorous tennis gallery but one more like a World
Team Tennis crowd today.   Shouts, vulgar remarks, loud cheering and much commotion, both within and without the club
enclosure, would continue until the end of the match, with
Helen appearing to be a good deal less affected by these conditions than Suzanne.

Serving the first game, Suzanne won it at love by out-
steadying Helen from the baseline.   Helen held serve after being
down 15-40, and then broke Suzanne to lead 2-1, hitting hard
and deep to Suzanne's backhand.   Momentarily surprised by the
pace of Helen's shots, Suzanne counter-attacked by running
Helen back and forth along the baseline and then hitting a
sharply-angled short ball to the sideline.   This pulled Helen out
of position, enabling Suzanne to then pass her down the other
line.   With these tactics she took two love games in succession
and then got to 30-love on Helen's serve for a total of ten straight
points.   Helen then won two points, but Suzanne took the next
two for a 4-2 lead.   Helen broke Suzanne in the next game, but
Suzanne easily broke back with the loss of one point, and then
held service, Helen again getting only one point, for the set, 6-3.

Up to the eighth game this first set looked as if it could go
to either player, and although Suzanne did win the last two
games decisively, the effort needed to win the set had clearly
put a considerable strain on her nerves and powers of endurance.
She had several times indicated her annonyance with the noisy
gallery and the commotion made by the persons outside, and
when she changed courts to begin the second set paused at the
umpire's chair to sip cognac.

Serving very strongly in the first game of the second set,
Helen won it at love.   She was now hitting her groundstrokes
harder than ever, and Suzanne, who appeared to let down somewhat, was put on the defensive and fell behind 3-1, with Helen's
serve to come.   But now when she was in a position to gain a
commanding 4-1 lead, instead of continuing to hit out strongly,

Helen began to play more cautiously, trying to outsteady
Suzanne rather than to force her into error, thereby violating a
cardinal law of tennis strategy that one should never change a
winning game.   With Helen playing less aggressively, Suzanne,
who had taken more brandy, began winning most of the rallies,
losing only one point in the fifth game and one more in the sixth
to tie the score at 3-all.

In the seventh game, usually the most crucial one in a set,
Helen was down 15-40 on her serve, but she was once again
hitting out with great power and finally held after four deuces
to go ahead 4-3.   In the next game, Helen would have been at
break point, 30-40, on Suzanne's serve, had not Cyril Tolley
failed to call a Lenglen drive out that was clearly several inches
over the baseline.   The gallery on Helen's side of the court shouted "Out" in a chorus, and Helen, who had made no effort to return the ball, asked Tolley if he was sure it had been in.   When
he told her "yes" she threw up her hands in a despairing gesture.
Suzanne won the next point and the game when Helen returned
weakly into the net, but recovering her poise, Helen served and
drove well in the next game to win it for 5-4.   Needing only to
break Suzanne's serve for the set, which she had demonstrated
she could do by playing aggressively, Helen for the second time
grew cautious and tried to outsteady Suzanne.   The result was
a series of long rallies in the next two games, with Suzanne losing
only two points to go ahead 6-5.   Although visibly fatigued,
Suzanne lost only one more in the next game to get to 40-15,
giving her two match points.   Suzanne then hit what looked like
a point-winning serve, but Helen got it back, and there followed
a long, suspenseful driving exchange, with Helen finally getting
a short return which she hit with all the power of her forehand
to Suzanne's forehand corner.   The ball appeared to hit squarely
on the line, but there was a call of "Out."   Suzanne ran to the
net to accept Helen's congratulatory handshake, and the spectators poured out of the stands onto the court.   It was not Lord
Charles Hope, the line judge, however, who had made the call but
someone in the stands.   Making his way with difficulty through
the persons crowding the court to the umpire's chair, he informed Commander Hillyard of this fact, and that the shot had
definitely hit the line.

It took some minutes to make the gallery understand what
had happened, to restore order, and to resume the match.   It was
certainly not a happy occurrence for Suzanne, who had shown

signs of being under considerable physical and mental strain in the second set, and now she appeared to falter as she lost her second match point to Helen and then two more points to make the score 6-all. Nevertheless, she came back strongly to get to love-forty on Helen's serve, only to have Helen fight back to deuce and then to her advantage. One more point for Helen would have given her a 7-6 lead, but Suzanne held firm, winning the next three points and the game. Serving the next game, Suzanne reached 30-15, but Helen won the next two, and needed only one more to break serve and again tie the score. Suzanne took the points to get to match point, but then served a double fault, something she did so rarely it appeared that with victory in her grasp she had finally succumbed to nerves. Such was not the case. Reaching her fourth match point after a Wills' error, she won it after an exchange of drives by drawing Helen out of position and then hitting a clean winner.

With a cry of joy, Suzanne threw her racket high in the air and, after a second handshake from Helen, slumped onto a chair by the umpire's stand, where she fell to weeping as she was surrounded by a throng of well-wishers, some of whom pressed bouquets and baskets of flowers upon her. Outside those encircling Suzanne stood Helen, whose feelings at this moment she later described as follows: "So interested was I in the hubbub and general mass of gesticulating people that I did not become aware, until some moments later, that I was standing entirely alone on the court. Turning my thoughts upon myself, I found that I did not feel so sad as I really should have, but at the same time I began to feel rather overcome at being in the middle of the court by myself. Then suddenly a young man vaulted over the balustrade from the grandstand at the side of the court, and came over to me. He said, 'You played awfully well.' It was Mr. Moody."

Helen had indeed played well and had been unlucky not to win the second set. It was probably her tactics and not her strokes that cost her the match. Molla Mallory, asked to comment on its outcome, said she had almost been on the point of sending Helen a cable telling her "to knock the cover off the ball. That was what Tilden told me to do when I played Suzanne in 1921. I was inspired by his advice, and I played every shot for a placement. That is the only way you can beat Suzanne." Had Helen continued to pound the ball after gaining the lead twice in the second set instead of letting up and trying to beat

Suzanne at her own game, she might have been able to demoralize Suzanne as Molla had done.

As for Suzanne, her victory demonstrated her courage as well as her greatness as a match player. For years no one had come anywhere near challenging her as Helen had in the second set. During it the realization may have come to her that she was no longer invincible. Such an awareness does not seem to have occurred to her mother, however, who greeted her after the match, not with congratulations, but with "How could you lose so many games to Helen Wills? How can we explain to papa?" Replied Suzanne, "There will come a time when I cannot explain losses of games, or even of sets, matches, and championships."

A couple of hours later Suzanne and Helen took the court again to play the doubles final. Suzanne had the stronger partner in Didi Vlasto, and this was fortunate for her since she was obviously still tired from the singles, even though she had spent the interval between matches resting in bed at the Carlton. The doubles couldn't help being something of an anticlimax, but it was just as close and almost as exciting as the singles, Suzanne's side winning 6-4, 7-5. Helen was the best player on the court, while Suzanne came near to collapse in the second set and fainted after its conclusion. Suzanne was still the queen of the courts, but in repelling her brilliant young challenger, she had been made to suffer a great ordeal in order to achieve a great triumph.

The hard-serving, net-rushing Californian R. Lindley Murray
defeated Bill Tilden in the final round of the
1918 U. S. championship.
Courtesy of International Tennis Hall of Fame at the Newport Casino

R. Norris Williams, a brilliant shot maker, was the U. S. singles
champion in 1914 and 1916, and was national doubles
champion with Vincent Richards in 1925 and 1926.
Courtesy of International Tennis Hall of Fame at the Newport Casino

Brian I. C. Norton of South Africa, who was unlucky not
to beat Bill Tilden in the Wimbledon final of 1921.
Courtesy of *World Tennis*

Bill Tilden had several different forehands—flat, slice, topspin.
Here he is hitting a fairly flat shot with an Eastern grip.
Courtesy of William M. Fischer Lawn Tennis Collection,
St. John's University

Billy Johnston, unlike Tilden, always hit the same forehand,
a heavily topped shot using a Western grip.
Courtesy of *World Tennis*

The Tilden backhand drive is rated as one of the best
in the history of the game.
Courtesy of William M. Fischer Lawn Tennis Collection,
St. John's University

Billy Johnston's backhand lacked the power of Tilden's,
but it was a well-produced, consistent stroke.
Courtesy of William M. Fischer Lawn Tennis Collection,
St. John's University

Vincent Richards executes a half volley. He was a master
at making this shot, perhaps the most difficult in tennis.
Courtesy of United States Tennis Association

The Australian Norman Brookes was Wimbledon champion
in 1907 and 1914. At age 43 he lost hard-fought matches to
Tilden and Johnston when the U. S. won the Davis Cup in 1920.
Courtesy of William M. Fischer Lawn Tennis Collection,
St. John's University

Tilden and Johnston winning the Davis Cup doubles from
Brookes and Wilding, Auckland, New Zealand, 1920.
Courtesy of United States Tennis Association

President Harding with the 1921 U. S. Davis Cup team
before an exhibition match played on the White House grounds.
Julian S. Myrick, USLTA president is second from the left.
The four players (L. to R.) are Watson Washburn, Wallace
Johnson, R. Norris Williams and William T. Tildon.
Courtesy of United States Tennis Association

The American Olympic tennis team of 1924 won all five tennis events. (L. to R., seated) Edith Sigourney, Eleanor Goss, Marion Zinderstein Jessup, Hazel Hotchkiss Wightman, Helen Wills, Lillian Scharman. (standing) Watson Washburn, Dr. Sumner Hardy (President, California LTA), Vincent Richards, Frank Hunter, R. Norris Williams, Julian Myrick.

The 1928 U. S. Davis Cup team sails for Europe aboard the *Ile de France.* (L. to R.) Wilbur F. Coen, Jr., George Lott, Samuel Peacock (manager), Bill Tilden, John Hennessey.
Courtesy of United States Tennis Association

René Lacoste was the greatest of the Four Musketeers
(the others were Jean Borotra, Henri Cochet and Jacques
Brugnon) who won the Davis Cup for France from the U. S.
in 1927 and dominated tennis for the rest of the decade.
Courtesy of International Tennis Hall of Fame at the Newport Casino

Henri Cochet, the most talented of the French Musketeers,
executes a low backhand volley, one of his favorite shots.
Courtesy of *World Tennis*

Suzanne Lenglen was noted for her acrobatic volleying.
Courtesy of Keystone Press Agency, Ltd.

Dorothea Lambert Chambers
was many times a Wimbledon champion and
runner-up to the youthful Suzanne Lenglen in 1919.
Courtesy of United States Tennis Association

Molla Bjurstedt Mallory was eight times U. S. women's
champion. Her backhand was dependable but it was
her powerful forehand that brought her victory.
Courtesy of William M. Fischer Lawn Tennis Collection,
St. John's University

Helen Wills in 1921
when she won her first national girls' championship.
Courtesy of United States Tennis Association

Helen Wills in 1929.
Courtesy of United States Tennis Association

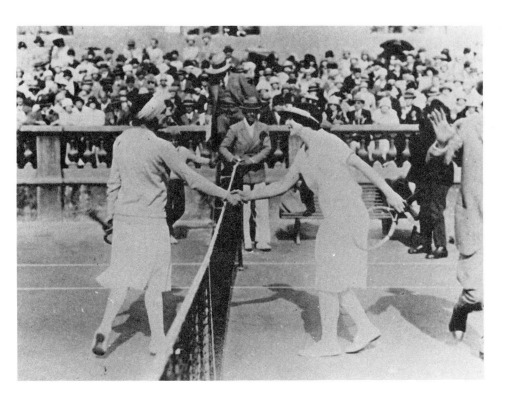

Suzanne Lenglen is congratulated by Helen Wills
after winning their match at Cannes, 1926.
Courtesy of Wide World Photos

Helen Jacobs, the other Helen of American tennis
in the late 1920's and 1930's, pioneered in wearing shorts.
Courtesy of United States Tennis Association

Tilden and Richards won the U. S. Professional Doubles
Championship in 1945, twenty-seven years after they won
their first U. S. doubles title, when Richards was only fifteen.

Courtesy of United States Tennis Association

(L. to R.) R. Norris Williams, Mary K. Browne, Hazel Hotchkiss
Wightman and Maurice McLoughlin were inducted into the
International Tennis Hall of Fame at Newport, Rhode Island in
1957. James H. Van Alen, founder of the Hall, is on the right.
Johnston and Mallory were inducted in 1958, Tilden and Helen
Wills Moody in 1959, and Vincent Richards in 1961. Lacoste,
Borotra, Cochet and Brugnon were inducted in 1976.
Courtesy of International Tennis Hall of Fame at the Newport Casino

René Lacoste with the steel racket of his design, 1965.
Courtesy of *Business Week*

CHAPTER NINE

SUZANNE TURNS PROFESSIONAL

That Helen and Suzanne would play each other again seemed assured when both announced the day after their match that they would enter the singles in a second tournament at Nice, scheduled for the second week in March. Then a couple of days later came another announcement from the unpredictable Suzanne. She would not play at Nice after all, her physician having forbidden her to play another "hectic" match for four months because her nerves would not stand it. Helen, she added, would still have a chance to play her in the Hard Court Championships in Paris and at Wimbledon, where the conditions would also be more favorable to Helen than those on the Riviera.

Now as popular a Riviera attraction as Suzanne, Helen went about winning more tournaments in her usual business-like manner. Hawkers in Nice sold replicas of her eyeshade, and a record crowd watched her play at Monte Carlo. She literally supplanted Suzanne as queen of Riviera tennis, the latter having abdicated by going to the Lake Como region in Italy to rest and recuperate, and also, said some unsympathetic American journalists, because fear of Helen had driven her there.

Except for her loss to Suzanne, Helen's Riviera campaign was a resounding success. In seventy days of play she defeated some forty opponents in singles alone, a number of them several times over, and in the nine tournaments she played in she won eight singles trophies. The match with Suzanne had strengthened her confidence, and her play got even better. There was no question but that she would be a most dangerous rival to Suzanne at Paris and Wimbledon.

After her last Riviera tournament late in March, Helen spent several weeks in Italy playing exhibitions and sightseeing in Milan, Florence and Rome. Seeing the Colosseum by moonlight in the company of Fred Moody, she felt a cold breath of night air that made her shiver, but fortunately she did not contract the Roman Fever that carried off the American heroine of Henry James's *Daisy Miller* after a similar visit. A few weeks later in Paris she was not so fortunate, suffering an acute attack of appendicitis after winning a first-round match in the Hard Court Championships. The surgery was successful and Helen's recovery rapid, but instead of the eagerly-awaited Lenglen-Wills final match that Parisian fans had looked forward to, they saw Mary K. Browne, three times an American champion over a decade earlier, lose to Suzanne, 6-1, 6-0, bringing to four the total number of games lost by Suzanne in the entire tournament.

Helen's operation, it turned out, precluded any further championship play for the season. A spectator at Wimbledon, she was accorded the rare honor of being invited to sit in the royal box. Dressed more fashionably than formerly, as a result of her stay in Paris, where she had also had her hair bobbed, she was seen freqeuntly in the company of Fred Moody, and since she was wearing a pearl ring on her engagement finger, it was rumored that they were engaged, which Helen denied. After returning to America she thought herself ready to resume tournament play, but losses to Elizabeth Ryan and Molla Mallory convinced her that her physical condition was not good enough for strenuous match play, and she went home to Berkeley instead of defending her U. S. singles title.

The Wimbledon of 1926 was a Jubilee tournament in celebration of the fiftieth anniversary of this now famous international sporting event. In keeping with the British fondness for tradition and ceremony, it was observed by the presentation on the Centre Court by the King and Queen of commemorative medals to thirty-two former men and women champions, and by an exhibition doubles match in which, somewhat surprisingly, the supposedly invincible team of Lenglen and Ryan were defeated by Mrs. Godfree (the former Kathleen McKane) and Kea Bouman, the Dutch champion, 8-6, this last being a portent of further unhappy things to come for Suzanne.

Parenthetically, King George V and Queen Mary were quite keen tennis enthusiasts and did much better throughout the years in attending Wimbledon than has their granddaughter, Queen Elizabeth II. Well-known as a horse-racing buff, she has made only three visits to Wimbledon in a quarter of a century, the third in 1977, fifteen years after her second, being almost obligatory since this was the year not only of the twenty-fifth anniversary of her reign, during which she made numerous public appearances, but also that of Wimbledon's Centenary. Appropriately, the Queen, who attended on the second Friday to watch the final of the ladies' singles, found herself at its conclusion presenting the winner's trophy to Virginia Wade, an Englishwoman who won her first singles championship after sixteen years of trying.

Suzanne, who the previous year had won the triple Wimbledon crown of singles, doubles and mixed doubles for the third time, was, of course, once again the star attraction in 1926, but the show she put on for the Wimbledon fans turned out to be of quite a different sort than they had expected. In her first-round match, Suzanne found herself again opposed by Mary K. Browne, who dealt something of a blow to her ego by winning five games, one more than Suzanne had lost in the whole of the 1925 tournament in singles. Suzanne was also drawn to play her first-round doubles against Miss Browne, who was paired with Miss Ryan, Suzanne having been ordered by the French Tennis Federation to give up her long-standing partnership with Ryan to form an all-French team with Didi Vlasto.

This important match was scheduled for 4:30 P.M. on the day following Suzanne's singles with Miss Browne, but it seems that she did not learn until almost noon of that day, while still in her London hotel, that she had been scheduled belatedly to play a second-round singles at 2 P.M. against Mrs. Dewhurst, a lesser English player unlikely to give her much, if any, competition. Suzanne, who described herself as suffering from a "horrid" cold, sent a message to the Wimbledon referee, saying she had a doctor's appointment and could not play at 2 P.M., but would arrive in ample time for her doubles. Apparently the message was never received, and to make matters worse, the King and Queen, having been informed of Suzanne's schedule, said they would have an early lunch and arrive in time to see her play singles. When Suzanne arrived at 3:30, believing herself an hour early for her match, the King and Queen had departed after receiving profuse apologies from the president of the All England Club and Jean Borotra for Suzanne's nonappearance. Severely rebuked by the tournament committee, Suzanne went into hysterics and secluded herself in the ladies' dressing room. The only man known to have entered such sacred precincts, Borotra, who was her partner in the mixed doubles, was sent in blindfolded and led by Didi Vlasto to entreat her to take the court for her doubles, but nothing he could say would persuade her to play that day.

To disappoint British royalty was a heinous crime in the eyes of their subjects, and when Suzanne, her composure somewhat restored, left the Wimbledon grounds by motor car a couple of hours later, she was hissed and booed by some of the crowd who witnessed her departure. In reporting the incident, the London papers subjected Suzanne to much unfavorable comment. *The Morning Post,* under the caption, "A Spoiled Darling," said she should have been defaulted, an action the tournament committee had considered but decided against after lengthy discussion. Other papers contrasted her with Miss Ryan, who was also scheduled to play singles before the doubles and had done so, and they also recalled for their readers how Suzanne had walked off the court when she played Mrs. Mallory at Forest Hills in 1921.

The doubles match, played the next day, was also an unhappy experience for Suzanne, she and Didi Vlasto losing to Miss Ryan and Miss Browne after having three match points in the second set. While playing she showed signs of being unwell and was reported to have fainted afterward in the dressing room. The next day she won her singles from Mrs. Dewhrust, and the day after that a mixed doubles match with Borotra, but on both occasions the Centre Court gallery was cold and unfriendly, despite some clowning antics on Borotra's part in an effort to win it over. Affected adversely by this and by the attacks on her in the press, she declared herself too unwell to play and withdrew from the tournament altogether.

A few days later Suzanne also gave ill health as the reason why she would be unable to appear for her presentation to the Queen at the Court of St. James, an event scheduled for the week after Wimbledon, and for which Suzanne had brought along a diamond-trimmed dress from Paris. Her illness was described as a severe attack of neuritis for which she was taking electrical treatments and having to wear her arm in a sling. Like some of the reports in the past dealing with the state of Suzanne's health, this one had the appearance of being somewhat exaggerated, since she was well enough to attend Wimbledon toward the end of its second week where, sitting in the royal box, but on the opposite side from Queen Mary, she saw Jacques Brugnon, one of her favorite mixed-doubles partners, lose an exciting five-set semi-final singles match, after having five match points, to the Californian Howard Kinsey, who later lost in the final to Borotra.

With both Suzanne and Helen Wills out of the tournament, the women's singles final was won in three close sets by the durable and steady Kitty McKane Godfree over the more talented but not as consistent Lili de Alvarez, a Spanish girl who was again the Wimbledon runner-up in 1927 and 1928, both times to Helen Wills. In her tennis style a kind of feminine R. Norris Williams, Senorita de Alvarez liked to hit daring shots of great speed and pace off rising balls and this accounted for her frequent unsteadiness. As beautiful as Helen Wills and as vivacious and graceful on the court as Lenglen she might have become an equally great player had not her temperament and her interest in other sports made her unwilling to devote herself as seriously to the game as they did. Of their Wimbledon matches, which produced some of the most brilliant women's stroking ever seen on the Centre Court, Helen Wills said: "There would have been little hope of winning from her except that about halfway through the set she would try to make a winner when the risk was too great. Then the demands of match play would suddenly become wearisome to her."

Suzanne Lenglen's unhappy experience at Wimbledon could have had something to do with her turning professional only a little more than a month later. This came about through the efforts of C. C. ("Cash and Carry") Pyle, an enterprising American promoter, who had begun negotiations with Suzanne while the Riviera season was still in progress. The preceding fall Pyle had signed Harold "Red" Grange, a star University of Illinois football halfback to a contract to be managed by him and to play for the Chicago Bears professional team. Grange, who was in his senior year, left school after his final college game and played with the Bears in a series of late-season games. At this time professional games, in contrast to the big college games, seldom drew more than ten to fifteen thousand fans, but against the New York Giants, Grange played before a crowd of 70,000, and games in Washington, Columbus and other cities, despite some bitterly cold weather, brought out fans in record-breaking numbers. Professional football needed a Red Grange just as tennis needed a Bill Tilden to develop into a big-time spectator sport.

As with Grange, Pyle saw in Suzanne another sports superstar with great drawing power, this having been demonstrated, as Damon Runyon, the journalist and popular author of short stories about New York underworld characters, pointed out to him, by the tremendous amount of publicity given to the Lenglen-Wills match. Assuming that Suzanne might balk at giving up her amateur standing, he sent a representative to Nice to offer her two choices: $250,000 to turn professional, or $100,000 and a guarantee that she would be able to remain an amateur. The second offer, which Suzanne and her father tentatively accepted, was a scheme of Pyle's to bring Suzanne to America to play exhibitions as an amateur and remunerate her through the device of giving her a contract to make a movie. The USLTA soon indicated, however, that it would not grant sanctions for any matches Pyle might arrange between Suzanne and American amateurs at which admission was charged, and Suzanne, apparently having concluded she could not tour America for money without becoming a professional, disavowed any intention of going there, saying: "I am perfectly content with existence in Europe and have no desire to go to a country where many people deliberately malign and misinterpret my very nervous Latin temperament."

Three months later, however, early in August, Suzanne exercising her prerogative as a woman to change her mind, did turn professional. It was not reluctance to give up her amateur standing, said Pyle of his negotiations with Suzanne, which took place at Pourville near Dieppe where she was summering, that caused her at first to hesitate, but her fear that the stigma of being a professional would cause her to lose friends and social position, but in the end Pyle's argument that money never hurt anyone's social standing, supported by a substantial advance cash payment to bind their bargain, prevailed. "The nightmare is over," Suzanne told an Associated Press correspondent. "I have escaped from bondage and slavery. No one can order me about any longer to play tournaments for the benefit of club owners. Now I will be able to make some money, have some fun, and see the world."

There were those who were not convinced, as her statement seemed to suggest, that this was the first opportunity Suzanne had been given to reap some pecuniary benefit from her tennis. Suspecting that Suzanne had been playing for something more than mere love of the game, they were inclined to view her turning professional with some cynicism, as did one John Benson, who published the following little piece of light verse on the subject in a Detroit newspaper:

Suzanne, you shock us, you really truly knock us
    By being a professional in sport!
To think they're paying a girl like you for playing,
    Who long have been your family's support!

My goodness, dearie aren't you a little leery
    Of being a professional like Grange?
When you have changed your rating can you keep people waiting
    Won't customers feel it's a little strange?

Suzanne, start thinking! There is no use in blinking
    A point on which a lady must make sure.
The course that you are taking, will you at that be making
    As much as when you were an amateur?

Suzanne's action evoked varied reactions. The president of the French Tennis Federation called it "deplorable." The official organ of the British Lawn Tennis Association, in an obvious reference to the Wimbledon contretemps involving Suzanne, said that although she had been a great ornament to the amateur game her leaving it was no loss, because her temperatment and long supremacy had made her almost impossibly difficult to deal with by tournament officials. "Lenglen Turned Pro for Love of Luxury" was the headline of a New York *Times* article, which said that the current depressed value of the franc plus Suzanne's expensive tastes had influenced her to succumb to Pyle's offer. The *Times* also commented that Suzanne's exhibitions would be good for the game from an instructional point of view and should also make it more popular. Most of the American players and tennis officials who expressed an opinion were skeptical about the tour and its chances for success, and everyone wondered, since the USLTA had said it would not approve matches between amateurs and Suzanne, whom she would play against. Frank Menke, a sports columnist for the King Features Syndicate, predicted that the USLTA would change its mind. He wrote: "It's about 1000 to 1 that the USLTA won't bar amateurs from mingling with Suzanne for the very elaborate reason that to do so would knock about $50,000 right out of the grasping hand of the USLTA. But in allowing Wills, Mallory, Tilden and others to play, it will demand a huge portion of the gate receipts. So after all, there will be only one radical difference between the 'holier-than-thou' USLTA and the promotional Mr. Pyle. He will 'cut' part of his end with Suzanne, whereas the USLTA will keep ALL its share for itself." Menke was proved wrong, but his comment is worth quoting because it is indicative of the lack of esteem in which the Association was held in some quarters and, particularly, by some members of the sports-writing fraternity.

Pyle would not say who Suzanne's opponents would be except that they would be "world-renowned" players. He denied having a "business arrangement," as had been rumored, with any member of the U. S. Davis Cup team, but he did say he would approach several leading American players after the Challenge Round and National Singles Championships were completed. Pyle needed most of all a strong American woman to match against Suzanne, and his prospects for securing one did not seem very good. In Berkeley, Helen Wills, who had withdrawn from competitive tennis for the season as a result of her operation, said that she definitely would not turn professional. Certainly there was very little reason why she would want to. She didn't need the money, she was still very young with the prospect of a brilliant career before her, and despite her already impressive record she had not yet achieved her ambition to win at Wimbledon. Molla Mallory had played amateur tennis too long and successfully and enjoyed it and the social life that went along with it too much to want to give it up, and having a wealthy husband there was no financial pressure for her to do so. It would, she declared, take an offer of $500,000 to induce her to consider turning pro, and even then she probably wouldn't.

Fortunately for Pyle, the situation was different with the one other former American champion who would make a suitable opponent, indeed an excellent one, since she had, as has been noted, given Suzanne a good match in singles at Wimbledon and had actually defeated her in doubles. Early in September, Mary K. Browne, who said she had spent ten days coming to a decision, signed with Pyle for a reported $50,000 to tour with Suzanne, giving as her reasons that she needed the money and felt it more honest to play tennis as a professional, the second statement being one which would be repeated by more than one later amateur champion who turned professional. Miss Browne, having reached the age of thirty, may well have felt also that she had gained all the amateur honors she could hope for. An excellent golfer as well as tennis player, she had the unusual distinction, in addition to winning three national women's singles and doubles titles in a row back in 1912, 1913, and 1914, of being the runner-up in 1921 in both the national women's golf and tennis championships.

That Pyle intended to include men players in the Lenglen touring troupe was indicated a few days later when he announced he had signed Paul Feret, the fourth-ranking player of France. Feret, who had beaten Vincent Richards during the summer in a France-United States team match, issued a statement saying it was better for players to accept openly their share of tournament receipts rather than "secret advantages which both giver and receiver deny afterward." He did not know, he added, of a single leading tournament player, man or woman, who could be called a true amateur. He had not, however, turned pro for the money since he had an income that enabled him to live comfortably. His young wife had recently died, and he had accepted Pyle's offer to tour with Suzanne believing that the travel and diversion it would offer might help him better to overcome his feeling of loss.

But Pyle obviously needed another man player in addition to Feret, one of at least equal reputation, who would serve both as an opponent in a men's singles and as a fourth in mixed doubles. It was rumored that Pyle had signed two other Frenchmen, but, if so, they were surely not any of the four French Davis Cup team members—Lacoste, Cochet, Borotra and Brugnon. The French had lost to the United States in the Challenge Round, but Lacoste had beaten Tilden, and later in the U. S. Singles Championship, all four members of the American team—Tilden, Johnston, Richards and Williams—had gone down before the French players, with Lacoste beating Borotra for the title. Confident of success, Lacoste and his teammates were firmly committed to again seeking to wrest the Cup from the United States in 1927.

There also seemed little chance of Pyle being able to induce an American Davis Cup player to turn professional. Tilden was said to have told Pyle he would refuse any offer the promoter might make. Johnston said that he had turned down an offer of $50,000 from Pyle. Williams, now past his prime as a singles player, had always regarded his tennis as purely an avocation, and it seemed most unlikely that Vincent Richards, now the main hope for continued American tennis supremacy, with Tilden and Johnston aging, would seriously consider giving up his amateur status.

Pyle, however, had a surprise up his sleeve, and, clever showman that he was, revealed it in dramatic fashion. When Suzanne arrived in New York on the liner *Paris* toward the end of September, Pyle had "Red" Grange on hand for publicity purposes to welcome her at the pier, and the next evening gave a banquet in her honor for two hundred persons in the grand dining room of the *Paris,* with Big Bill Edwards, the president of the American Professional Football League, as toastmaster. There were two vacant seats at the speaker's tale, and just before the diners were served they learned who would occupy them when Vincent Richards and his attractive young wiife made a stage-like entrance, and Richards announced he had signed with Pyle to make a four-month tour with Suzanne.

Why did Richards turn professional at the age of twenty-three when he had not yet in all probability reached his peak and had good reason to believe he could establish himself as the leading American amateur and perhaps even a world champion? He had been the only American to reach the semi-finals of the National Singles, Tilden and Johnston both losing in the quarter-finals, and he had beaten Tilden with such frequency during the season that he could almost surely count on being ranked number one nationally, an honor actually accorded him by the ranking committee of the USLTA, but later denied him at the Association's annual meeting when it was voted not to include in the ranking list any player who was a professional prior to the time the rankings were submitted to the delegates for approval. This was a small-minded and punitive action, and Bill Tilden, although he became its beneficiary by being moved up from the number two position, to his credit protested it strongly, pointing out that, besides being manifestly unfair to Richards, who had not turned professional until after the conclusion of the regular season of which the rankings were a record, to drop him would render that record inaccurate and incomplete.

"I had to turn professional in justice to myself and my wife," Richards told the guests at the Lenglen dinner. He did not say how much money he had been guaranteed by Pyle, but it was probably in the neighborhood of $35,000, a not inconsiderable sum at that time for a young man who seems to have found that subsisting as an amateur expected by the USLTA to play for love of the game and not for profit was not the easiest thing in the world to do. For the first time in tennis history, a young player like Richards had the opportunity to capitalize openly and far more substantially than he could as an amateur on his tennis skills and reputation. Professional tennis, as Pyle had been enthusiastically proclaiming, could well be an idea whose time had come, and Richards, in company with the great Lenglen, would be a pioneer in its development.

In addition to Richards, Pyle augmented his troupe with two more men players so he could add a men's doubles to his card and also use them to fill in on occasion in singles and mixed doubles. One was Harvey Snodgrass of Los Angeles, a former high-ranking amateur recently turned teaching professional, who played a strong serve and volley game, the other was Howard Kinsey, the chop-stroke artist and doubles specialist from San Francisco. Kinsey was national doubles champion with his brother Robert in 1924, was ranked fourth nationally that year behind Tilden, Johnson and Richards, and on an overseas tour with Richards during the summer of 1926 distinguished himself by winning the International Hard Court Doubles with him and, as already noted, by being runner-up to Borotra at Wimbledon.

Professional tennis made its debut in the United States on Saturday evening, October 9, 1926, when Pyle's troupe opened its tour in New York City's Madison Square Garden before a crowd of 13,000, who paid $1.50 to $5.50 for seats. Suzanne beat Mary K. Browne, 6-1, 6-1, Richards defeated Feret, 6-3, 6-4, and the spectators were also treated to two sets of doubles, Lenglen and Richards defeating Browne and Kinsey, 6-2, and Richards and Snodgrass beating Feret and Kinsey by the same score. The USLTA, although it did not go so far as to urge its members to boycott the event, did forbid any of them to serve as officials. There were some bad calls by the inexperienced linesmen Pyle had to recruit, but in all other respects the proceedings, according to Allison Danzig, who gave them full coverage in the New York *Times,* were highly successful. The big crowd appeared to consist, for the most part, of real tennis fans, and they were highly appreciative of the play of Lenglen, who was in excellent form, and of her fellow-players as well, all the matches, said Danzig, being as competitive and hard-fought as if they were in a tournament rather than merely being exhibitions. One of the most enthusiastic and approving spectators was Bill Tilden, who, when introduced along with other dignitaries in attendance, got a big hand from the crowd.

Suzanne and company played again the next night in the

Garden before 5000, with Bill Tilden again in attendance, and, during the next ten days, before crowds averaging better than this figure in Toronto, Baltimore, Boston, and Philadelphia. Paid attendance for the first six matches, according to Pyle, amounted to almost $85,000, and he estimated that at this rate the total gross receipts for the tour would come to around $700,000. The four-month, forty-city tour took the troupe to other large cities in October and November—Montreal, Buffalo, Cleveland, Pittsburgh, Columbus, and Chicago. December saw them in the Pacific Northwest and California, and January in Cuba, Florida, and elsewhere in the Southeast. Back in the Northeast in February, after matches in New Haven, Newark, and Brooklyn, the tour ended in Providence on February 15, and Suzanne sailed for home a few days later.

Playing Suzanne over and over again made Mary K. Browne, she said later, a much better player than she had been before, but even so she could not win a single one of their matches, and in only two did she take a set, although she was several times within a point of winning another. She remained a good loser, however, and there was some consolation for her in that whenever she forced Suzanne to a close set Pyle gave her a $100 bonus. Richards also dominated the other men players in singles, but in doubles the teams could be more evenly matched, and Lenglen and Richards now and then found themselves on the losing side. Critics of the tour liked to maintain that because they were exhibitions and because it was almost a foregone conclusion that Lenglen and Richards would always be the singles winners the matches necessarily lacked the interest of tournament play. What they failed to mention was that Pyle's troupe besides putting Lenglen on view, which would seem to have provided interest enough, gave the great majority of the thousands who saw it perform their first experience of what top-flight tennis was like.

Financially, the tour was by no means the failure those who took a skeptical or antagonistic attitude toward professional tennis had predicted or hoped for, Pyle reporting the gross receipts, including royalties for advertising, as $500,000. With her guarantee and percentage of the gate receipts, Suzanne earned $100,000, Mary K. Browne and Richards about $35,000 each, and the others players $10,000 to $20,000. Pyle himself profited to the extent of $75,000. Edward C. Potter, a tennis historian, in his *Kings of the Court,* calls these figures "grossly exaggerated," but he gives no evidence for this except to say that Howard Kinsey later sued Pyle to collect on a note the promoter had given him. One feels that had Lenglen not received the sum Pyle said she did she would most certainly have made that fact known. It was evident that USLTA officials did not want to believe that Pyle's venture could have been successful, and Potter appears to reflect this Establishment view, one which, rather interestingly, has been perpetuated in a 1977 advertisement for the Virginia Slims Women's Tennis Circuit, which not only called the Lenglen tour a "resounding failure" but also inadvertently reversed an illustration of Lenglen, who, of course, was right-handed, making her appear to be left-handed. So much for truth and accuracy in advertising!

Shortly before Suzanne's departure from the United States, late in February, Pyle announced that he had no plans for another tennis tour, his reason being that the player's financial demands, especially Suzanne's, were too great. A second tour would also need not only Lenglen but almost certainly, if it were to be successful, a new star or stars to go along with her, and these apparently being impossible for Pyle to obtain except at an exorbitant cost, if he could obtain them at all, he turned to other promotions. The most notable of these was a transcontinental marathon, nicknamed the "bunion derby," in 1928, with 55 out of 199 runners who had started from Los Angeles finishing 3422 miles and 84 days later in Madison Square Garden. Fifteen million persons, it was estimated, saw the runners, and Pyle took in enough revenue from contestants' entry fees, advertising, and civic groups anxious to have his caravan pass through their towns to cover his expenses and turn a tidy profit. A second marathon the next year, this time from New York to Los Angeles, and with 274 runners, collapsed before the finish, leaving Pyle heavily in debt. Undismayed, he later recouped his fortunes with a "Believe It or Not" concession at the Century of Progress Fair in Chicago. Pyle, who died in 1939 at the age of 56, in some of his less respectable promotions, recalls the old-time American pitchman and hustler, but he deserves a place in American sports history for the impetus he gave to professional football and tennis through his promotions of Grange and Lenglen.

After returning home, Suzanne, having put herself under the management of Baldwin M. Baldwin, an aspiring young promoter with a millionaire father, whom she had met in California, announced that after a European tour she would make a second American one. She had enjoyed America greatly, she told French reporters, and felt she had done much to stimulate tennis interest there. The galleries had been enthusiastic and appreciative, the California climate was particularly delightful, and, despite prohibition, she and her mother had had as much in the way of alcoholic beverages to drink, except in the Middle West, as they were accustomed to having at home.

More tours did not, however, materialize. Baldwin found that he could sign no European amateurs with crowd-attracting reputations without guaranteeing them impossibly large sums and long-term contracts. Plans to have Suzanne play extensively on the Riviera and to tour in Germany and other countries were abandoned. She did play a brief series of exhibitions in London in July, but this was the end of her career as a touring professional. Although she played little from then on, she did keep up her interest in tennis and for several years during the 1930's was the director of a government-sponsored tennis school.

Helen Jacobs tells a story of how, while she was playing in the French Championships in 1933, Suzanne volunteered to give her a lesson in tennis tactics. Still the idol of the French, Suzanne attracted a large number of spectators from the stadium where Borotra was playing to the outside court where she rallied with Helen for an hour and a half. The two concentrated, at Suzanne's suggestion, on drilling Helen, who was the current American champion, in hitting the kind of short, sharply-angled shots Suzanne had employed in defeating the now Helen Wills Moody at Cannes seven years earlier. "Helen," said Suzanne, "does not run quickly up and back," and if Helen Jacobs could master the short-angled shot, she would have a better chance of successfully defending her title against Mrs. Moody, as she would probably be called upon to do later that summer at Forest Hills. Helen Jacobs, who was more than willing to learn having lost to the other Helen five times in straight sets, found Suzanne amazingly accurate and consistent, never once committing what was for Suzanne the worst of tennis crimes—hitting the ball into the net.

Her health never of the best, Suzanne died at 39 of pernicious anemia. As befitted a national sports heroine she was given a semi-state funeral and awarded the Legion of Honor posthumously. Jean Borotra delivered the funeral oration, and flowers from persons and tennis clubs from all over the world filled several automobiles in the funeral procession. She lived long enough to see the professional tennis tour, of which she had been the pioneer, become a regular annual occurrence, with such great champions as Tilden, Vines, Cochet, Perry, and Budge relinquishing their amateur status during the 1930's to follow her lead, as did Kramer, Gonzales, Laver, and other amateur champions later on before open tennis became a reality in 1968 and tennis became a professional game.

CHAPTER TEN

THE FOUR MUSKETEERS

Suzanne Lenglen was not the only glory of French tennis during the 1920's. Her exploits were matched, if not surpassed, by her four compatriots: René Lacoste, Jean Borotra, Henri Cochet, and Jacques Brugnon. Called the "Four Musketeers" (It was Henry W. Slocum, Jr., the national champion in 1888 and 1889, and later a prominent tennis official, and not, as might be supposed, a sports-writer, who first so referred to them at a USLTA dinner in their honor, having in mind Alexandre Dumas' classic tale of the dashing D'Artagnan and his three comrades—Athos, Porthos, and Aramis—all Musketers in the service of the French King), the quartet won the Davis Cup six straight years between 1927 and 1932, defeating the United States five times and Great Britain once.

Although a Frenchman, Yvon Petra, won at Winbledon in 1946, France has had no players since their day to compare with Borotra, Cochet, and Lacoste. For six years, beginning in 1924, they made the Wimbledon singles final an all-French affair, except in 1926, when Borotra beat the American Howard Kinsey. Borotra defeated Lacoste in 1924, Lacoste turned the tables on Borotra in 1925, Borotra lost in 1927 to Cochet, who lost to Lacoste in 1928 and won from Borotra in 1929. Brugnon, although he won no major singles championships, was seven times a Wimbledon doubles finalist, winning the title twice with Cochet and twice with Borotra. The Musketeers' six Wimbledon singles in a row is a record for non-English players, the United States and Australia tieing for second with five straight. Five Americans, beginning with Jack Kramer, won from 1947 through 1951, and between them Rod Laver (1968, 1969) and John Newcombe (1967, 1970, 1971) accounted for five in a row. Also , since then, Bjorn Borg has won five consecutive Wilbledons. In 1976, the four Musketeers, all still living, were inducted into the International Tennis Hall of Fame, the only non-Americans up to that time to be so honored except for the Englishman Fred Perry, and at the Wimbledon Centenary ceremony in 1977, Borotra (age 79), Cochet (76), and Lacoste (72) received commemorative medals as former singles winners, and Brugnon (82), as did Elizabeth Ryan (85), received a medal for "representing all the doubles champions." They were also present (except for Brugnon who died in March, 1978) to receive the tributes of their own countrymen at the fiftieth anniversary ceremonies held in conjunction with the French Open Championships at Stade Roland Garros, which was built for the Musketeers' 1928 defense of the Davis Cup after they had won it from the United States.

Although France had no players before the advent of the Musketeers who were of their caliber, tennis had become a well-established sport in that country before the turn of the century. British players like the Renshaw brothers, both Wimbledon champions, brought tennis to the Riviera, a court being laid out at the Hotel Beau Site in Cannes as early as 1875. The first French national championship was held in 1891, and France was a challenger for the Davis Cup as early as 1904, a competition begun in 1900, and in which only the United States and Great Britain had previously participated. Three outstanding pre-World War I French players were Max Decugis, André Gobert, and William H. Laurentz. Decugis was French singles champion eight times between 1903 and 1914, and with Gobert won the Wimbledon doubles in 1911. Gobert also won the Olympic singles in 1912, and had some good wins at Wimbledon, one being over the Australian Gerald Patterson. Laurentz, who died young of pneumonia, when only sixteen defeated the great Anthony Wilding and won the World Hard Court Championship in 1920.

Jacques "Toto" Brugnon, born in Paris in 1895, and the oldest of the Musketeers, although his singles play was not on a level with that of the other three, had a special talent for doubles. Like the Americans George Lott and John Van Ryn, two other outstanding doubles players during the late Twenties and early Thirties, he had a fine topspin forehand return of serve which was so acutely angled and dipped so sharply after it crossed the net that it often evoked an error or a weak return from the incoming server. His backhand was less dangerous, but his anticipation was so good and he was so quick of foot that he could usually run around it to make a forehand return. His serve and overhead were forceful and consistent, and he was a fine volleyer. He and Lacoste made a formidable team, but it was when he partnered either Borotra or Cochet that his talent for setting up shots for them to volley or smash away became most evident. Brugnon was also Lenglen's favorite mixed doubles partner.

Three years younger than Brugnon, Jean Borotra was born in Biarritz in 1898. Slender and of medium height like Brugnon, but without the latter's moustache and with sharper, more angular features, he was known as the "Bounding Basque," because of his dynamic play and the beret he wore in all his matches. Borotra did not begin to play tennis until he was a young lieutenant in the army, but he came to the game with sharp reflexes and considerable racket dexterity developed through playing the Basque game of pelota, from which Jai Alai was derived. Borotra's service and groundstrokes were not particularly strong, or at all graceful, being made with a somewhat cramped and jerky motion, but they were adequate to get him to the net, which he sought at every opportunity. There, with his great agility and keen anticipation, he would dive to make winning volleys off his opponent's passing shots, or leap high in the air to kill lobs with spectacular overhead smashes. In a day when the footfault rule was more stringent than now, it was not infrequently alleged that Borotra was able to get to the net so quickly behind his serve by frequently committing with impunity such violations as jumping off the ground and swinging his back foot over the baseline before his racket made contact with the ball.

Borotra's acrobatic, net-rushing style of play required the expenditure of a great deal of energy, and though he no doubt would have been happier playing today when best of three set matches are more often the rule than best of five, and a tie breaker prevents a set from going on interminably, he was expert at pacing himself and conserving his strength in long matches. An intelligent player with a fine sense of tactics, he was also a master gamesman who, through slowing down the play, if not stalling outright, and through other tricks such as feigning utter exhaustion or declaring himself hopelessly beaten by an opponent far too good for him, often succeeded in breaking an opponent's concentration or lulling him into a false sense of security, whereupon Borotra would launch a furious net attack that would frequently bring him victory.

Borotra was both a showman and a show-off, par excellence. He was a great gallery favorite, although not so to his opponents, especially Bill Tilden, who said that Borotra annoyed and irritated him more than any other player he ever met. Bill may have disliked Borotra not only because of his sportsmanship which bordered on the questionable but also because Borotra was an even better actor on the court than Bill. Borotra was an energetic and hardworking businessman, a salesman of gasoline pumps and related equipment, as well as tennis player—his business and tennis travels in 1926, for instance, resulted in his spending 187 nights in sleeping cars and staterooms—and he would commute to Wimbledon and other British tournaments by airplane from Paris, often making a dramatic appearance just in time for his match after changing into his tennis clothes in a taxi on the way from the airport. Duncan Macaulay, for a number of years the All England Club secretary and a referee of many English provincial tournaments, has described how Borotra, competing in the Midland Counties Championship at Edgbaston, "generally enlivened the proceedings by arriving by air on Tuesday and being prepared to play three or four rounds running Wednesday to get level. Naturally this was a great thrill for the crowd."

Borotra's longevity as a tournament player, like that of such later-day players as Pancho Gonzales, Gardnar Mulloy, and Ken Rosewall, was amazing. Long after his three compatriots stopped playing competitive tennis, Borotra was still at it, playing Davis Cup matches as late as 1947, when he was in his fiftieth year. Borotra has been credited in his old age with having invented the game of half-court tennis singles played on half the doubles court, the center service line (and its imaginary extension to the baseline) and the doubles alley line being the boundaries. It makes a good game not just for older players and very young ones who have difficulty covering the whole singles court, but for anyone wanting to improve his accuracy.

In contrast to the volatile, extroverted Borotra, Henri Cochet was reserved and almost taciturn. Born in 1901 in Lyons, he became a ball boy at the local tennis club managed by his father and was playing tennis regularly by the time he was ten. He began to play in tournaments after the war, and by 1922 had become one of the leading players of Europe by virtue of final-round victories over Borotra in both the World's Covered Court Championship at St. Moritz and the French Hard Court Championship, and also by winning the World's Hard Court Championship that year at Brussels.

Whereas Borotra did most of his playing at the net and Lacoste almost all of his in the backcourt, Cochet did much of his in the middle of the court, the so-called "no-man's land" a player is supposed to avoid, taking the ball on the rise and using the half-volley deliberately as an attacking shot rather than as the involuntary and semi-defensive one that it is for most players. Cochet could do this successfully because he used a short back-swing and because his touch and timing were so good. Although he was rather short of stature, it was difficult to lob over him since his low volleying was so good that he could play far enough back to cover the deepest lobs and dispatch them with his power-ful overhead. A marvelously gifted player whose strokes were made so easily and effortlessly that they did not appear as good as they really were, he could be a little lazy and nonchalant sometimes in his matches and lose to almost anyone if he was off form. Laziness also seems to have kept him for several years from working to improve a relatively weak serve and backhand. Finally overcoming his procrastination in this regard, he de-veloped in the late twenties into as great a player as Borotra or Lacoste, some said even greater.

Born in 1905, Jean-René Lacoste, the youngest of the Musketeers, did not begin playing tennis until he was sixteen. His father, a wealthy automobile manufacturer, wanted him to go into business, but acceded to the son's request that he be per-mitted to concentrate on tennis for a period of no longer than five years—which proved to be sufficient—in an effort to make himself a champion. Of medium height and with dark hair, an olive complexion, and a rather large nose, he did not have a par-ticularly strong physique and at times his health was none too good, but he worked diligently to improve his game, studying books on tennis, being coached by the famous French profes-sional Darsonval, grooving his groundstrokes by hitting against a wall or using a ball-throwing machine of his own invention, and keeping notebooks with comments on the strengths and weaknesses of his tournament opponents and how to play them. Bill Tilden liked to point to Lacoste as a good example of his strongly felt belief that champions were the result of long hard work, although it took Lacoste only about half as long as it did Bill to make himself one.

Lacoste had none of the Gallic dash of Borotra, and he lacked the natural talent and grace of Cochet, but his ground-strokes, made with a Continental grip, were smooth and classic in their execution and were so consistent and accurate that his play was often described as machinelike. Lacoste could serve, volley, and smash adequately, but it was from the baseline that he won his matches, being both an attacker and a counter-puncher from that position, much like the great Ken Rosewall of a later era. Rosewall, however, although he was three times a runner-up, was never able to win Wimbledon, and Bjorn Borg, with his post World War I record of five straight victories from 1976 through 1980, is the only true baseliner since Lacoste who has been able to do so.

Reminiscing about how he got the nickname, "The Croco-dile," Lacoste said that while the French Davis Cup team was in Boston in 1923 to play against Australia, he happened to see a traveling bag made out of crocodile leather which took his fancy in a shop window, and the team captain agreed to buy him the bag if Lacoste won his match. Lacoste didn't win, and he didn't get the bag, but a sports writer who heard the story wrote in his account of the match that Lacoste was so steady that he was as hard to kill as a crocodile. Lacoste was so taken by this com-parison that he had a large crocodile emblem embroidered on the breast pocket of his white flannel blazer and smaller ones on the short-sleeve polo shirts he wore in his matches. Some years later, after he retired from tournament play, he got the idea of market-ing the shirt, and for more than three decades the "Chemise Lacoste" has been a world-wide favorite for sports and leisure wear, not to mention having spawned many imitations. The crocodile emblem, or alligator, as it is often erroneously called, has also been licensed to manufacturers of other apparel for men and for women and children as well.

Meticulous and methodical in everything, Lacoste was par-ticularly so in regard to his equipment. He wore specially de-signed, made-to-order tennis shoes with very light crepe rubber soles, and he always had at hand ten rackets strung at varying tensions so he could pick the one he believed best suited to the temperature conditions. Lacoste had observed that Norman Brookes, who played with a very loosely strung racket, usually played better on a cold day. On such a day the ball bounced lower and felt heavier off the racket, and Lacoste would use a lower-tensioned racket because its greater elasticity required him to use less force and effort in his stroking than a higher-tensioned one. Following Lacoste's example, a present-day champion like Bjorn Borg will travel to a tournament with thirty or more rackets strung at different tensions to anticipate different conditions in court surface, weather and balls.

On one of his earlier visits to the United States, Lacoste tried out a new racket with a metal head fitted to a wooden handle and strung with twisted steel strings designed by William A. Larned, the former national champion, and manufactured by the Dayton Steel Racket Company. The Dayton racket was durable and relatively inexpensive—a low-priced model cost $7.00, the deluxe model, $12.50—and Lacoste was impressed by it, although, like Tilden and most of the other leading American players who had tried it, he did not consider it to have the feel of a good wood racket. Although it never caught on with tournament players to any extent, the utility of the Dayton racket gave it appeal for the average player. It sold well during the 1920's and 1930's and continued thereafter to be the only racket of its type available until a steel racket designed by Lacoste and introduced by the Wilson Sporting Goods Company in the United States in 1967 began the present-day vogue of the metal racket.

Lacoste spent fifteen years perfecting the design of his racket. Made of chrome plated steel tubing with an open throat, it has an ingenious string-suspension system consisting of wire anchors inside the frame that hold the strings instead of their being passed through holes in the frame. This makes for a whippy racket with a trampoline or sling-shot effect. Its flexibility makes it easier on the arm than a stiff wooden racket and gives more speed of shot with less effort, although less control, some maintain, than a conventionally strung wooden or metal frame. This does seem to be the case when some players use it, but Jimmy Connors, who has done exceedingly well playing with it for the past several years, can hardly be said to have any problems in this respect. And Billie Jean King, though she has since gone back to wood, won Wimbledon with it in 1968. In its various models it was for several years the largest selling metal racket.

Also on the subject of rackets, the racket with an oversize head that became popular in the 1970's, especially with many older players, had its forerunner too in the 1920's, a British player by the name of Donnisthorpe having designed one that he asserted enabled him to volley better, an advantage also claimed by many of the users of today's big-head rackets. And the tennis balls that come today in pressurized cans to keep them fresh and lively were first packed that way in 1927 by the Pennsylvania Rubber Company.

When Lacoste was named to the Davis Cup team for the first time in 1923, the four Musketeers were complete. Borotra and Cochet had played the year before, and Brugnon had been on the team since 1920. Although beaten by Australia in 1922 and 1923, it had become clear by 1924 that the French had the makings of a team that could eventually win the Cup. In that year, because of the increased number of entries, the challenging nations competed for the first time in one of two zones, France defeating Ireland, India, Great Britain and Czechoslovakia to win the European Zone, and Australia coming through in the American Zone. Once again, however, the Australians were France's nemesis, winning the Interzone Final played at the Longwood Cricket Club. Lacoste won both his singles matches over Gerald Patterson and Pat O'Hara Wood, but Borotra, who earlier in the summer had beaten Lacoste to become the first Frenchman to win at Wimbledon, played poorly to lose both of his, and France also lost the doubles.

History repeated itself, up to a point that is, in 1925, France and Australia again meeting in the Interzone Final, at Forest Hills. This year it was Lacoste, although he had turned the tables on Borotra to win Wimbledon, who did not play well, losing the opening match to Patterson. Borotra, however, saved the day by beating both Patterson and James O. Anderson, and he and Lacoste won the doubles over Patterson and J. B. Hawkes at 10-8 in the fifth set. The final singles was not played because of rain.

So the French had finally gained the Challenge Round, but their chances of winning even one match against one of the strongest teams in all Davis Cup history seemed very slim. The mighty Tilden had gone undefeated in a long succession of American tournaments, except for one in which he had lost to Vincent Richards, a loss offset, however, by several victories over the same player. Tired after losing his third final-round match in a row in New York area tournaments to Tilden, Richards announced he would rest from tennis for two or three weeks, but not so Tilden, who was scheduled to play in the Nassau, Long Island tournament the next day, and in succeeding weeks in the Rhode Island State at Providence, the National Clay Courts at St. Louis, and the Illinois State, one of Bill's favorite tournaments, at Skokie, a suburb of Chicago. Wrote Allison Danzig, who made his debut as tennis writer for the New York *Times* this year: "Where Tilden will go after that is uncertain at this time, but it can be said that he will go some place he can play tennis. The Champion loves his game too well to desert it for a moment and will start a tournament of his own if necessary."

Herbert Warren Wind, who writes perceptively about sports for the *New Yorker* magazine, in contrasting the tennis of the twenties with the open tennis of the seventies, makes the valid point that tournament players fifty years ago led a much more leisurely existence than nowadays, competing usually in no more than fifteen or so tournaments a year instead of the forty or more that many touring professionals now play. Mr. Wind might also have noted, however, that Bill Tilden was a notable exception. Bill did not just play in the Eastern grass court circuit of tournaments (Seabright, Southampton, Rye, Newport, and several others), the Nationals, and perhaps three or four sectional and state tournaments, as practically all the other leading players did. He found indoor tournaments to play in in the Winter, and tournaments large and small all Summer long. During the twenties he probably averaged somewhere around thirty-five tournaments and Davis Cup and other team matches a year besides playing a goodly number of exhibitions. In 1930, his last year as an amateur, he played in over a dozen Riviera tournaments during the Winter and early Spring, followed this with major and minor tournaments and Davis Cup matches in Europe and England, and, then returned to America for the big tournaments culminating in Forest Hills, which added up to nine months of almost continuous play. And as a professional during the 1930's, Bill followed a schedule perhaps even more rugged than most pros do today, playing three or four and sometimes more one-night stands a week, often having to drive considerable distances between cities to do so (with effects perhaps not too different from the jet lag that today's pros have to endure. On one tour they made in 1934, Bill and Ellsworth Vines played 136 matches in 180 days). It is true that Bill would quite often have easy early round matches in the amateur tournaments in which he played, something that the leading pros in this day of so many fine players don't often experience, but on a pro tour he always had a tough opponent—a Kozeluh, Richards, Vines, Perry, or Budge. Bill, without a doubt, would have thrived on the life of a pro today and enjoyed every minute of it.

In the Challenge Round the Musketeers also had to contend

with Billy Johnston, who was back on the American team after having been displaced by Richards in 1924. His tournament schedule had been much more limited than the indefatigable Big Bill's, but he appeared to be as formidable as ever on grass. Richards and Williams, the American doubles team, had won the National Doubles at Longwood with a decisive final-round victory over Patterson and Hawkes, to whom Borotra and Lacoste had narrowly escaped losing the Interzone Final.

There were some signs, however, that Bill Tilden might not be quite the invincible champion of previous years. In winning his fifth National Clay Court title over young George Lott of Chicago he had been forced to the limit, Lott leading by two sets to one and having a lead of 5-4 and 30-love in the final set before Bill finally pulled it out at 8-6. In the Illinois State the next week he was again in dire straits when the Californian Howard Kinsey gained a lead of 5-2 in the fifth set of their semi-final match. When the players changed courts at this point, although it was a cloudy day with a chilly wind blowing off Lake Michigan, Tilden pulled off the sweater he had worn throughout the match, poured a pitcher of ice water over his head and proceeded to engineer another of his famous rallies, winning four games in a row and finally the set at 8-6.

This was only a prelude to even more spectacular come-from-behind tennis against both Borotra and Lacoste in the Challenge Round at the Germantown Cricket Club. Against Borotra, Bill trailed almost all the way, but pulled out the match, 4-6, 6-0, 2-6, 9-7, 6-4, largely because of his greater staying powers, Borotra's constant net rushing leaving him exhausted and helpless to resist at the end. He was, however, unlucky not to win the fourth set, having Bill down 15-40 on serve at 4-all before Bill held. Later he broke Bill's serve to lead 6-5, but Bill, playing carefully, but hitting for winners when he had the opportunity, broke back. In the fifth set the leg-weary Borotra, whose angled volleys had been brilliant throughout the match, managed to hang on to 4-all, but Bill won the next two games for the match with drop shots which drew Borotra to the net and lobs over his head which he was too exhausted to leap for.

Johnston then beat Lacoste in four sets, and when Richards and Williams won the doubles the next day the United States had retained the Cup for another year. The final two singles had no bearing therefore on the outcome, but Tilden and Lacoste played a bitterly fought match in which Bill appeared hopelessly beaten before he made perhaps the most sensational of his many dramatic comebacks to win, 3-6, 10-12, 8-6, 7-5, 6-2. An upset stomach and his hard match with Borotra left Bill feeling weak and uncertain in the first part of the match, and hitting with pace and precision, Lacoste ran him from corner to corner. At 4-0 against him in the third set, Bill took a large revivifying draft of aromatic ammonia, and managed to pull up almost even. Finally Lacoste got to 5-6 and 15-40 on Bill's serve, double match point, but Bill forced him to err off the backhand, and then made a winning volley to bring the score to deuce. Twice more in this game Lacoste had match point, but he erred both times through being over-anxious, and Bill pulled out the game. In the fourth set Lacoste was within two points of victory in the tenth game, but in the final set, Bill's staying powers, still fortified by the ammonia, were superior to those of his tired opponent, and he was the victor after two hours and forty minutes of play. In contrast, in the final match, Johnston won over Borotra 6-1, 6-4, 6-0 in forty minutes.

Bill Tilden played with great courage and determination in winning over Borotra and Lacoste, but he was clearly not the player of 1924, when he stood in a class by himself. He appeared to have less stamina and to have suffered some loss of control, exhibiting a tendency at times to miss easy set-ups. His cannonball service, instrumental so often in the past in getting him out of difficulties, also appeared less effective. Nevertheless, he was the favorite to win the National Singles beginning the following week, although it was conceded that Johnston, Richards, Lacoste and Borotra were dangerous rivals. As it turned out, Bill was in no danger from the Frenchmen, Borotra going down to an inspired Dick Williams in the third round, 6-2, 6-2, 6-2, and Lacoste losing to Richards in straight sets in the quarter-finals. In the semi-finals, Bill defeated Richards in four sets, being in top form and playing with great concentration throughout, and Johnston beat a very off-form Williams in straight sets. In the final, in spite of a sore shoulder which forced him to use his cannonball only sparingly, Bill once again demonstrated how great a five-set player he was, winning 4-6, 11-9, 6-3, 4-6, 6-3. Johnston had three set points in the second set and led 2-1 and 40-15 in the final set, but lost the game, Bill rising to his greatest heights when pressed the hardest. It was an even more frustrating loss for Johnston than his five-set one to Bill back in 1922, since he wanted to win and retire. The closeness of the match was indicated by the fact that Bill won only two more points than his opponent, 191 to 189. Bill's victory was his sixth consecutive one, and it was the last time he and Little Bill would play each other.

CHAPTER ELEVEN

BIG BILL DETHRONED

Encouraged by having pushed the great Tilden to the limit in the 1925 Challenge Round, undiscouraged by their later defeats in the National Championship, which could be attributed to a let down after their strenuous efforts in the Cup matches, and exhibiting no lack of persistence, three of the Musketeers— Lacoste, Borotra, and Brugnon—crossed the Atlantic again in February of 1926 to play in the American Indoor Championship and to engage Bill Tilden and Vincent Richards in an international team match.

In the Indoor Championship the invaders carried all before them. On the same day, in the fourth round, Tilden lost to Borotra, Richards to Lacoste, and Frank Hunter to Brugnon. The loss to Borotra was Tilden's first in singles in a national championship since his final-round defeat by Johnston at Forest Hills in 1919. Borotra's net-rushing game was especially well suited to the fast board courts of the Seventh Regiment Armory in New York City, where the tournament was held, and he volleyed away many of Bill's best passing shots to win 13-11, 6-3, but in the final Lacoste's groundstrokes were too strong for him and he lost in four sets. Bill, however, got some compensation for his singles defeat by pairing with Fred Anderson, a tall New Yorker, whose hard serve and fine net game made him a formidable indoor player, to beat Lacoste and Borotra in the doubles semi-final, 6-4, 6-4, and Richards and Hunter in the final at 12-10 in the fifth set.

After their successes in the Indoor Championships, the Musketeers had high hopes of winning the international team match, which was played along Davis Cup lines with four singles and a doubles, and they began auspiciously with Lacoste playing brilliantly to beat Tilden in straight sets, 6-4, 8-6, 6-3. Bill, who could not stand up to Lacoste's hard driving or break Lacoste's greatly improved service even once, said his opponent's play was the best he had ever seen indoors. Richards, however, beat Borotra in four sets, and he and Bill beat Lacoste and Brugnon at 7-5 in the fifth set to give the U. S. a 2-1 lead. In the first of the final two singles, Lacoste, playing every bit as well as he had against Tilden, easily overcame Richards 6-3, 6-1, 6-3, but Bill saved the day for the United States, getting revenge on Borotra for his Indoor Championship defeat by a score of 6-4, 8-10, 11-13, 6-1, 6-3.

Although the French had lost the team match, Lacoste's fine play gave cause to wonder if the end of Tilden's reign as the world's greatest player might not be in sight. Observed Allison Danzig, "Today, you can say practically everything in praise of Lacoste's game that has been said for six years about Tilden's." Lacoste, however, did not achieve as much success subsequently as might have been expected. He lost to Cochet in the final of the French Championship, and, his health being none too good, he followed his doctor's orders and did not defend his title at Wimbledon, where Borotra won his second championship. In the Davis Cup Interzone Final against Japan (Australia did not challenge for the Cup in 1926), which France barely won 3-2, Lacoste also sustained a defeat, as did Borotra, at the hands of Takeichi Harada, a hard hitter who never temporized in his shot making and who had to his credit a 1925 Davis Cup victory over Gerald Patterson.

In the opening singles matches of the Challenge Round, played at the Germantown Cricket Club, both Lacoste and Borotra were off form. Lacoste could not get good length or pace on his drives, especially on the forehand, against Billy Johnston, who time and again drove Lacoste's short returns into the corners for outright winners to win 6-0, 6-4, 0-6, 6-0. Tired by his murderous driving in the first two sets, Johnston let the third set go to regain his strength, this accounting for the unusual score. Borotra, who had come so close to beatint Tilden the preceding year, was this year completely at Bill's mercy. "I was bad," he said, referring to his volley being off, "but it was largely because Tilden did not let me play better. He killed me." Bill won 6-2, 6-3, 6-3.

The next day the U. S. won the Cup for the seventh straight year when Richards and Williams defeated Cochet and Brugnon, whom they had also beaten earlier in the National Doubles, in straight sets, 6-4, 6-4, 6-2. The Musketeers were bitterly disappointed, and Pierre Gillou, their non-playing captain was so unhappy over their performance that he sailed for France instead of accompanying them to Forest Hills for the National Singles Championship, never dreaming that they would achieve brilliant victories there over their American rivals. Gillou was also unhappy, as he reported later to the French Tennis Federation, that the Challenge Round was played at Germantown since the cost of erecting and dismantling the temporary stands, amounting to some $15,000, had reduced by $4,000 the amount the French would have received had the matches been played in the West Side Stadium at Forest Hills. This was no mean sum, representing about half the expenses of the French team for their transatlantic travel and a month's stay in the United States.

Although the Cup had been won, a crowd of over 8000 turned out on the third day to watch Johnston beat Borotra 8-6, 6-4, 9-7, and Bill Tilden, who had won fifteen Davis Cup singles since 1920, suffer his first defeat, Lacoste winning 4-6, 6-4, 8-6, 8-6. Had it not been for some bad luck, however, Bill might have remained unbeaten. At set point for Bill in the third set, Lacoste hit a drive which appeared to land a good six inches beyond the baseline, but which the linesman did not call out. Then at set point for Lacoste, Bill, in an unsuccessful dash to the forecourt to return a drop shot, twisted his left knee, causing the semilunar cartlage to slip out. This was no novelty for Bill, the same thing having happened in another important match when he had played the Japanese Shimizu at Wimbledon in 1920, at which time he had been compelled to pull up his trouser leg and push the cartilage back in place as the Queen gazed down from the royal box. All the tennis Bill had played since that time had made the knee weaker and more susceptible to being reinjured. The knee trouble might have been corrected by surgery, but Bill would not risk an operation because if it failed there was a chance he would be left with with a permanently stiff knee.

Since the match with Lacoste amounted to no more than an exhibition, Bill should probably have defaulted, as he was advised to do by a doctor. Dick Williams, that year's Davis Cup captain, after watching Johnston make the score four matches to none for the U. S., seems to have decided his presence was no longer necessary and had gone off to get in some tennis himself on a Germantown back court. Perhaps he would have ordered Bill to retire but apparently no one thought to apprise him of what had happened, and Bill continued to play but with a pronounced limp. Sometimes after the cartilage had been pushed back in, to go on playing would cause Bill considerable pain, sometimes not. This time it obviously did, but even so, after Lacoste had got to 4-2 and 40-15 in the fourth set, Bill put on one of his characteristic rallies and actually reached set point before Lacoste, who was punishing Bill mercilessly with drop shots and lobs, finally prevailed.

In talking to Al Laney some ten years later about the match, Bill said he thought at the time that his knee injury had been responsible mainly, if not entirely, for his losing. With the passage of time, however, he had come to realize that Lacoste had already exhibited both the strokes and the tennis intelligence which had been responsible for Bill's defeat.   Even though Lacoste had come within a point of beating him in their 1925 Davis Cup match, Bill had always felt confident of winning, and Lacoste's play had not told him, as it should have, that with his astuteness and phenomenal steadiness Lacoste could become one of the game's finest players. Lacoste's strategy, which was to get Bill to beat himself, had been essentially the same in both 1925 and 1926. It hadn't quite worked the first time, but with some refinement and improvement it had the second. Lacoste took advantage of the balls getting heavier from the moisture on the grass court by mixing up the pace and length of his shots and waited for Tilden's errors, which came more frequently than usual because Bill tried to hit too hard to Lacoste's virtually impregnable backhand, a stroke Lacoste had improved with the help of Edwin Faulkner, the Germantown Cricket Club professional, who served as a practice partner. Faulkner, who also coached the U. S. team in 1925 and 1926 and then the French team in 1927, suggested that Lacoste try opening the face of the racket on his backswing instead of turning it down, as had been his habit, and this had given the shot increased power and accuracy. Also at the time Bill had been inclined to underestimate Lacoste's serve, which he had actually made a very effective weapon by serving a slow but heavily sliced and sharply-angled ball to Bill's forehand that Bill, in trying to punish, often overdrove or put into the net. In short, then, it was Bill's over-confidence and short-sightedness more than his knee injury that brought about his defeat.

Despite his knee injury and the fact that he had lost twice during the year to Lacoste, three times to Richards, and once to Borotra—his worst record in six years as champion—it was assumed by nearly everyone that Bill would again be the winning finalist against Billy Johnston in the National Championships. His knee still giving him some trouble, Bill got through three rounds, his third round match against Arnold Jones, a former protégé, going to five sets, to reach the quarter-finals. This stage of the tournament found America's four Davis Cuppers pitted against the four Musketeers: Tilden versus Cochet, Williams against Lacoste, Johnston versus Borotra, and Richards against Brugnon. In a shocking succession of upsets all the Americans except Richards were eliminated. Appropriately, someone called this day of upsets "Black Thursday."

Cochet, who at twenty-four was almost ten years Tilden's junior, was not nearly as well known to American tennis fans, nor as highly regarded by them, as Lacoste and Borotra, and this served to make his defeat of Bill all the more unexpected and shocking. He had visited the United States only once before, in 1922, when France had lost to Australia in the Davis Cup Interzone Final, and this was his first American singles championship, whereas it was Borotra's third and Lacoste's fourth, the latter having been a quarter-finalist in both 1924 and 1925.

Cochet, who had beaten Richards in the French Championship and again at Wimbledon, where he also forced Borotra, the eventual winner to a 7-5 fifth set in their semi-final, played cool, crafty and phenomenally steady tennis against Bill to win 6-8, 6-1, 6-3, 1-6, 8-6. Cochet's unusual steadiness resulted in the umpire inadvertently calling out the score on one occasion as "Advantage Lacoste." It was a mistake that evoked laughter from the gallery but was certainly excusable so rock-like was Cochet's defense. Bill, whose defeat made column one of page one of the New York *Times,* fought fiercely to the very end, evoking a wild demonstration from the gallery of 9,000 when he rallied from 1-4 down in the final set to tie the score at 4-all and then get to double break point on Cochet's service in the ninth game. But Cochet refused to crack at this point, or later, when Bill was serving for the match at 6-5. Bill's cannonball service did not have quite its former sting, and Cochet was able to take it on the rise and put all his returns into play, two of them for outright winners, to take the game easily. He then held his serve at love and broke Bill once again for the match. As for his feelings when Bill led him 6-5, Cochet wrote later: "At this time I was shaken by a great chill. For several instants I knew nothing of what was transpiring about me, but as time passed I realized that he was no less excited than I, and at 15-40 he proved this by making a double fault. It was entirely through morale that I triumphed over a man whom I considered invincible. The match will remain the match of my life."

It was natural that Bill's loss to Cochet should be attributed in large measure, as had been his defeat by Lacoste, to his being handicapped by his bad knee. There were those who felt, however, that even with his handicap the Tilden of a year or two earlier, after rallying magnificently to get within one service game of victory, would never have failed to close out the match. The losses to Lacoste and Cochet could be regarded as having been suffered by a Tilden who had come to a turning point in his career, a player who had begun, though still almost imperceptably, to pass his prime. Bill, incidentally, had some company in the dethroned-champion department. The same week Bobby Jones was defeated in the National Amateur Golf Championship, and a week later Jack Dempsey lost his heavyweight boxing title to Gene Tunney.

With Bill out of the tournament, Billy Johnston, who was scheduled to play Borotra later in the afternoon, appeared to have an excellent chance to regain the title he had held in 1915 and 1919. He had never lost a set to Borotra, he had beaten Lacoste decisively less than a week earlier, he had never lost to Cochet, and he had almost always been able to beat Richards in their numerous past encounters. Borotra had found it difficult in their Davis Cup match to make winning volleys off Johnston's hard-hit, sharply-dipping topspin drives, and this was again the case in the first two sets, which Johnston won 6-3, 6-4. But Borotra persisted in coming to the net on everything, and, to use Bill Tilden's description, "out-stalled, out-thought, out-talked, and out-volleyed" Johnston, whose control fell off as he lost concentration, to win the last three sets, 6-3, 6-4, 6-4.

Both semi-finals were bitter struggles, Richards getting to within three points of the match at 6-5 and 15-love in the fourth set before Borotra, employing much the same tactics he had against Johnston, won at 3-6, 6-4, 4-6, 8-6, 6-2. Cochet, favored to take the title after his defeat of Tilden, volleyed brilliantly to take the first two sets from Lacoste, who then counterattacked by coming to the net himself behind forceful deep drives to win 2-6, 4-6, 6-4, 6-4, 6-3. Cochet's second serve, which was soft and not very well placed, also contributed to his defeat. As long as an opponent didn't smear the second serve, Cochet got his first serve in quite regularly, but when Lacoste started to hit it back for winners in the third set, Cochet's first serve began to fail him frequently because of his anxiety to get it in. Bill Tilden, who called a line during the match, had he employed this strategy more consistently might well have been opposing Lacoste rather than occupying a linesman's chair.

Lacoste was also the clever strategist against Borotra, taking advantage of him where he was most vulnerable. The morning of the final, Lacoste practiced lobbing for a full hour, and so accurate was he with this shot during the match that time and again Borotra had to chase lobs over his head back to the baseline. Already tired from his two five-set struggles with Johnston and Richards, and faced with an opponent who knew him too well to be lulled into a sense of false security by Borotra's oft repeated "Ah, René, I am so exhausted and you are much too good for me!" he succumbed, 6-4, 6-0, 6-4.

So, although France had failed to win the Davis Cup, America could scarcely be regarded any longer as the number one tennis nation. Lacoste was now both the indoor and outdoor champion of the United States, Borotra held the Wimbledon championship, and Cochet that of France. With Tilden and Johnston both aging and clearly no longer invincible, with Richards singularly unsuccessful in his encounters with the Musketeers, and with no young American players of sufficient promise to be a threat to them, the Musketeers had every reason to believe that the Cup would not elude them in 1927.

CHAPTER TWELVE

FRANCE BECOMES THE CHAMPION NATION

Back in February of 1926, after Bill Tilden had been beaten indoors first by Borotra and a few days later by Lacoste, Suzanne Lenglen, who cordially disliked Bill, for reasons we have seen earlier, expressed elation over his defeats, saying: "I'm glad to have lived to see Tilden beaten twice in a week by two different Frenchmen right in his own country. Tilden cannot evade the issue now. He must come to Paris in May and June and there get defeated again in the hard court championships."

Helen Wills, who was also at this time on the Riviera where she had recently lost her epic match with the great Lenglen, but where she would triumph over all her other competition, was reported as saying she thought Bill would want to come abroad to avenge his defeats and that she hoped she might play mixed doubles with him at Wimbledon. Bill, queried by a reporter at the Mayfair Theatre in New York City, said he was flattered that Miss Wills should want him as her doubles partner but that both business and personal considerations were likely to prevent his playing abroad, and besides it was ridiculous to think he would want to pursue Borotra and Lacoste across the ocean merely because he had lost to them in America.

Bill was not seeing a play at the Mayfair Theatre; he was acting in one, and the "business and personal considerations" he referred to had to do largely with acting ambitions he had harbored ever since he had first taken part in amateur theatricals in Germantown many years earlier. Late in January of 1926, Bill had made his Broadway debut playing a supporting role in *Don Q Jr.* Described as a "whimsical comedy" by its producers and dealing with the trials and tribulations of a newsboy hero who has a heart of gold, it was considered by almost all the New York critics as pretty awful. Tilden's performance was also regarded without enthusiasm since he greatly overacted his part, a tendency which he continued to exhibit in later dramatic performances. Before going on stage Bill was usually so nervous he could drink only a little egg and milk mixture whereas his stomach gave him no problem before a big tennis match if he called on it only an hour or so before to accommodate a big meal consisting of steak, fried potatoes, pie and ice cream. When *Don Q Jr.* closed after two weeks, Bill, who would not until some time later concede that the critics were right, insisted on keeping it alive for two weeks more, moving it to the Mayfair, which he rented at considerable expense to himself but which was so small that even if the play had been a success it still could not have met expenses.

Quite possibly Bill's stage activity at this time affected adversely his play against Borotra and Lacoste, although he did not think so. Although he had been upset by Borotra in the Indoor Championships, he could point to the fact that he had beaten him in the deciding international match, the starting time of which, incidentally, had to be put back an hour so Bill could finish a performance before the footlights, a kind of illumination which, it was suggested, might have bothered his vision in the match, but which Bill denied. And he had not played badly against Lacoste, a player who had now clearly arrived at the height of his powers and who had been in top form.

During the Spring of 1926, however, Bill had played indifferently in several Southern tournaments, losing twice to Vincent Richards, at Jacksonville and White Sulfur Springs, and almost losing the final of the South Atlantic Championships at Augusta, Georgia to his protégé, Alfred Chapin. Early in June he did actually lose the Connecticut State final in straight sets to Chapin in New Haven, where he was also appearing nightly in a play as well as guest lecturing to Professor William Lyon Phelps's Yale drama class. A week later, however, his acting over for the time being, Bill trounced Chapin in straight sets in the final of the New England Championships at Hartford.

Late in July, still preoccupied with the idea of being a thespian as well as a tennis player, Bill had told the Associated Press that he expected to return to the stage the middle of August, and since his dramatic work would have priority, this might keep him out of the season's remaining tournaments and even prevent his playing in the Davis Cup Challenge Round and the National Singles. Happily, since Bill was far better qualified to delight tennis galleries than theatre audiences, the producer of the play in which he was to appear decided that the humid summer weather of late August and early September would not be propitious to successful theatrical presentation, and Bill was not called on to sacrifice his tennis on the altar of his dramatic ambition.

His return to the boards came about in October, when he appeared in another short-lived Broadway production into which he again poured a good deal of his own money. A so-called comedy entitled *They All Want Something,* its involved and none-too-credible plot called for Bill to play the leading role of a tramp who is really an heir to a fortune and who after he is hired as a butler is called on to impersonate a famous author who fails to show up for a party in his honor. Once again the critics had few kind words to say about either Bill's performance or the artistic merits of the production.

It was shortly after the play closed that Bill announced he had returned down an offer from C. C. Pyle to turn professional. He would remain an amateur, he said, because he wanted to aid the United States to regain its tennis supremacy, and to this end he would be invading France and England in 1927, as well as attempting to regain the American singles championship. Even so Bill had no intention of deserting the stage. He would appear in more plays later on, including *Dracula* (in which, although it hardly seems possible, he managed, according to the testimony of his loyal friend, Frank Hunter, and others to overplay the title role), but now for the time being he had the motivation to concentrate on his tennis.

Now that Bill Tilden was no longer world champion, his popularity with tennis fans was greater than ever before, according to S. Wallis Merrihew, the *American Lawn Tennis* editor. "Am pulling for and expecting a big year for Big Bill," was a sample, said Merrihew, of numerous letters expressing support of Bill that the magazine had received. Perhaps Bill's most ardent supporter was a reader by the name of John H. Kaiser who sent in the following versified tribute:

To Bill Tilden

I wandered today to the game, Bill
And watched the scene below.
The stroke and the pace were the same, Bill
As they used to be long ago.
The pep has not gone from your pins, Bill

Though knee be slightly sprung,
The ball from your racket ever spins, Bill
As when you were sprightly and young.

They have tried you of late to replace, Bill
With sundry and divers recruits;
But they are shy of filling the space, Bill
And rattle around in your boots.
You have been on the job many years, Bill.
The world your praises have sung,
And I find you are getting the cheers, Bill.
As when you were sprightly and young.

They've said you were feeble with age, Bill,
That your shots lacked the ginger of yore.
They said that and work on the stage, Bill
Would keep you from playing any more.
We find you are the King of the Sport, Bill,
Though many a heart you have wrung,
And you are still holding the Fort, Bill
As when you were sprightly and young.

Toward the end of 1926, Bill announced that he would be going abroad to play on the Riviera in February and March. George Agutter, the teaching professional at the West Side Tennis Club since 1913, when it moved to Forest Hills (and who would continue in that position until his retirement in 1959 at the age of 73), and his assistant, Paul Heston, at about the same time had journeyed at their own expense to Cannes to play in the French professional championships. The English-born Agutter, before coming to America in 1904 as the personal professional of a wealthy international lawyer, had been a professional at the Tennis Club of Paris and elsewhere on the Continent. The trip gave Agutter, still a very good player though he had turned forty, and the younger Heston a chance to test their skill against such great European professionals as Karel Kozeluh, Albert Burke, and Roman Najuch, who turned out to be too good for them, and also provided Agutter the opportunity to look into the current situation of professional tennis teaching abroad. The number of American teaching professionals was increasing, and Agutter and others among them looked forward to some kind of organization, one which did come into being soon after with the formation of the Professional Lawn Tennis Association in September, 1927.

John Tunis, who was covering tennis on the Riviera that

winter for the *New Yorker* magazine and other publications,
hearing that Bill Tilden would soon be putting in an appearance
there, was moved to draw a contrast between the two West Side
professionals, who had made their trip with the blessing of the
USLTA but with no financial support from it or anyone else,
and Bill, who presumably would be getting his way paid for him
and a good deal more besides. Apparently quoting either Agutter
or Heston, Tunis wrote: "An acute professional playing in the
French Professional Championship at Cannes in December of
1926 made this distinction between a professional and an amateur. 'See,' he said, 'it's like this. A professional tennis player
is a simp who pays his own expenses from New York to Cannes
to play in a tennis tournament. Whereas an amateur player is a
gentleman (or lady) who comes from New York to Cannes to
compete in a tennis tournament, has all expenses paid, is lodged
at Grand Palace hotels, and eventually goes home with fifty thousand dollars picked up on the side by the sale of his (or her) very
valuable name'." All the competitors in the French professional
championship, said Tunis in conclusion, "made their living openly, honestly, and legitimately out of tennis."

Another contribution to the discussion of "shamateurism"
in tennis at this time was a *Saturday Evening Post* article by
Vincent Richards. He was glad, he said, that he had become
an honest professional by signing with C. C. Pyle to tour with
Lenglen since there was no such thing as an honest amateur.
Richards' article was the forerunner of a number of pieces that
would be published in later years on the same theme by high-
ranking amateurs who turned professional, among them George
Lott, Jack Kramer, and Lew Hoad. Richards also sent a clever
Christmas card for 1926 to his friends. It showed him smiling
broadly as he sat on bags of gold and stacks of banknotes
dumped out of a wheelbarrow by Pyle. The card read:

Vincent Richards
hopes he does not
jeopardize your
amateur standing
by wishing you a

Merry Christmas
and a
Happy New Year

Instead of journeying to the Riviera, Bill Tilden decided to postpone his European invasion until April, but kept in shape by competing, as he had the previous Winter, on the Southern tournament circuit, his main competition coming from George Lott, the promising twenty-year-old Chicagoan, whose fine play during the year, including a victory over Lacoste at Southampton, gained him the number three national ranking for 1927. Lott did beat Bill in five sets at Ormond Beach in Florida, but lost to him at Augusta, Georgia in four sets and again at Pinehurst, North Carolina in three.

The USLTA was all for Bill going abroad and at its annual meeting in February approved sending him and a partner of his choice to officially represent it in a series of team matches in Germany, France, Belgium, Holland, England, and Italy and to compete in the French Championships and at Wimbledon. The trip would provide a good indication as to the strength of French Musketeers and how dangerous a threat they would be in the Davis Cup. The Association also expected to benefit financially from Bill's trip, as indeed it did, the tour returning a profit of some $10,000 to its treasury after all expenses.

At first Bill was at a loss as to whom he should ask to play with him, none of his Davis Cup teammates being available, since Richards had turned professional, and neither Billy Johnston nor Dick Williams was interested in making such an extensive trip. Then one day several weeks before Bill's scheduled departure, Frank Hunter, whom Bill had known for a long time, although the two were not close friends, invited Bill to have lunch with him and volunteered himself as Bill's partner. Bill described his reaction in his autobiographical *My Story* as follows:

> I practically passed out on the spot. Many years before I had earned the title of World's Worst Doubles Player. I had been awarded said title by those great experts of the Tennis Association and had brilliantly defended it against all comers. Hunter, however, was one of the few who could successfully threaten my hold on the honor—and here he was claiming that together we could be a doubles team. The man was mad!
>
> Before I could say anything, Frank went on, "I'm in a position to go to Europe this year and unless you've already selected your partner or have a distinct preference for some other player, I wish you would consider me. I

think my game will suit yours and we can make a really
dangerous pair." It was a revolutionary idea, but the
more I thought about it the more I realized that Frank
might have something there.

That Hunter was not really being presumptuous in pro-
posing himself as the great Tilden's teammate can be demonstrated by briefly reviewing his tennis history, which went back
to 1920 when he first began playing the tournament circuit after
graduating from Cornell University where he had been captain of
the hockey team. He broke into the first ten of the national
rankings in 1922, and the next year he moved up to number 5,
right below the top four of Tilden, Johnston, Williams, and
Richards. This was all the more remarkable since Hunter was
virtually a one-stroke player, relying on the crushing power of
his forehand drive to win matches. But to compensate for his
lack of a well-rounded game, Hunter, who had a stocky physique
more suited to a fullback than a tennis player, had great determination and fighting spirit and was noted for winning
matches after he appeared hopelessly beaten, a notable example
being his five-set upset of Vincent Richards in the 1923 National
Championship after being down seven match points in the fourth
set. As for Hunter's doubles ability, about which Bill had spoken
mock-deprecatingly, he and Richards had made an outstanding
team, winning the Olympic and Wimbledon doubles in 1924, as
well as a number of lesser tournaments. In addition, Hunter
had distinguished himself by reaching the Wimbledon singles
final in 1923, losing to Billy Johnston.

As for Bill's ability in doubles, although he was fond of
putting himself down as a terrible dub, especially ever since, as
recounted earlier, his doubles intelligence had been impugned by
Harold Hackett of the Davis Cup Committee when Bill played
with Dick Williams in the 1923 Challenge Round, his doubles
record through 1926 could hardly have been more impressive—
four national championships, the first of these with the fifteen-
year-old Vincent Richards, three national indoor championships,
three mixed doubles championships and victories in three out of
four Davis Cup Challenge Round doubles.

Bill, it was true, was notorious for his poaching, invariably
trying to play most of the court with partners he could domi-
nate, such as the boy protégés with whom he often paired. When
he and Richards first played together, Bill insisted on playing

three quarters of the court and, if he could get to it, would not hesitate to run over and snatch a ball from directly in front of Richards. They also played one up and one back, and their victories were usually due to Bill's brilliant driving and lobbing. Against first-rate teams, however, this method made victory uncertain, if not impossible. Richards was never able to convince Bill that they should develop better team work, and after winning the National Doubles for a third time in 1922, the two split up, Tilden winning again in 1923 with B. I. C. Norton, the South African, and Richards with R. Norris Williams in 1925 and 1926. Almost two decades later, their differences with each other settled long before, the two got together one more time on the same side of the net to win the United States Professional Doubles.

Bill, of course, was the dominant player in the Tilden-Hunter partnership, but with their opponents usually playing as much as possible to Hunter as the weaker player, and with rigorous practice sessions with Bill during the European tour (five sets of singles in the morning and another five in the afternoon every day they did not have a team match!) bringing Hunter's backhand and volley up to very nearly first-class standards, it turned out that Hunter would usually pretty much carry his fair share of the load. Not a doubles team in the true sense, as were Brugnon with Borotra or Cochet, or George Lott with John Doeg or Lester Stoefen, they were essentially two singles players on a doubles court. "They played a doubles game all their own," said Lott, who often faced them across the net. "Court position meant nothing, but win they did." Tilden's tactics, touch and all-round game plus Hunter's fighting spirit, forehand, and otherwise greatly improved strokes would make them the premier doubles team of 1927 by virtue of winning Wimbledon, the U. S. title, and the Davis Cup Challenge Round doubles.

After being honored at a dinner to wish them bon voyage and success abroad, hosted by none other than Bill's old bête noire, Julian Myrick, Tilden and Hunter sailed for Europe late in April. Bill took along three dozen Spalding Top-Flite rackets, one dozen being strung with a special "World Champion" gut made specially to his order and packed in moisture-proof mahogany boxes made for him by Spalding. The other frames would be strung for him after he reached Paris, and there would also be two dozen additional frames awaiting him in London. Bill didn't really need nearly this many rackets for his own use, but he liked to be able to give one away now then as a souvenir.

The Top-Flite was an innovation in racket making, being the first wooden frame to have an open throat. Bill may have been induced by Spalding to use it in part because of its presumed superior playing qualities, but it may have been profitable otherwise for him to do so as well. Bill had been playing for a couple of years previously with a handsome all-white "California" racket made by a San Francisco manufacturer, who advertised the racket using an action photo of a player seen from the rear who was unmistakably Bill, with the caption underneath: "Of course, you'll want what the champions use." Bancroft, whose "Winner" racket Bill had forsaken for the California, tried to compensate for their loss by vigorously promoting for a time a "Tilston" racket. This was something like an English firm which violated the spirit, if not exactly the letter, of the amateur rule prohibiting the use of a player's name on a product when it brought out a Len-Glen tennis shoe for women.

He had two ambitions in making his first trip abroad since 1921, said Bill in an interview he gave when the liner bound for Bremen docked briefly at Plymouth, England: the first was to win Wimbledon again, the second was to appear in his play, "They All Want Something," on the London stage, his hope being to find a theatre manager who would provide him with the necessary theatre. Bill, who loved performing in this play every bit as much as he did on the court, had acted in a stock company production of it early in the spring in Miami while at the same time commuting to Palm Beach to compete in the Florida State Championship. Arrested one morning for speeding on the Dixie Highway, he was brought before a judge who seems to have fancied himself as something of a humorist since he released Bill with the warning, "not to get his courts mixed in the future." Bill would eventually win another Wimbledon, but unhappily from his point of view, if not from that of London playgoers, the only stage he would have on which to display his histrionic talents, or lack thereof, would be Wimbledon's Centre Court.

Winning their team matches in Berlin, Amsterdam, and Brussels, as expected, Tilden and Hunter arrived in Paris the middle of May where they were put to sterner tests, first in a Franco-American team match against Borotra, Lacoste, and Brugnon, and following that in the French Hard Court Championship. In the former Hunter lost to both Borotra and Lacoste, and Tilden and Hunter to Borotra and Brugnon, but Bill defeated Lacoste 6-4, 7-5, and Borotra 6-0, 6-3. Bill, highly pleased, said, "I think I played like my old self again and feel sure I will be able to do even better in the five-set matches in the tournament next week," this last being a reference to his having worked hard to get himself in good condition and to strengthen his knee through rigorous exercise and practice. Stamina, as well as strokes, would be needed to win over his younger French opponents.

In the Hard Court, which had to compete for the attention of Parisians with Charles Lindbergh, who landed at Le Bourget Airport on Saturday, May 21, the end of the first week of the tournament, after his solo flight across the Atlantic, Bill got revenge for his 1926 Forest Hills loss to Cochet, beating him in the semi-finals, 9-7, 6-3, 6-2, the loser declaring emphatically that he had never seen Bill play better. Lacoste, who put out Hunter and Borotra, was the other finalist, but Bill was definitely the favorite to win the title, since he had beaten all three of his French rivals in the space of little more than a week, and without the loss of a set.

Meanwhile, the rumor spread that Lindbergh planned to attend the final between Bill and Lacoste, and this, along with the natural drawing power of the match, resulted in 7500 persons packing the stands at St. Cloud to overflowing, and hundreds more being turned away. Played on a very hot day over a period of almost four hours on a court made soft and slow by heavy watering, which the French were reputed to do intentionally before Tilden's matches in order to slow down his cannonball serve and to make it more difficult for him to achieve the speed of shot he needed on his groundstrokes to keep Lacoste on the defensive, the match turned into an endurance contest almost as much as a battle of skill.

In the first set, which was characterized by many long rallies, Bill led 4-2, but Lacoste, using a sharply spinning, medium-paced serve to the forehand, off which Bill had difficulty making an aggressive return, held serve twice and broke Bill twice to win 6-4. Bill retaliated by taking the second set by the same score and the third at 7-5 from a Lacoste whose mobility toward its end was hampered by leg cramps. After the rest period, by rule restricted to ten minutes, but which was extended to a half hour without any objection from Bill so that his opponent might fully recover from his cramps with the aid of massage, Lacoste came back to win the fourth set 6-4, setting the stage for a final set full of excitement and suspense in its later stages, twenty games being required for its outcome.

With Bill behind at 3-4 on his serve, the footfault judge, an expatriate American by the name of Allan Muhr, who had been the non-playing French Davis Cup captain in 1922 and 1923, and who thus might have been suspected of partisanship, suddenly called three successive footfaults on Bill, one on a second serve which, of course, cost Bill the point. Serving again at 4-5, and smarting with resentment, Bill jeering called on Muhr to watch his feet closely. He then served a sizzling cannonball and put away Lacoste's weak return with a winning placement. Three more scorching first serves followed to make it a love game for Bill.

Whether or not he was justified, Muhr apparently had little precedent for his action, footfaulting in the Hard Court appearing to be the last thing the officials worried about. S. Wallis Merrihew, after attending the 1927 tournament, reported that although footfaulting was quite common it seemed to cause no concern. He noticed that Lacoste sometimes served with his left foot touching the baseline and let his right foot swing over it before his racket made contact with the ball, while Borotra, rushing the net behind his serve, had a habit of jumping slightly off the ground as well as swinging over his right foot prematurely. A number of other players were guilty of similar violations, but no one was ever penalized for them.

The heat was almost as scorching as Bill's serve, but rejuvenating himself, as was his habit in a long, hard match, by pouring pitchers of drinking water over his head when changing courts on odd games, Bill got to 9-8 and 40-15, two match points. What happened then Bill recalled as follows:

> I felt it was now or never; for I, like Lacoste, was verging on complete exhaustion. I really wound up on my service, cannonballing a serve that travelled perhaps as fast as any shot hit in the entire match. The ball fell either on the outside edge of the side line of the service court, or missed it by a fraction of an inch, just which I'm not positive. At the time I thought it had touched the line. It flashed past Lacoste and with a sigh of relief I relaxed, thinking the match was over. In the same instant Henri Cochet, who was calling the side line, shouted "Fault."

Nowadays it is not at all uncommon for a player to question a close call, with the linesman in some cases changing his call, or the point being played over. Nowadays also one would certainly not expect to see a player like Cochet serving in such a capacity, since it would be something like having Arthur Ashe's Davis Cup teammate, Stan Smith, call a line when Ashe played Tom Okker of Holland in the final of the 1968 U. S. Open (this does not mean that Smith would make calls that would unfairly benefit Ashe). Bill gave no indication he thought it might be wrong, but he was shaken by Cochet's call and missed an easy set up on his second match point. Lacoste won the game and the next two as well for the match, Bill double faulting to give him the final point. Cochet told Bill in the dressing room after the match that the serve had just missed the line, and Bill replied that he saw no reason to question Cochet's judgment. Whether correct or not, Bill was sure that Cochet sincerely believed he had made the right call. Borotra called Bill on the phone the next day to tell him he had won many friends as a result of his good sportsmanship in accepting Cochet's call, to which Bill replied that he wished he had made one less friend and one more point.

Despite the loss to Lacoste, Bill was favored to win at Wimbledon, especially after he swept through five opponents to reach the semi-finals against Cochet, who just barely survived his quarter-final match with Hunter, after being down two sets to none. Playing what he later called the best tennis of his life, Bill was overwhelming against his French opponent during the first two sets and up to 5-1 in the third. Cochet won only nine points in this set and seemed thoroughly beaten. Then at 15-all in the next game, three points from victory, Bill inexplicably hit a successsion of wild shots, most of them far out of court, and the surprised Cochet found himself with a reprieve when he was expecting execution. Bill lost seventeen points in a row and could not win one until the score was 5-all and 30-love for Cochet. He was able to win only three more points, all in the last game, before Cochet won the set, 7-5. In the fourth set, teased by Cochet's soft, cautious returns, Bill continued to be erratic in his driving, and though he got to 4-all by a tremendous effort he could not keep Cochet from winning the next two games for the set. Making a supreme effort in the final set, Bill managed to get to 3-2, with his service to follow, but he had shot his bolt at this point and could put up virtually no resistance, Cochet winning the next four games for the match. In the final, Cochet, still living a charmed life, won his first Wimbledon title by beating Borotra, the conqueror of Lacoste, after Borotra was seven times at match point, five times in one game!

No one, not even Bill, who thought the heat might have affected his coordination, could satisfactorily explain how he lost. Cochet did not suddenly rise to great heights when faced with defeat nor did he change his tactics, as he had in coming from behind to defeat Hunter, forsaking baseline play to storm the net. Instead, from start to finish, he played mostly a safe baseline game more reminiscent of Lacoste, allowing Bill, after he had lost his control to beat himself. Bill pooh-poohed the idea that he had lost his concentration because he had thrown away the game when ahead 5-1 in the third set so that he could treat King Alfonso of Spain, a great tennis enthusiast, who had just entered the royal box, to a spectacular closing out of the match with his cannonball service in the next game. Such dramatic reversals of form are uncommon, but they do happen, and, oddly enough, Cochet was similarly afflicted in the final of the doubles. Against Tilden and Hunter, he and Brugnon, the defending champions, led two sets to none and 5-3, 40-15 on Cochet's serve, at which point his game fell apart, enabling Tilden and Hunter to fight off the two match points, run out the set, and then win the next two for the championship.

Returning to America the middle of July, Bill appeared in fine physical condition and full of energy, not at all, as Allison Danzig put it, "the tottering shell of the courts who had lost to both Lacoste and Cochet," that the tennis officials and newspaper reporters who met him at the pier expected to see. Any other player, said John Kieran, the New York *Times* sports columnist, would surely have taken a rest from tournament play, but not Bill. Pausing only briefly in New York City to attend a dinner tendered to him and Hunter by the Davis Cup Committee, to whom he reported that the French would indeed be a serious threat to the U. S. hold on the Cup, he was off to Providence to play doubles with his protégé Sandy Wiener in the Rhode Island State Championships. Then it was out to the Middle West to capture a seventh National Clay Court title in Detroi and a fourth Illinois State Championship in Chicago. From there it was back to the East to win three grass-court tournaments in a row at Seabright, Southampton, and Newport. During this period Bill played as well as he ever had. His old knee injury appeared completely mended, and the French would surely find him a formidable opponent in the Challenge Round.

That they would find Billy Johnston, who was expected to be the other singles player, equally formidable there was some reason to doubt. In contrast to Bill Tilden, who played all year round, it was Johnston's usual habit, after returning to California at the close of the tennis season in the East, to put away his rackets until the next May. He would practice and play in several California tournaments during the early part of the summer and go East about the first of August, which enabled him to play in at least two or three grass-court tournaments before the National Singles and Doubles and the Davis Cup Challenge Round. In 1927, however, because he did not want to leave a clientele he had worked hard to build up in a new position as a stockbroker any longer than he had to, and because he did not want to go through the rigors of grass-court singles play during the heat of August, the Davis Cup Committee allowed him to delay his arrival from California until just in time for the National Doubles, only a little more than a week before the Challenge Round. He had always been able to shift quickly from California asphalt to grass and did play well in the Doubles, reaching the final with Dick Williams, where they lost in three close sets to Tilden and Hunter. Another good sign for U. S. Cup hopes was the elimination of both French doubles teams in the quarter-finals by two promising young American teams, Cochet and Brugnon losing to George Lott and the Californian John Doeg, and Lacoste and Borotra to John Hennessey and Lucien Williams, who, like Lott, were Middle-Westerners.

Nevertheless, the French were confident they had a good chance to win the Cup, and some American sports writers, among them Al Laney, who had followed their play closely abroad, were predicting, at least cautiously, that they would do so. The American team of Tilden, Johnston, Hunter, and Williams was an "old" one with an average age of 34½; the French team was considerably younger, it had three equally strong singles players instead of only two, and it had a doubles specialist who could play equally well with any of his colleagues. If they were to be successful, the French believed, much depended on the draw. There was a distinct possibility, they felt, that the Cup could be won by taking two singles from Johnston and the doubles, but their hope also was that Lacoste, who along with Cochet, had played singles in the Interzone Final, in which the

Japanese had been easily defeated, would not have to play a fresh Tilden on the first day, giving him the advantage of a day's rest before he met a Tilden who would be playing for the third straight day, assuming that he would play doubles as well as singles, as he was almost certain to do, and who might not, therefore, be up to winning the kind of long, tiring match Lacoste was capable of subjecting him to.

Fortune did favor the French; Johnston and Lacoste were drawn to play the first match, with Tilden and Cochet to follow. Also, the misgivings of those who feared Johnston might be undertennised and thus incapable of maintaining his undefeated record against the French in Cup play were borne out almost from the very first game. Throughout, Lacoste was both too forceful and too steady, winning 6-3, 6-2, 6-2. Johnston's famous western forehand was not the attacking weapon it had been in his 1925 and 1926 Cup victories over the French, and he could not get to Lacoste's well-placed shots with the same speed of foot as formerly. He still had his famous fighting spirit, but it could not save him from being sadly outclassed.

With Johnston succumbing to Lacoste a Tilden victory seemed imperative, and there was also reason to fear that the memory of his having lost his touch against Cochet at Wimbledon might affect his play. But if Bill felt any pressure on either of these counts, it did not prevent him from defeating Cochet, who said he played better than he had at Wimbledon, 6-4, 2-6, 6-2, 8-6. Bill, understandably jubilant after the match, indicated that he did have his experience at Wimbledon against Cochet on his mind, saying: "Once you let down against him, you never know whether he will ever let you come up again." Given hindsight, however, Bill's victory was one of those battles which, although they are won, also serve to contribute to the losing of a war. As much as possible he had played to conserve his energy, letting the second set go after falling behind, but he could not afford to do so again in the fourth against a much younger opponent who had a genius for winning fifth sets.

A day's rest would have restored the considerable amount of energy Bill had been obliged to expend, but he was needed to play doubles against Borotra and Brugnon, which would not have been the case had Vincent Richards still been an amateur, he and Williams having won the doubles from the French the preceding two years. Before playing doubles Bill also found himself engaged in a contest of wills with the Davis Cup Committee, which at first named Johnston as his partner instead of Hunter, even though Tilden and Hunter were the logical choice by reason of having won not only Wimbledon but also four American tournaments, including the National Doubles. Only after Bill said he would not play at all if he could not play with Hunter did the Committee, a bare three hours before the match was scheduled to begin, definitely decide to select them. This put great pressure on Hunter, who felt he must play well, which he was able to do, to vindicate Bill's faith in him, and also on Bill, who said later that he was obsessed by the feeling that if they didn't win, and the Cup lost as a result, he would have been held responsible. But Bill also played well, serving powerfully and lobbing effectively, and the Americans won in five sets, the first four being very close and hard fought, but the final one going to them at love.

When he came out to play Lacoste on the third day, Tilden had thus played a total of nine sets on the two preceding days. The day was hot and humid as had been the two before it, and Bill knew he had little chance of outlasting Lacoste in a long match. He knew also that if he lost France was almost certain to win the Cup since Johnston, barring some kind of miracle, would never be able to beat Cochet. So, trying for a quick victory he began hitting hard from the outset, but, although he served a dozen aces and made some brilliant groundstroke winners, Lacoste was too steady for him, winning the set 6-4. Bill's control improved in the second set, but Lacoste forced him to expend much energy before Bill won it 6-2, and in the third set, after gaining a lead of 3-2, he could win only four more points as Lacoste took the next four games for the set. The rest period did Bill little good; Lacoste won the fourth set pretty much as he pleased, 6-2.

Billy Johnston made a game fight against Cochet, winning the second set and pulling up in the fourth from 2-5 to 4-5 and love-30 on Cochet's service. The stands were in a continuous uproar during Johnston's rally. Cochet had two match points in the eighth game, but after losing both and finally the game he looked obviously worried. Making some bad errors he lost the ninth game at love and the first two points of the tenth. At this point, however, he got a grip on himself, and it was Johnston's turn to become overanxious after Cochet passed him at the net for the third point. Three Johnston errors followed—two shots hit out, a backhand drive and a high volley, and a forehand into the net—giving the match to Cochet and the Cup to France. Both Little Bill and Big Bill had given of their best to hold on to the Cup they had defended successfully for so long, but their adversaries had been too young and too strong for them. In the case of "Grand Bill," as the Musketeers called him admiringly, it had taken the collective effort of all four of them to wear down and overcome him and thereby gain the prize they had so long and persistently striven for.

France's victory was one of the memorable events that made 1927 a great year in sports history—Babe Ruth broke his 1921 record of 59 home runs by hitting 60, Gene Tunney survived the famous "long count" knockdown to beat Jack Dempsey for the second time, Bobby Jones won the British Open for the second year running and the third of his five U. S. amateur titles, Walter Hagen won his fifth PGA championship and his fourth in a row, Helen Wills won her fourth U. S. singles title and her first at Wimbledon—and the jubilation and national pride of the French knew no bounds. Carpentier, their boxing champion, may have lost to Dempsey, but their Davis Cup team had restored French athletic prestige, and every Paris newspaper had front-page accounts of the great victory. Ten thousand Parisians would file past the Cup when it was placed on exhibition in the Louvre, where it would remain for six years until the French lost it to Great Britian in 1933. There was further cause for rejoicing when the news came not much more than a week later that France could boast of the number one player in the world, Lacoste having won his second successive U. S. Singles title by again demonstrating his mastery over Tilden.

He did so against a Tilden who played as well and as confidently as perhaps he ever had at Forest Hills, and yet Bill could not take a set, losing 11-9, 6-3, 11-9. In the quarter-finals, Bill had beaten Borotra 6-1, 3-6, 10-8, 6-1, Borotra having had seven set points in the third set. Then in the semi-finals against Hunter, who had beaten John Hennessey, who had upset Cochet, Bill had pulled out two long deuce sets to win 14-12, 6-1, 4-6, 9-7, but although he fought heroically, urged on by the cheers of a partisan gallery, he could not repeat the performance against a Lacoste whose defense was so impregnable on all the crucial points that it made no difference that Bill, besides leading 3-1 in the second set, looked to be an almost certain winner of the other two, leading 7-6 and 40-love in the first and 5-2 and two set points in the third. Borotra summed it all up when he said after the match, "If René keeps playing tennis like that, how is anyone ever going to beat him?"

CHAPTER THIRTEEN

FRENCH SUPREMACY MAINTAINED

What steps should be taken to regain the Davis Cup, as the USLTA for financial as well as patriotic reasons of course wanted to do? Being a challenging nation instead of a defending one made for a whole new ball game. Bill Tilden, as might be expected, had some ideas on the subject andnaturally was not hesitant about presenting them to Association officials when they met in convention at Chicago in February of 1928. Having a couple of months earlier suggested that the United States challenge in the European Zone instead of the American, an idea the Executive Committee of the USLTA had turned down, he now proposed that there be two U. S. teams. One of these would play in and could be expected to win the American Zone over the not very strong opposition provided by such countries as Japan, Cuba, Canada, and Mexico. The other would go to Europe early enough to become thoroughly accustomed to playing conditions in preparation for the Interzone Final and, if that were won, for the Challenge Round. This second team would actually be the "first" team and would consist of Hunter and himself with the addition of certain members of the other team after it had won the American Zone.

Bill argued unsuccessfully for a resolution directing the Davis Cup Committee to adopt the two-team plan, but the delegates did vote that it be given further consideration. They also approved the ranking committee's recommendation that he be ranked number one nationally for the eighth straight year. Another action supportive of Bill was reported in a dispatch from Chicago to the New York *Times* as follows:

> The American privilege of glaring at officials, whether it be in baseball, boxing or tennis, was saved to the tennis players of the land, it was learned today, when this right was on trial at the U.S.L.T.A. meeting here last Saturday.

Advocates of the English code offered a regulation for-
bidding the players' glaring at the officials. Tilden rose
with some choice remarks and some very impressive
glaring, and the rule against "dirty looks" was voted
down.

Bill Tilden had long been notorious for protesting what he
considered to be bad line decisions, his favorite trick being to put
his hands on his hips and glare at the offending official. As a
result more than one angered or humiliated umpire or linesman
had quit in the middle of one of Bill's matches. In justifying his
protests, Bill once said: "It's quite simple. There are many occasions when I am in a perfect position to see better than they
just what happens. Suppose, for example, I take a chance on
hitting one down the sideline and I play one of my best strokes.
I see the ball strike inside by an inch or half an inch. Surely I
can't stand by quietly and hear the ball called 'out' by some official, either not in a position to see perfectly or incompetent to
judge correctly."

Bill also would often embarrass linesmen by throwing the
next point when he believed his opponent had got a bad line
call, and although he advocated, in *The Art of Lawn Tennis* and
elsewhere, that this should be done unobtrusively he did not always practice what he preached, sometimes doing so in a most
conspicuous manner. Many young players of Bill's day and later
were influenced to follow this practice of his, believing that good
sportsmanship required them to thus throw points. Don Budge
has told how he followed Tilden's example in this regard until
he played Wimbledon for the first time in 1935 and was convinced by Gottfried Von Cramm, to whom he lost in the semi-
finals, that in making a great show of giving away a point because
he thought a call had wronged his quarter-final opponent Budge
had really been a bad sport because his action had embarrassed a
poor linesman in front of 15,000 people. Nowadays, like Bill,
most of the top pros do not hestitate to question what they consider to be bad calls against them, but only Manuel Orantes, the
very likeable Spaniard, has been known to have purposely
missed a shot after his opponent has clearly been the victim of a
bad call. He has said, "I'm friends with everybody. We all play
for money and we all know each other. If the other guy gets a
bad call, it's going to bother me. I want to beat him because I
play better, not because someone made a mistake. If I didn't

miss the next shot my game would be affected. I'll think I'm taking advantage of him."

Perhaps with the idea that half a loaf would be better than none, Bill, when he got back East from Chicago, said he stood ready to compete in the American Zone after all, and that what he had in mind in presenting the Chicago resolution was that he and Hunter would play one or two American Zone matches with the other members of the team playing the remainder, leaving Tilden and Hunter free to go abroad early enough to become fully acclimated. It did seem that the U. S. team would have enough depth to win the American Zone without the full services of Tilden and Hunter, but the Cup Committee not wanting to take any chances nor to assume the extra expense that would be incurred decided otherwise.

Bill accepted the decision without protest and also appointment as team captain, even withdrawing from a play in which he was appearing so that he could join several other players, among them George Lott and John Hennessey, who had been ordered to Augusta, Georgia on March 19 for a week of practice and test matches to determine the makeup of the team that would go the following week to play Mexico in Mexico City.

Some of these players were college students. John Doeg was at Stanford, John Van Ryn at Princeton, Wilmer Allison and Lewis White at the University of Texas, and Edward Chandler, twice national intercollegiate champion while at the University of California, was a first-year law student at Harvard; and apparently the Cup Committee did not realize that it might be laying itself open to criticism in asking these players to interrupt their studies well before the end of the school year. When Dr. Sumner Hardy, the president of the California Tennis Association, and unlike his brother Sam no friend of Bill's, learned that Doeg was taking a leave of absence from Stanford to go to Augusta, he denounced Tilden and the Committee, saying: "It's all wrong to put tennis first. Doeg cannot afford to take nine months off. He would miss the final exams of the Winter Quarter and all the Spring Quarter and would not get back until October if he played through the whole Davis Cup season. Take the whole Davis Cup squad, with the exception of George Lott, who does nothing, and Tilden, whose business is tennis, and you will not find a single one who should not be in school or business." One could hardly dispute the correctness of Dr. Hardy's statement about Bill, but he was not being accurate concerning Lott, who, although he did play considerable tournament tennis, actually had been in attendance at the University of Chicago and had played no tennis during the winter. Once he finished school Lott did merit Dr. Hardy's description by becoming a self-confessed "tennis bum," a phrase he himself was credited with coining.

Charles S. Garland, who had been on the 1920 Davis Cup team and was chairman of the Selection Committee, telegraphed Dr. Hardy that the players had been "invited," not "ordered," to report, and that there was no intention they should put tennis before their college work, although how this could be, given the circumstances, he did not explain. Garland also wired Doeg, although not in his official capacity, advising him not to come, but Doeg, having arranged to obtain credit in two of his courses without examination and being assured he could make up the other two, did so anyway. The other college players also reported except for Van Ryn, to whom it was more important to finish his senior year at Princeton and graduate. Chandler took part in the trials but then returned to law school.

The team Bill picked at the conclusion of the trial matches included in addition to Hennessey, Allison, and himself, two of his protégés, Arnold Jones and Wilbur F. Coen, Jr., a former national boys' champion, who was named as a reserve. This looked like favoritism, but actually Bill did carry out his promise to the players that his selections would be based solely on the outcome of their matches. Lott, who was short of practice lost to both Allison and Jones, as well as to Tilden. Hennessey played unbeatable tennis in all his matches inflicting on Bill his one singles loss. Coen, whom Bill had got included in the trials on the grounds it would give him valuable experience, made Bill's heart glad by beating Doeg, who, like Lott lost all his matches, and also Chandler and Jones. Allison Danzig, covering the matches for the New York *Times,* reported that Coen's play was so good that he had a chance of becoming a regular member of the team.

It was John Hennessey, however, who gave the most hope that the U. S. might have a team strong enough in 1928 to have at least an outside chance of winning back the Cup from the French. Off the court, the twenty-seven-year-old Hennessey, who was from Indianapolis, with his tall, rangy physique, rugged features, and unruly shock of brown hair, looked more like a middle-western farm boy than a tennis player. His stroke equip-

ment consisted of a very strong western forehand drive, an excellent serve, volley and overhead, and a backhand hit with an
awkward, corkscrew motion somewhat reminiscent of Gerald
Patterson's which was nevertheless a reliable, if rather unlovely
looking stroke. Hennessey ranked fifth nationally in 1927,
having beaten Cochet, the reigning Wimbledon champion, at
Forest Hills at 6-1 in the fifth set. He had the reputation of
being cocky and a clever gamesman—his victory over Cochet
seems to have been achieved in part by lulling the Frenchman
into a false sense of security—and he took particular delight in
doing and saying things that would annoy Bill Tilden. Before the
tryouts even began he inquired of Tilden where they would be
staying in Mexico City, implying that he had no doubt about his
making the team. To bring the cocky Hennessey down a peg,
Bill changed the tryout schedule so that he would play
Hennessey first. Hennessey countered by appearing for the
match—it was a cold spring day in Augusta—attired in a half
dozen or more sweaters, three of them letter sweaters borrowed
from his collegiate teammates. At intervals during the match,
Hennessey would remove a sweater with great ceremony which
gave the sizable crowd that had turned out for the afternoon
tryouts considerable amusement. Tilden grew more and more
annoyed over Hennessey's antics, and his game was adversely
affected. The match went to five sets and Hennessey won the
last one 8-6.

The Davis Cup tie with Mexico was no contest, the U. S.
team winning all five matches easily. Tilden and Hennessey
played the singles and Tilden and Jones the doubles. Feeling
that the Mexican fans ought to have more for their money, Bill
played Hennessey in a singles exhibition, and he and Coen played
Hennessey and Jones a doubles match. Bill also got in a plug for
his young partner in an inspirational talk he gave to the several
hundred students of various nationalities attending the American
School of Mexico City. Urging them to work equally hard at
their studies and sports, he said: "Coen is a shining example of
what I am advising. He is only sixteen years of age, but he is the
most remarkable tennis player of his age the world has seen,
and he is the leading student in his class at a Kansas City high
school. He is also captain of the basketball team. And all this
he has accomplished by hard work and training himself to concentrate." As he grew older, Coen remained a superior student,
making Phi Beta Kappa in college, but on the tennis court, like

Bill's other boy protégés, he never fulfilled the high hopes Bill had for him. It was not Bill's departure from the amateur ranks at the end of 1930, that caused Coen to give up serious tournament a couple of years later, as Bill tried to make himself believe, but rather Coen's coming to the conclusion that his slight physique and his inability to develop a strong serve and volley to go with his excellent groundstrokes were limitations that would keep him from reaching the top flight.

Coen still has the distinction of being the youngest American player ever to participate in a Davis Cup match. His victories in further tryout matches played in St. Louis warranted Bill's naming him as a regular on the team, as did those of George Lott, the two replacing Allison and Jones. The next match, against China, would be played in Kansas City, Coen's home town, and how fitting it would be for Coen to play in the doubles with Bill before his proud fellow townsmen. The only trouble with this idea was that Lott and Hennessey were a much better team, having twice beaten Tilden and Coen decisively in the St. Louis tryouts, and twice more in practice matches, which were closer, in Kansas City, Coen by this time having got used to being stationed at the net while Bill covered all the rest of the court. Since Bill had named Lott and Hennessey to fill the singles spots, they had no objection to Bill and Coen playing the doubles. The Chinese, Gordon Lum, who had learned his tennis in Australia, and Paul Kong, who had been in the United States for some time attending Columbia University, were both nice young men, but they were so sadly outclassed—out of the twelve sets played in the four singles matches Lum and Kong together lost half at love—that Lott and Hennessey were probably just as happy not to have had to play them in doubles as well. Against Tilden and Coen the Chinese could win only six games, losing 6-2, 6-1, 6-3.

Early in June, Tilden and company disposed of Japan handily in the American Zone final in Chicago, and by the middle of the month were in England in time for a week of practice before beginning play at Wimbledon. Here they were joined by Frank Hunter, who had been playing abroad since early in May, it being his and Tilden's idea that if the USLTA would not send both of them abroad as early as they believed necessary to get thoroughly accustomed to foreign conditions, Hunter, at least, being a wealthy business man, could go at his own expense and get properly acclimated.

The results of Wimbledon did not augur well for America's Davis Cup chances. The irrepressible Hennessey, who created a minor sensation by appearing for his first round match in striped white flannels, lost in the quarter-finals (wearing plain white trousers by official request) to Cochet, and Bill Tilden, after beating Borotra in the same round in four sets, lost for the fourth straight time to Lacoste, 2-6, 6-2, 2-6, 6-4, 6-3, Bill in the fourth set needing only one point for a 4-1 lead. Lacoste then won his second Wimbledon title by beating Cochet in four sets. In the doubles Tilden and Hunter could not repeat their victory of the year before, being upset by Patterson and Hawkes in a marathon five-setter in one semi-final, while in the other Lott and Hennessey lost in four sets to Cochet and Brugnon, who went on to win the title.

It should be noted that Lacoste had only recently lost the final of the French Championships to Cochet, and his victory at Wimbledon came about because he was able to correct a weakness in his stroke equipment which had made him vulnerable to Cochet's volleying attack in their earlier encounter. Lacoste's forehand cross-court return had not been good enough to pass Cochet at the net at crucial points in the match, and before and during the Wimbledon meeting, and even for a couple of hours on the morning of the final he worked assiduously to perfect a sharply angled drive that would dip quickly out of reach of the incoming volleyer. With his patience and persistence and his keen tennis intelligence it was no wonder Lacoste was so formidable an opponent.

In 1928, for the first time in over a quarter of a century of Davis Cup competition, the defending nation would be a country other than Australasia, Great Britain, or the United States; for the first time also the Challenge Round would not be played on grass, but on the slow red clay courts of the Stade Roland Garros in the Paris suburb of Auteuil. Bill Tilden put the American team through a week of hard practice on these courts which he pronounced "splendid," where the Interzone Final against Italy would be played on July 20, a week before the Challenge Round.

Deeming the facilities at St. Cloud, where the French Championships had always been played, inadequate for defending the Cup, the French Tennis Federation had begun construction late in 1927 on the Stade Roland Garros, named in memory of a famous French aviator killed in action in World

War I.   Situated on the southern edge of the great city park known as the Bois de Boulogne and not far from the Auteuil race course, it had a singularly beautiful tree-shaded setting. A handsome old country house was converted into a club house, and seven red clay courts, joined by winding flower-lined walkways, were laid out around the grounds in an irregular pattern rather than in rows side by side.   An eighth court, *le cour central,* was enclosed by a cement stadium in the shape of a rectangle and open at the top. Its seats were quite steeply pitched, giving the 10,000 persons they could hold, as they looked down on the players below, a feeling of being very close to the play, more so than was the case in the arena-like enclosures at Wimbledon and Forest Hills.

On July 18, Bill announced that he and Lott would play singles against the Italians and Lott and Hennessey the doubles. The next day he was informed that the Amateur Rule Committee of the USLTA had declared him ineligible for Davis Cup play "for having violated the amateur rule by writing current newspaper articles for pay or a consideration covering the Wimbledon tournament in which he was a competitor." The action, the result of a complaint by the California tennis official, Dr. Sumner Hardy, whom the reader has already met, and who, like Julian Myrick, was one of Bill's most inveterate enemies in the USLTA, was taken without giving Bill any warning or any opportunity to answer the charge, and without consulting with or even notifying in advance Samuel Collom, the president of the Association, or Joseph Wear, the chairman of the Davis Cup Committee, both of whom were in Europe at the time.

One particular article written for the Philadelphia *Ledger* Syndicate, a general description of the first week's play at Wimbledon which included references to some of Bill's own matches, provided the chief basis for his suspension. Bill had written similar articles on Wimbledon the year before to which the USLTA had made no objection, and he contended now that what he had written "consisted of comment" and thus did not violate the player-writer rule which prohibited daily reports on tournaments by a participating player.   Bill was still in the tournament, however, when he wrote the article, and Dr. Hardy, having read it in his San Francisco paper and finding references to matches played less than two days earlier (the rule called for an interval of forty-eight hours before publication) argued that it was a "current" report.

Bill's face was pale and his lips trembled when he appeared at Roland Garros to read a prepared statement categorically denying the charges and volunteering, although barred from playing, to continue to give advice and assistance to the team. The assemblage of reporters, tennis officials, and fans who heard him gave him an ovation, and from Lacoste and the other Musketeers, who were also present, he received expressions of sympathy. "Pauvre Beeg Beel," the French now called him, and he was looked on as something of a martyr, a role Bill was more than happy to play in his relations with the press and public. American opinion also appeared to be almost entirely on Bill's side, and the New York *Times* gave him its editorial support. Collom and Wear publicly expressed disagreement with the ruling, and the latter announced that he would resign from the Davis Cup Committee when the team returned home. The other members of the team, led by Lott, threatened to strike, but were dissuaded by Tilden, who told them: "Personalities do not count in this affair. Let's go to work to win back the Davis Cup first. We will settle personal matters later on." It was also agreed that although Wear would have to replace him as captain Bill would continue to coach the team unofficially.

For the first time in nine years of Davis Cup competition, Tilden was a spectator, albeit a pleased one, as he watched Hennessey and Hunter score singles victories on the opening day of play against Italy. The gallery of only five hundred or so—meagre, no doubt, because Bill was not playing—cheered him when he entered the stadium and again when he gave Hennessey a congratulatory hug after the latter defeated de Morpurgo, the star of the Italian team and one of Europe's best players, in four sets.

As the French and everyone else expected, the U. S. defeated Italy four matches to one, Hunter losing to de Morpurgo, and now there was the distinct possibility, which was almost unthinkable to the French, that they would be defending the Cup without being challenged by the great Tilden. Said Lacoste, who was greatly upset over the Tilden disqualification: "We would rather lose the Davis Cup than retain it when there may be some excuse in the absence of Tilden." Not only would a French victory be a hollow one, but there was also the matter of the gate if Tilden did not play. Many tennis fans would assuredly stay away, and packed galleries were needed to help pay for the new stadium.

The French Tennis Federation expressed its concern in a cablegram sent to the USLTA, the meaning of which was clear enough even though its English was somewhat unidiomatic: "Without desiring to interfere in your interior regulations, we would be very happy if you could, by way of exception, authorize Tilden to play in Davis Cup, as his absence takes away from game great part of regularity." No reply was forthcoming, but there were rumors that other moves were being taken to get Bill reinstated. Collom was reported to have advised Association officials in New York that he reserved the right to play Tilden in the Challenge Round, and it was revealed that he had made a two-hour transatlantic telephone call, trying to get the Amateur Rule Committee to reverse its decision. At the rate of $16.25 per minute his call had cost a total of $1,950.

Failing to get any support from back home, Collom announced that the ban on Tilden would stand. Then, two days later and not much more than twenty-four hours before the Challenge Round would begin, at the urging of American Ambassador Myron T. Herrick, whom the French had asked to intercede, Collom reversed himself, saying that "on my own responsibility," and "in the interest of international good feeling," he was declaring Tilden eligible to play, although Bill would have to answer to the charges against him later. The USLTA, apparently having finally become aware that Bill's suspension had been a bad idea as far as the French were concerned, as well as being highly unpopular with nearly everybody else, issued a statement giving grudging assent, and which gratuitously went out of its way to condemn Bill for breaking his written promise to observe the player-writer rule.

Drawn against Lacoste in the opening match, Bill who was short of practice and emotionally drained by the prolonged uncertainty as to his situation, was hardly in any condition to make good on the promise he had made to his opponent after their gruelling Wimbledon semi-final, "I'll beat you yet, René" (Bill always pronounced it "Rainy"), and the opening set, in which he could win only a single game, and that on his service after Lacoste had had game point four times, seemed clearly to bear this out. Bothered by a strong wind that swirled about the court and lacking in confidence, he could not get his hard-hit drives under control and his service was equally unreliable.

Following the match-play precept that you should always change a losing game, Bill, at the beginning of the second set, eschewed his hard hitting, resorting instead to slices and chops and to frequent drop shots. As he said later, this seemed to be the worst possible tactic to employ against a player as steady as Lacoste, since the long rallies that could be expected to result would turn the match into an endurance contest that would be to the decided advantage of the younger player. But instead the varied spins that Tilden put on the ball gave Lacoste considerable difficulty in judging its bounce, broke up his rhythm, and made his timing uncertain, so much so that Bill was able to win the second and third sets, 6-4, 6-4. Then, for some reason, perhaps because he felt he could not go five sets—George Lott described him as looking "plain beat" during the rest period after the third set—and must try to finish off Lacoste quickly, if at all, he went back to hitting hard, thereby violating the match-play principle that you should never change a winning game, and as his errors again piled up, Lacoste soon made it two sets all.

But Bill had something in reserve, and going back to his chopping and slicing game, he got to 4-3 in the fifth set after Lacoste had twice almost broken his serve. At 15-all in the next game, with Lacoste serving, during a long rally Bill hit a short ball which Lacoste returned with a deep approach shot to Bill's backhand. Bill replied with a slice down the line which Lacoste volleyed sharply cross court, but Bill, anticipating such a return, was already racing to his right and, drawn far out of court, hit a stunning passing shot which passed outside the net and into Lacoste's backhand corner to win the point. It was a shot like the one Bill had hit to win a crucial point when he defeated Billy Johnston in the 1921 Singles Championship, and the one Don Budge hit on match point in his famous 1937 Davis Cup victory over Gottfried Von Cramm. Lacoste was so unnerved that he served a double fault on the next point, missed an easy shot to give Bill 15-40, and then lost the game when Bill hit a winner for 5-3, after which Bill won the next game on his serve for the set and match.

Bill's victory evened the score with Lacoste in Cup play at two matches each. It could also be considered the finest victory of his career. He may have played better tennis on other occasions but never a better match. He had out-maneuvered, out-spun and out-steadied a frustrated but admiring opponent who had every reason to believe he knew how to beat Bill. "Now," Lacoste told Al Laney after the match, "I do not know any more. Now on my own court he beats me. Is he not the greatest player of all?"

John Hennessey, like Johnston the year before, although he gave a better account of himself than expected, was not strong enough to come through in either of his singles matches. Against Cochet on the first day he almost gained a two-set lead before losing 5-7, 9-7, 6-3, 60-, and he also had a close four-set match with Lacoste, going down 4-6, 6-1, 7-5, 7-3.

Although the 1927 Challenge Round had seemed to demonstrate that three straight days of hard play against the French was too much to ask of Tilden, instead of Lott and Hennessey being named to oppose the French team of Cochet and Borotra, Bill was again called on to assume the added burden of the doubles. He and Hunter had won the year before, but this time they lost in five hard-fought sets, 6-4, 6-8, 7-5, 4-6, 6-2. It was a wonder that Bill was able the next day to extend a Cochet at the top of his game to the extent he did. Cochet had to fight off three set points in the first set and seven in the second before winning 9-7, 8-6, 6-4.

The USLTA did not want anyone to get the idea that in permitting Bill to play in the Challenge Round it had done anything more than lift Bill's suspension temporarily, and even before he got back to America early in August, it was announced that Bill would be given a trial by the Association's Executive Committee to be held on the twenty-fourth of the month. The use of the word "trial" rather than "hearing" could well have been a reflection of USLTA animosity toward Bill, and he sarcastically commented that its use was "very amusing." Bill's *fidus Achates,* Frank Hunter, sent telegrams to ranking players and to clubs around the country in an effort to get a campaign going to put pressure on the USLTA to postpone the trial until after the close of the tennis season, but it took place as scheduled, with the result that Bill was found guilty and barred from amateur play indefinitely. At the same time that this verdict was being reached in a six-hour meeting in New York City, Bill, who said he could not be present because of "business reasons," was on a theatre stage in Boston doing a vaudeville monologue before an audience that included Cochet, Borotra and Brugnon, who had recently arrived in the United States, hoping to add the national championship to their Wimbledon and Davis Cup triumphs.

With Tilden barred from playing and with Lacoste not defending his title (he had announced even before the Challenge Round that he would not come to America), Forest Hills was somewhat of an anticlimax. Cochet, as expected, came through to win the championship, but it was Frank Hunter who was the star of the tournament. He beat Borotra in five sets in the quarter-final round, Lott in four in the semi-finals, and against Cochet he led two sets to one and almost took the fourth before losing 4-6, 6-4, 3-6, 7-5, 6-3. It was perhaps the finest match Hunter had ever played, and it reflected credit on Tilden as well, since it was the coaching and practice Hunter had received from Bill that had been instrumental in large measure in enabling him to develop his game to such a high level.

CHAPTER FOURTEEN

THE END OF AN ERA

The day after Bill Tilden's suspension went into effect, he announced that he would apply for immediate reinstatement when the Executive Committee of the USLTA met again in September. He resented, he said, the accusations and insinuations of the Committee, and added: "I am willing to stack my services to American tennis up against that of any individual official on the committee which barred me and let the public choose which has been and is of more value to the game. I am far more amateur in spirit than some of the men who have run tennis for years with an eye to the gate and have exploited me for its advancement."

Others besides Bill considered tennis officials as something less than amateur in spirit, among then John Tunis, an astute and sensitive commentator on the current sports scene who was particularly knowledgeable about tennis. Wrote Tunis in an article published early in 1928 in *Harper's* magazine, entitled "The Lawn Tennis Industry," "The plain fact is that ninety percent of the regular tournament players and probably the same percentage of tennis officials are no more concerned with the furthering of amateur sport than is Mr. Tex Rickard or Mr. C. C. Pyle. They are in tennis—the sport which was formerly a sport for amateurs —for what they can get out of it."

While conceding that a tennis official like Julian Myrick— certainly one of the men Bill was referring to in his statement quoted above—had made an immensely valuable contribution to the development of the game, Tunis also suggested that the publicity Myrick and his flourishing insurance business had received from Myrick's association with tennis had been immensely valuable to him. Myrick sold insurance without having to call on customers, and Tunis quoted another insurance executive as saying, "At a conservative estimate, I figure the publicity Mr. Myrick has received is worth $50,000 a year." He also believed that in the decade since 1918, when Myrick became vice president of the USLTA, that Myrick's tennis connection had probably enabled him to profit to the extent of at least $300,000.

As for Bill Tilden, wrote Tunis, "he professes tennis as a doctor professes medicine or a lawyer professes law. Life to Mr. Tilden is tennis. He eats, breathes, sleeps and thinks tennis. How anyone could be more of a professional in this sense than he I am at a loss to understand." But Tilden and other leading players could hardly be blamed for opposing such restrictions as the player-writer rule put on them by the USLTA when they could observe the overlords of the game—bond dealers, real estate men, and insurance salesmen—reaping profits out of the game well beyond their reach. If a player like Tilden could command a thousand dollars for an afternoon match he should be allowed to do so, "freely, frankly, openly." There was no more disgrace in making money out of tennis than out of business. The disgrace of tennis was its false amateurism.

The Executive Committee took no action in September on Bill's suspension, and at its next meeting in December referred the matter to the Amateur Rule Committee which was instructed to confer with Tilden to determine if he was "chastened in spirit and willing to promise that he would conform to both the letter and the spirit of the player-writer rule." Bill never expressed the contrition, at least publicly, that this seemed to demand of him, but at the annual meeting of the Association in February his reinstatement was nevertheless approved. He was also given the number one national ranking for the ninth time, which surpassed the record of eight held by William A. Larned. There were some who questioned whether he should be ranked at all since he had not played in the national singles, but his Davis Cup victory over Lacoste carried sufficient weight to overcome their objections.

Bill's suspension also appears to have given him both the inspiration and opportunity to begin writing *Glory's Net,* a novel about tennis he published early in 1930. Unlike his earlier tennis stories, it seems to have been intended more for the adult than the juvenile reader, and to have been written out of a need Bill felt to justify continuing his existence as a tennis player should his suspension be lifted. There was certainly nothing about the novel to suggest that such leading novelists of the day as Hemingway, Fitzgerald or Sinclair Lewis had any need to fear Bill as a rival, but it did get some favorable notices, one reviewer describing it as "an enthralling romance interwoven with an exposé of the amateur-professional tennis situation."

Bill's protagonist is young David Cooper, "the darkest of dark horses ever seen at Forest Hills," who wins the National Championship on his first try. A small-town boy from Illinois and a fine all-around athlete in high school, he had been attracted to tennis, even though it was regarded as a sissy game by the other boys, and "had a natural instinct for hitting the ball correctly much like that which had marked the games of Vincent Richards and Junior Coen in their early years."

After becoming champion, David marries his boyhood sweetheart, Mary Jones, and goes to work for Randolph Harper, a New York investment banker and prominent tennis official, his job, like the sinecure Bill once had in Providence selling insurance, leaving him ample time for tennis. David finds their new existence most agreeable—the Manhattan social life, with its atmosphere of affluence and sophistication, the traveling to tournaments at home and abroad with all expenses paid, the adulation he receives from tennis fans—but Mary, who commendably, we are to believe, has retained her small-town ways and values, decides after a time that their way of living has turned her husband into a "tennis gigolo and parasite," and when he refuses to give it up she goes back to Illinois alone after uttering these parting words: "Live this life, David, live it as long as you wish. Come to me if you feel I am right and that you want to come. If you do not come it will not change my love, it will only fill my heart with regret at the loss of a man."

In addition to such melodramatic speeches, the formula for Bill's equally melodramatic plot—the beautiful daughter of his employer almost succeeds in her efforts to win David away from Mary—called for a happy ending. David eventually comes to realize that without Mary true happiness does not result from living in New York and winning victories at Wimbledon and over Lacoste and Cochet in the Davis Cup. Back he goes to Illinois to find that not only has Mary borne him a son but also that, having seen the error of his ways, he can have Mary and his tennis too. When he tells her, "I've played my last match," she replies, "No, David, you must play. You owe it to your country, to the game, to us. . . . You are an artist in your line. Any artist belongs to the country and to the world." This, in effect, is what another Mary, Bill's good friend and loyal tennis fan, Mary Garden, the famous opera singer, had told Bill after his straight-set loss to Lacoste, despite having set points in two of the sets, in the 1927

Forest Hills final, which, coming after two earlier heartbreaking losses that year to Lacoste at Paris and Cochet at Wimbledon, had so discouraged Bill that he was almost ready to give up the game. Mary Garden had reminded Bill that he was a tennis artist and as such must never lose faith in himself. "Win or lose, right or wrong," she had told him, "be true to your art."

Even before he was reinstated, Bill was making plans for another European invasion with Frank Hunter. The American Zone, said Bill, could undoubtedly be won without them, and they would, of course, be available for Interzone and Challenge Round play. The Davis Cup Committee concurred in this view, and before his departure early in May, the USLTA, apparently seeing no irony in so doing, commissioned him to write for its official magazine, *Tennis.* A circular sent out to potential subscribers urged them not to miss the special feature of the May issue, which was "a complete forecast and analysis of Davis Cup play in 1929, prepared by William T. Tilden, 2nd., one of the greatest international tennis players of all time."

Abroad Bill, unfortunately, could not match his performances of the year before against the Musketeers, much less improve on them. In the French Championships, tired from a gruelling five-set match the previous day with Baron de Morpugo, he lost in the semi-finals to Lacoste, 6-1, 6-0, 5-7, 6-3. Lacoste then won the championship at 8-6 in the fifth set over Borotra, who had put out Hunter and Cochet. At Wimbledon (Lacoste did not play there nor in the Davis Cup because of ill health), Bill lost for the third straight year in the semi-finals, being decisively beaten by Cochet, 6-4, 6-1, 7-5, who went on to beat Borotra for the title, also in straight sets.

In contrast to Bill Tilden, there was no question as to Helen Will's invincibility. At Paris she won for the second straight year, and at Wimbledon for the third year in a row. In winning she lost only sixteen games in six rounds of play, defeating the young Californian Helen Jacobs, 6-1, 6-2 in the final. At Forest Hills later in the summer where she won the American championship for the sixth time, she was even more dominating, losing only eight games, six of them to her final-round opponent, the Englishwoman Mrs. Phoebe Watson. In the semi-final, Helen smothered Molla Mallory 6-0, 6-0, losing only five points in the first set and fifteen in the second. The one-sided victory was all the more remarkable since Mrs. Mallory had been a straight-set quarter-final victor over Betty Nuthall, the young English girl who had carried Helen to an 8-6, 8-6 match in the Wightman Cup a few days earlier.

In the Wills-Mallory match, each time the players changed courts on odd games and Mrs. Mallory walked toward the baseline to serve or receive, the gallery applauded her with great fervor. In the second set when she was within a point of winning a game on two different occasions only to fail by the narrowest of margins, the crowd groaned in sympathy. It was not just that the always popular Mrs. Mallory was the underdog that the gallery was all on her side. Rather it was because of the emotionless, merciless way in which Helen Wills cut down her opponents. She was a killer who played the game without seeming to get any pleasure out of it, and whose only purpose seemed to be to dispatch opponents summarily.

Against Phoebe Watson, who actually kept Helen on the defensive much of the time, but who lost because she made a good many more errors, the crowd loudly cheered the shots of the Englishwoman but greeted Helen's best shouts with comparative silence. On the other hand, Bill Tilden, after he had won his seventh national championship several weeks later in the same stadium, was cheered to the echo by the largest gallery of the year. At Wimbledon, the gallery gave Helen only polite applause after she had won the final point. In the same tournament, as already noted, Bill was badly beaten by Cochet, and yet, as he picked up his sweater and extra rackets to leave the court, the crowd rose and cheered him in what old-time observers said was the most remarkable demonstration Wimbledon had ever witnessed. No doubt the gallery felt sympathy for Bill because he had fallen from his place as the greatest tennis player in the world, but he had never been nor was he now a truly popular champion. What brought Bill the admiration and support of fans was their instinctive realization, as one tennis commentator put it, "that the game is his life and that he has given himself to tennis, that he loves it, revels in it, that on the court he is the artist supreme."

In the Challenge Round against France, represented by a two-man team of Cochet and Borotra, Bill suffered the most crushing defeat of his international career, losing to Cochet on the opening day, 6-3, 6-1, 6-2, although he came back two days later to beat Borotra in four sets. Fitz-Eugene Dixon, the American non-playing captain, had recommended by cable to the Davis Cup Committee that Frank Hunter be the second singles player against the French, Hunter having won both his singles in the American victory over Germany in the Interzone Final, but Dixon was ordered to play George Lott, on the theory that the twenty-two year-old Lott had a better chance of gaining a singles win than the veteran Hunter, and in any event should be given the experience.

The young Chicagoan, one of the two best players ever to come out of the Midwest, the other being John Hennessey, was ranked number three nationally in 1927 and 1928, right behind Tilden and Hunter, and he had tournament victories over both these players. A western-grip player, which hampered him somewhat in hitting strongly off the backhand, he was an astute and determined competitor. His quick reflexes, fine net game, and the guile and delicate touch with which he could make openings for a partner's put-away shots had already brought him the first of the five American doubles championships and the two Wimbledon doubles titles he would ultimately win with four different partners. One of the great doubles specialists of all the time, it was not Lott's destiny to achieve championship rank in singles, but at this point in his career there was considerable justification for the USLTA belief that he might eventually do so.

As it was to Tilden, Lott's selection was a great disappointment to Hunter, but being a good team player he accepted it with good grace, saying, "If they thought Lott had a better chance than I, it's quite all right with me. I'll be there rooting for George." Lott needed more than rooting to win, but he did creditably, forcing both Cochet and Borotra to close four-set matches. The U. S. won the doubles, the two other young members of the team, Wilmer Allison and John Van Ryn, who had earlier won the Wimbledon doubles, doing themselves proud in beating Cochet and Borotra 6-1, 8-6, 6-4, but the French had taken three singles matches, giving them the Cup for another year.

With Cochet and Borotra content to rest on their laurels, and Lacoste, threatened with tuberculosis, having decided to retire from international play, no Musketeers competed in the American championships, and Bill Tilden, in their absence, won his seventh national singles title, equalling the record of Richard Sears and William A. Larned, but not before being severely tested by young John Doeg in the semifinals and again by Frank Hunter in the finals. Bill was down two sets to one in both matches, but proved that he still had great staying powers and the ability to raise his game to great heights when he needed to. Now well into his thirty-seventh year, he could still play the kind of tennis, wrote Allison Danzig, which had made him supreme from 1920 to 1926.

Bill's last year as an amateur—1930—was, he said, "enriched" (the word might be taken in another sense as well as the one Bill intended) by the "most delightful trip of my tennis life." He was referring to his playing the Riviera winter and spring tournaments, which he did at the invitation of George Pierce Butler, the American tobacco millionaire and patron of tennis who spent his winters at Monte Carlo. Butler had built a tennis club there overlooking the sea, and to it came famous international players at his invitation to play in the Butler Cup Doubles and other Riviera tournaments. Except for one inexplicable loss to a lesser English player by the name of Peters, whom he soundly trounced later, Bill won tournament after tournament, much as Helen Wills had done before him in 1926, his chief opposition coming from George Lyttleton Rogers, a six-foot, six-inch Irish Davis Cup player, Baron de Morpurgo, Jacques Brugnon, and Henry W. Austin, a British Davis Cupper.

Another opponent was the Czech Karel Kozeluh, generally recognized as the best of the European professionals. Kozeluh had shown up at the Beaulieu tournament as a spectator, and a match scheduled for the center court being delayed for some reason, Bill, to the delight of the gallery, challenged him to an impromptu match, ignoring, with impunity as it turned out, an International Lawn Tennis Federation ruling prohibiting matches between professionals and amateurs where admission had been paid. Bill was in fine form after some three months of Riviera play, which he needed to be to win 6-4, 6-4. Kozeluh was a veritable human backboard, but he was also more than a mere retriever since he could force with his groundstrokes and had fine touch on his drop shot and lob. Kozeluh had won the American professional championship in 1929, defeating Vincent Richards, and he and Bill had become well acquainted that same year when Kozeluh was hired as coach and practice player for the American Davis Cup team before the Challenge Round in Paris. They would become even better acquainted in 1931 after Bill turned professional, and the two toured the United States, Bill winning 63 out of the 76 matches they played.

In addition to all his singles triumphs on the Riviera, Bill won the championships of Austria, Italy, Germany, and Holland. In doubles, with Junior Coen as his partner most of the time, he won thirteen tournaments and another nine in mixed doubles playing with Cilli Aussem, their outstanding win being the French Hardcourt Championships, where they beat Borotra and Elizabeth Ryan in the semi-finals and Cochet and Eileen Bennett Whittingstall in the finals, both in straight sets. Cilli Aussem was an attractive and popular German girl who had the makings of a champion, but she also had a mother who so much wanted her daughter to be one that it put a great nervous strain on the girl. Bill perceived this and was able to talk the mother into returning to Berlin, leaving her daughter alone, but with proper chaperonage, on the Riviera for the rest of the season. With parental pressures removed and with Bill's coaching and partnering her to give her confidence and improve her game, Cilli proceeded to win ten singles tournaments. In the French Championships and at Wimbledon her performance was second only to that of Helen Wills Moody, and the next year when Mrs. Moody did not return to Europe, Cilli won both of those championships. Not long afterward she married and retired from tournament play. None of Bill's protégés may have become champions but in Cilli Aussem he had a protégé who did.

Had the circumtances been different, Cilli Aussem would no doubt have had strong competition from Helen Jacobs, who had accepted an invitation from the French Tennis Federation to play on the Riviera. The young Californian was expected to be a star attraction, having reached the Wimbledon final against Helen Wills the year before on her first trip abroad. Unfortunately, she came down with quinsy upon her arrival in Nice in February, and even after a couple of weeks in bed could not regain enough strength to play anything like her usual game. Bill Tilden had been interested in Helen's tennis development ever since 1924, when she had won the National Girls' Championship, the final match of which had been played at Bill's suggestion, as a curtain-raiser on the first day's play of the Davis Cup Challenge Round at the Germantown Cricket Club. To Bill's coaching, Helen owed her fine forehand slice which often served her better than her forehand drive, especially as an approach shot in taking the net.

The way Helen's slice came into being was typical of the kind of enthusiastic and energetic assistance Bill was in the habit of providing promising young players. In 1925, Helen, while

still only a seventeen-year-old junior player, competed in the
National Women's Championship for the first time and got to
the round of sixteen before being eliminated. On the day of the
final while she and her mother were lunching with Mr. and Mrs.
Sam Hardy, Bill Tilden came into the hotel dining room and
sat down with them. He had seen some of Helen's matches and
didn't like the way she hit her forehand drive. Not satisfied with
trying to explain what she was doing wrong, he suggested that
Helen and Sam Hardy meet him after the women's final at
Forest Hills and he would teach her a slice. This they did, Helen
in tennis clothes and Bill and Sam Hardy in street clothes with
their shirt sleeves rolled up. Said Helen of her experience:
"While Mr. Hardy threw balls to me, Bill taught me the fundamentals of the slice, literally kicking my feet into position,
occasionally taking my racket from me in desperation to show
me what he meant." And this went on for two hours in the hot
sun. Since Helen would be defending her national girls' title the
following week, Bill explained that there was not time enough
to alter successfully her forehand drive, but that she could
use a slice in its place, if necessary. This she did to good effect
in winning the final match of the girls' tournament, the slice
being particularly adaptable to the court which had been made
slow and slippery by a heavy rain the night before.

After watching an obviously unwell Helen Jacobs lose a
2½-hour match at Beaulieu to Mrs. Satterthwaite, an ultra-
steady Englishwoman, Bill, according to Helen, "kindly but
firmly informed me that unless I left for Paris that very day
he would forcibly remove me from Riviera tennis. I knew he
was in earnest. He never swore at me unless he was, and his
choice of oaths was both varied and admirably suited to the
occasion." Helen took his advice, and after resting until mid-
May reached the final of the French Championships, losing to
Helen Wills, now Mrs. Frederick Moody. At Wimbledon she
lost in the quarterfinals to Cilli Aussem, but when she returned
home poor health kept her out of the American tournaments.
Helen, however, was still only twenty-one, and during the 1930's
she would become Mrs. Moody's most formidable rival and the
winner of a Wimbledon championship and four championships at
Forest Hills as well.

Although they had similar backgrounds—both played at
the Berkeley Tennis Club, attended the same girls' preparatory
school and the University of California, and even lived at dif-

ferent times in the same house in Berkeley—and there was only three years difference in their ages, Helen Wills Moody and Helen Jacobs, during an eleven-year period (1927-1938) of playing each other in major championships, had something less than a friendly rivalry—some sportswriters given to hyperbole called it a "feud"—because, as the younger Helen explained it, each had different personalities and her own friends and because the older Helen's attitude toward tennis opponents "was definitely on the cold side."

Bill Tilden (in *My Story*) expressed a comparable view but far more strongly. Acknowledging that on the basis of her record Helen Wills could be regarded as the greatest of women players, even greater than Lenglen, he also wrote: "I regard her as the coldest, most self-centered, most ruthless champion ever known to tennis. Her complete disregard for all other players and her fixed determination to play tennis only when she wished to and felt it was to her advantage let her make little or no contribution to the advancement of the game or the development of younger players." Admittedly a Jacobs' partisan, Bill may have been unfair to the older Helen in judging her lacking in humanity and generosity of spirit while attributing an abundance of these qualities to her rival. There was perhaps some evidence, however, to justify him in the contrasting actions and demeanor of the two Helens in their three most famous matches.

For six years—from 1927 to 1933—Helen Jacobs endured a series of decisive defeats at the hands of the older Helen, including a final-round loss at Forest Hills in 1928 and final-round losses at Wimbledon in 1929 and 1932. Not once did she win a set, and only once did she win as many as four games in a match. In 1933, having won at Wimbledon earlier in the summer for the fifth time by defeating the English girl, Dorothy Round, who had put out Helen Jacobs in the semi-final, Helen Wills Moody was the favorite to gain her eighth American title with a final-round victory over the younger Helen, who was the defending champion, the older Helen not having competed the year before. After winning the first set 8-6, and losing the second 6-3, Helen Jacobs broke service twice and held her own to lead 3-0 in the final set, at which point the older Helen walked off the court declaring she could no longer continue to play. In a statement given out after the match explaining her default she said, "I felt as if I were going to faint because of pain in my back and hip and a complete numbness of my right leg." She added that she wished she had followed the advice given her not to play in the tournament by the orthopedic surgeon whom she had consulted about the recurring back pains she had experienced during the summer.   Inevitably, Mrs. Moody's default was compared with that of Suzanne Lenglen to Molla Mallory in their second-round championship match at Forest Hills in 1921, and there were some who believed, as was the case in the Lenglen default, that Mrs. Moody might well have been able to at least go through the motions of playing until the set had ended and that she should have done so.   Although happy to have retained her title, Helen Jacobs said that she was sorry to have the match end as it did, but that she did not see how anyone could dispute Mrs. Moody's statement as to why she had defaulted.

The two Helens met again in the 1935 Wimbledon final, where the younger player lost after leading 5-3, 40-30, match point in the third set.   Graciously she gave her opponent full credit for pulling out the match, whereas the usually impassive Mrs. Moody, it was said, appeared an excessively jubilant victor. Three years later, in the 1938 Wimbledon final, she was again the winner over Helen Jacobs, 6-4, 6-0, when the latter was rendered all but immobile at 4-all in the first set by an injured Achilles tendon.   Although urged to default by Mrs. Wightman, who came down from the stands to the court, the younger Helen played on, refusing to emulate the action of her opponent in their 1933 Forest Hills match.   At that time Helen had shown concern for Mrs. Moody's apparent physical distress, asking her if she would like to rest a while.   Now, however, Mrs. Moody did not avail herself of the opportunity to reciprocate.   Not only did she not express sympathy for her opponent's plight, she did not even indicate any recognition of it.   Made noticeably uncomfortable by this, the gallery did not give her the applause that might have been expected after her record-breaking eighth Wimbledon victory, and the next day she was attacked in the British press for lacking humanity.

Had it not been for Henri Cochet, "my nemesis in amateur tennis, the only man who ever beat me more times than I beat him as an amateur" (Cochet had seven wins to two losses, although Bill more than redressed this imbalance after the two turned professional), Bill Tilden would have remained invincible throughout his European safari of 1930.   They met in the final of the French Championship at Roland Garros, where Bill led by one set and 5-3 in the second before Cochet rallied to win

3-6, 8-6, 6-3, 6-1. Bill maintained he had never played better, and Cochet agreed, saying "Tilden played the best game he ever played against me in the last three years, but I am beginning to know his style."

However, what really won the match for Cochet, according to Bill, were two "miracle" shots in a row that Cochet made to save two set points against him in the second set. They were passing shots off forehand drives hit to his deep backhand corner which Bill had expected to go for clean winners. Bill's confidence was shaken and before he could recover, the match had turned around and Cochet was able to run it out. Bill credited another of Cochet's miracle shots, a perfectly disguised lob off a Tilden approach shot on set point for Bill in the second set as the turning point in his 1928 Davis Cup loss to Cochet, and he used these matches to document his assertion in *My Story* that "the great historic matches generally could go either way on a switch of three points—and often literally, are decided on one. The score never tells the whole story. Change the result of the vital points and the entire psychology of a tight match shifts, along with the victory."

Bill lost another close four-set match to Cochet in the Davis Cup Challenge Round, but he was not kidding anybody but himself when he continued to insist that he was playing as good tennis as he ever did in his life. "Cochet," he pronounced dramatically, "is simply too much for me. I could not have beaten him in his present form at any stage of my career. The strokes that stopped Billy Johnston cannot halt Cochet." To anyone familiar with the tennis scene of the 1920's, it was clear that Cochet was not being opposed by the Tilden of 1920-1925, the supremely confident Tilden who hit devastating forcing shots and made impossible gets with the greatest of ease, and who could dig himself out of a tight corner with parries that were offensive counter-thrusts. Bill was still a very great player, but now he was not always great when he needed to be, having lost in some measure his old mobility, combativeness, and confidence.

As in 1928, it looked for a time as if Bill would not play in the Challenge Round. The U. S. team, consisting of Lott, Allison, and Van Ryn, had come through the American Zone easily, and then taken the Interzone Final from Italy without difficulty, but it clearly needed the addition of Bill to have any chance of beating the French. Both Bill and the USLTA were well aware of this, and Bill, not at all reluctant to take advantage of the situation, said he would play only if the player-writer rule was waived so that he could cover the matches for his newspaper syndicate. At first the USLTA balked, but a few days before the matches were to begin a compromise was worked out which enabled both parties to save face. Bill would write advance articles immediately preceding the opening of play, but would not write reports on the three days of actual play, since this last would be in violation of the player-writer rule. So that Bill could write his articles a special rule adopted the year before barring an international team member from writing, giving interviews, or making radio talks while a member of the team was waived for his benefit.

Although Bill had agreed to play only pretty much on his own terms it really was, as he said, his "fondest hope" of being a party to bringing back the Cup a second time eleven years after he and Johnston had brought it back from Australia, but this was not to be. Bill had enough confidence and mobility, despite having turned an ankle in practice, to beat Borotra, if not Cochet, but Allison and Van Ryn lost the doubles to Brugnon and Cochet, and Lott, although he almost beat Borotra, lost both his singles, as he had the year before. Lott, who succumbed only at 8-6 in the fifth set, might well have defeated Borotra if he had not been the victim of a number of doubtful calls in Borotra's favor. Bill Tilden, who insisted he was not exaggerating, said that during the five sets he counted no less than twenty-eight miscalls on one line against Lott. It was a good illustration, said Bill, of the fact that in "certain European capitals" the benefit of the doubt was always given to the local player. Borotra, incidentally, was also the beneficiary of a horribly bad call on match point against him when he beat Allison in the 1932 Challenge Round. Borotra, who had the serve, hit his first ball into the net and his second serve fell so far beyond the service line that Allison did not even attempt to return it. The linesman, nevertheless, insisted the serve was good, and this was too much for an Allison who had had to endure the loss of three earlier match points, much Borotra gamesmanship, and a wildly cheering Gallic crowd urging on their hero. Allison's lead of 5-3 quickly evaporated, and Borotra ran out the set 7-5.

The outcome of the 1930 Challenge Round was especially disappointing to the Americans since they had done so well at Wimbledon a few weeks earlier, Allison and Van Ryn winning the doubles for the second year in a row, and Bill Tilden the singles for the third time, a full decade after winning his first title there. Allison, his final-round opponent, provided the sensation of the tournament, upsetting Cochet in the quarter-finals, 6-4, 6-4, 6-3. An outstanding doubles player, Allison was ranked only seventh in singles for 1929 and had the reputation of being unbeatable one day but erratic and lacking in confidence the next. Against Cochet, the blonde, twenty-five year-old Texan was very much the former, his strong American twist service, decisive volleying, and bludgeoning overhead smash, rated the best stroke of its kind in America, keeping his opponent on the defensive throughout.

In the final, however, Bill Tilden, now in his thirty-eighth year, played like the Tilden of five, six, or seven years earlier, and Allison could not get even one set, going down 6-3, 9-7, 6-4. But an even more impressive achievement was Bill's semi-final round victory over Borotra, whose brilliant play and super-gamesmanship tested Bill's endurance and powers of concentration and self-control to the limit. The unusual score of 0-6, 6-4, 4-6, 6-0, 7-5 was the result in part of Borotra's habit in a long match of going all out for a set and then playing in the next one to conserve his energy and regain his strength for another all-out assault in the following one, and so on, and also, as mentioned earlier in this narrative, by Bill's avowed intention of showing a partisan gallery that he could beat the perennial Wimbledon favorite by lobbing him to death, even though Borotra had one of the best overhead smashes in the world. To win merely by exploiting the weaknesses of an opponent who, Bill once said, "annoyed and irritated me more than any player I have ever met," would not be satisfying enough.

Bill had always preached playing to an opponent's strength, but only as a prelude to attacking his weakness at a crucial point, and not exclusively as Bill now persisted in doing in the first set. The lobs he threw up in game after game Borotra put away with powerful smashes, and Bill, making no effort to put pressure on Borotra with his service, but using it only to put the ball in play so that he could lob Borotra's return, lost all his serves as well as Borotra's to give the latter a love set. In the second set Bill continued his lobbing, but served with more pace and held serve throughout, breaking Borotra once, in the ninth game, by switching from lobs to passing shots. In the third set Bill kept Borotra dashing up and back, stretching to reach drop shots that barely cleared the net and chasing down lobs over his head. At its end, Borotra, although the winner, was clearly exhausted. There was no rest period after the third set at Wimbledon, and Bill, anticipating that Borotra would try to stall as much as possible while throwing the fourth set to regain his strength for the fifth, requested the umpire not to allow Borotra to delay play unduly. Borotra, who had been taking his time while toweling off, after the first game at once set off for his baseline, continuing to mop himself with one end of a huge towel while a very small ball boy trailed behind him holding the other end as if it were a royal train. The huge crowd that jammed the centre court yelled with laughter, but Bill was anything but amused. Borotra, quick to perceive this, repeated the antic on each succeeding court change, but Bill, his equanimity not seriously disturbed, concentrated on winning every point as quickly as possible and ran out the set in short order.

Borotra began the final set refreshed and full of his old élan, crowding the net to smash and volley, but Bill, mixing passing shots with his lobs, made him stretch and strain on nearly every point. Games went to five-all, both holding serve, with Borotra having to fight much the harder to keep from being broken. Then in the eleventh game, with Borotra down 30-40 and rushing the net behind his serve, Bill lofted a beautiful lob that sailed just over Borotra's outstretched racket to land on the baseline for a winner. Mentally and physcially spent, Borotra could offer no more resistance, and Bill easily held serve to win the set and the match.

This win over Borotra, perhaps even more than his Davis Cup victory over Lacoste in 1928, was Tilden's most memorable performance against his Musketeer opponents. In the preceding three years he had played against them at Wimbledon, he had lost to Cochet in 1927, defeated Borotra but lost to Lacoste in 1928, and lost to Cochet in 1929. His 1930 win, however, gave him three championships to the two won by each of the three Frenchmen, and although he was considerably older than any of them. not one of them would win another Wimbledon after he did. Tilden's record against the Musketeers in six years of Davis Cup play, 1925 through 1930, is also worth reviewing. He defeated Lacoste in 1925 and 1928, and lost to him in 1926 and 1927. He defeated Borotra in 1925, 1926, 1928, 1929, and 1930. He defeated Cochet in 1927 and lost to him in 1928, 1929, and 1930. Thus he suffered only five singles defeats while achieving eight victories. In doubles with Hunter he broke even, winning in 1927 and losing in 1928. No other Davis Cup player has ever done so well against such formidable opposition over such an extended period.

In 1930, twelve years after he lost to R. Lindley Murray in the 1918 final, Bill Tilden, ten times a finalist and seven times a winner of the title, was finally beaten by an American player in the national championships. To some extent, history appeared to be repeating itself, since John Doeg, Tilden's conqueror, was, like Murray, a left-hander who depended on a hard-serving, net-rushing style of game to win. Doeg, a blonde, powerfully built Californian from Santa Monica, who lacked three months of being twenty-two at the time of his victory, was ranked number three nationally in 1929 behind Tilden and Frank Hunter, having extended Tilden to five close sets in their Forest Hills semifinal. In 1930, at Wimbledon, where his aunt, May Sutton Bundy had been champion in 1905 and 1907, Doeg was a semifinalist, losing at 7-5 in the fifth set to Wilmer Allison.

George Lott, with whom Doeg won the national doubles in 1929 and 1930, was probably justified in saying that Doeg won at Forest Hills in 1930 with as little stroke equipment as any national champion ever possessed. Doeg's backhand was a slice or chop which he pushed rather than stroked, and since he had never succeeded in developing a dependable topspin forehand drive, he usually resorted to chopping off that side also. His chop was not very effective for use in backcourt exchanges or as a passing shot, but he could employ it to good effect in making forcing service returns and approach shots behind which he could move into volleying position. To offset the deficiencies in his ground game Doeg had a left-handed serve which had so much twist and spin that it looked like an egg in flight and was very difficult to return with any accuracy since the ball jumped off the racket before the receiver could stroke through on his return. The serve also had a wide break which pulled the receiver far out of position, leaving Doeg plenty of time usually to get to the net to volley the return, if there was one, to open court. Besides this almost unbreakable serve and his fine net game, Doeg had tremendous fighting spirit, and he never demonstrated this quality to a greater degree than in his semifinal and final round victories over Bill Tilden and Frank Shields.

Doeg had not played particularly well against Frank Hunter in the quarterfinals, trailing two sets to one before winning, and no one was prepared for the inspired tennis he produced against

Tilden. Advised by certain USLTA officials, who would be able to bear up bravely under a Tilden defeat, to go to the net at every opportunity, both on his serve and Tilden's Doeg assured them that he would go in "as long as I can stand up." So irresistible was his serve, so infallible his volleying, and so well did his supposedly defensive chop strokes hold up against Tilden's powerful drives that Bill could break serve only twice, once in the second set and once in the third. Winning by a score of 10-8, 6-3, 3-6, 12-10, Doeg made a total of twenty-eight service aces, twelve of them in the last set when he needed them most, since Bill, although he had taken a fall midway in the second set and played from then on with a limp, fought on so courageously and made such phenomenal recoveries of Doeg's best shots that he came within a hair of squaring the match.

In the final, Doeg again played in much the same fashion, except that he did not serve quite as well, to defeat the not quite twenty-year-old New Yorker, Frank Shields, another player with a powerful physique and who had superior groundstrokes and just as strong a serve, 10-8, 1-7, 6-4, 16-14. Doeg had to fight off four set points against him in the fourth set and was down 15-40 on his serve in the thirtieth game before pulling it out to win the match. As with Tilden, it was a heartbreaking loss for Shields, whose fate it was to be denied not only an American championship but a Wimbledon title as well the next year when he strained a leg muscle in beating Borotra in the semi-final round and had to default the final to his Davis Cup teammate, Sidney Wood.

At the time Bill played Doeg he had no idea that it would be his last amateur appearance. He would, he thought, be defending his Wimbledon title the following year and trying again for a record-breaking eighth American championship. Then one day early in October, a month or so after Forest Hills, a friend named Burt Cortelyou, a former theatrical producer, called him on the phone to ask if he would be interested in turning professional. Back in 1926, it will be recalled, Suzanne Lenglen had signed with C. C. Pyle, but Bill had declined to follow her lead. Bill had turned down an offer of $50,000 from Pyle for a six-month's tour, a sum equal to the annual salary of Babe Ruth, the highest paid player in baseball, prompting Pyle to say, "Mr. Tilden, I think you are a damned fool," to which Bill replied, "Mr. Pyle, I think you are right."

Now, however, Bill was definitely interested, and probably

for more than one reason. Said Vincent Richards concerning Bill's giving up his amateur status: "The Tilden exchequer was in bad shape when Bill decided to turn professional, but I believe the fact that the French had beaten us in the Davis Cup and Lacoste and Cochet were on the top of the heap had a great deal to do with his decision. Bill was no longer head man and he insists on being the main attraction." Bill was also greatly intrigued by the possibility, which Cortelyou had suggested, of getting a contract to make educational tennis movies. Cortelyou may have got the idea from hearing that Bobby Jones was negotiating with Warner Brothers to make a series of instructional golf films. The twenty-eight-year-old Jones, who had no worlds left to conquer, having won golf's grand slam in 1930—the U. S. Amateur and Open and the British Amateur and Open—did soon afterward sign a contract to do so, thereby automatically losing his amateur standing, and his action may have helped Cortelyou persuade Metro-Goldwyn—Mayer to make Bill a similar offer, which he accepted. Jones, it was said, received $180,000. Bill, who asked M-G-M not to reveal his remuneration, probably got a good deal less, but he was given assurances that he would be able to make tennis movies that had plots to them instead of merely instructional films, and there was the hope, as well, that this would be the prelude to further movie work.

On December 31, 1930, less than twenty-four hours after announcing his picture contract and ten years to the day after his first Davis Cup Challenge Round victory in Auckland, New Zealand, Bill signed a second contract, this one with Jack Curley, the sports promoter, to make a professional tennis tour with Karel Kozeluh as his opponent. So ended the amateur career of the game's first and perhaps greatest superstar, and with it an era which owed its character in large measure to his unique personality and tennis genius.

EPILOGUE

Although it is beyond the scope of this book a brief word should be added about Bill Tilden's role in the development of professional tennis. Little more than moribund after the Lenglen tour, professional tennis needed a Tilden in the Thirties to give it vitality even more than amateur tennis did in the Twenties. In his professional debut at Madison Square Garden in February of 1931, he defeated Kozeluh easily and went on to win the first 16 matches, 25 of the first 26 and 63 of the 76 they played in American and European cities, breaking attendance records in many of them. Jack Curley, who acted as booking agent, having an "in" at most of the big city stadiums through his boxing and wrestling promotions, pointed out to Bill that fewer Tilden victories might serve to increase the gate even more. But Bill, who retained over-all control of the tour, was determined that professional tennis, as long as he was concerned with it, would never suffer, as did boxing and wrestling, from the reputation of not always being on the up and up, and he gave Kozeluh no quarter, winning every match he could.

Bill also won all ten matches of a shorter, but equally successful tour—this one billed as being for the world's professional title—from Vincent Richards, and again beat Richards, who had eliminated Kozeluh, in the finals of the U. S. Professional Championship before a Forest Hills gallery of 4,000. From his touring, from endorsements (Spalding rackets, Dunlop tennis balls, Armour tennis gut, and so forth), and from syndicated newspaper articles commenting on the 1931 Davis Cup matches and other aspects of the current tennis scene, Bill cleared something over $100,000 during the Depression year, thereby rivaling the great Babe Ruth as a highly paid professional athlete. By the time he had completed six years of professional play Bill's earnings totaled at least a half million dallars.

Despite his great box-office appeal and his ability to play a brand of tennis much of the time very nearly as good as that of his best amateur championship days, Bill could not hope to keep on drawing the fans indefinitely by beating the same old opponents—Richards, Kozeluh, Nusslein and assorted other European pros—over and over. There had to be some fresh faces on the other side of the net. This need was satisfied in part in 1933 when Bill was able to persuade Cochet to turn pro. The next year Bill landed an ever bigger catch in the person of Ellsworth Vines, the American champion in 1931 and 1932 and Wimbledon titleholder in 1932. The twenty-two-year-old Vines made his pro debut in January of 1934 before a packed house of 16,000 at Madison Square Garden, the largest crowd ever to see a tennis match in the United States, losing to the forty-one-year-old Tilden, 8-6, 6-3, 6-2. Vines was too young and strong, however, over the long haul of one-night stands, and won their head-to-head tour 47 matches to 26. Another crowd attraction Bill devised this year was a series of nine U. S.-France, Davis Cup style matches played in New York, Chicago, and other large cities in which he and Vines opposed Cochet and Martin Plaa, a former European pro champion. The Americans won all the team matches and all but three of the singles, Tilden losing twice to Cochet and Vines once to Plaa.

Encouraged by the excellent response of the fans to this series, Bill, through his Tilden Tennis Tours, Inc., announced an ambitious plan to establish a professional tennis league in 1935, with teams in eight big cities playing a schedule of 100 matches during the summer months and the divisional winners meeting in a world's series. This World Team Tennis idea never got off the ground, however, probably because not enough good players could be recruited to man the teams. Two amateur players who did sign pro contracts for 1935 were George Lott and Lester Stoefen, the 1934 American and Wimbledon doubles champions. As for Bill, he continued to be indefatigable, the New York *Times* reporting that "far from being tired of tennis after his many years of campaigning Tilden looks forward with anticipation to his 78-match tour wtih Vines, Lott, and Stoefen beginning January 9 in Madison Square Garden." On this tour the format called for Bill to play Lott in the curtain raiser, followed by the feature attraction, a doubles pitting Bill and Vines against Lott and Stoefen, and concluding, if the doubles, which was usually three out of five sets, did not last too long, with a singles between Vines and Stoefen.

In 1937, the Englishman Fred Perry, a three-time winner at both Forest Hills and Wimbledon, defected to the pro ranks after turning down earlier offers on the grounds that he would have to pay half of what he made in British taxes and that he would be ostracized by all the clubs in Britain. (It turned out he knew whereof he spoke. After he turned pro he was asked to resign all his club memberships, even the honorary ones.) Perry and Vines drew 18,000 to their Garden opener, the largest crowd so far to see a professional match. Bill Tilden, however, got the greatest applause when he came out to play the supporting match. That Bill, now all of forty-four, could still pull in the spectators was demonstrated a few weeks later when he and Perry drew sixteen thousand to the Garden in their first confrontation on the court. Perry was the winner, but Bill was able to take two of the matches they played on a six-city tour.

His days as a pro headliner pretty much over, although he would still go on touring intermittently, Bill, from 1939 on, made his home in Los Angeles where he became a teaching pro, giving lessons to Hollywood personalities, as well as to more ordinary mortals. In 1941, no other worthy opponent being available, Bill was drafted to make an extended tour with Don Dudge, who had, in 1938, achieved the first grand slam of tennis by winning the Australian, French, Wimbledon, and American titles, and who had demonstrated his superiority over Vines and Perry after he turned pro in 1939. The tour had an added attraction in Alice Marble, who had dominated women's tennis with her hard-hitting, big-game style of play and who turned pro after winning her fourth American championship in 1940. But with America soon to be at war with both the men and women opponents mismatched, the tour played to small crowds. Bill could win only seven of their fifty-eight matches with Budge, although, according to Budge, Bill never got discouraged or stopped trying his hardest, and he often stole the show with his great repertoire of shots and his playing to the gallery. Mary Hardwick, a young English Wightman Cup player, who had remained in America after war broke out in Europe and who had reached the semifinals at Forest Hills in 1940, played a number of close matches against Marble but could win only three out of twenty.

After Pearl Harbor, Bill, with patriotic fervor, travelled all over the country, often paying his and the other players' expenses, staging exhibitions to benefit the Red Cross and to sell war bonds. During 1944 and 1945, he also played some two hundred matches for the Armed Services at camps, hospitals, and rehabilitation centers. Most of these exhibitions were played in the area around Los Angeles, and, in addition to a set or two of serious tennis, Bill and a Los Angeles pro named Walter Wesbrook would put on a comic act in which they dressed up as two old maids of the gay nineties, calling themselves "Miss Sophia Smearone" and "Miss Wilhelmina Shovelshot." The routine, which involved their bumbling through a set of doubles against two comely Southern California girl players, one of these often being Gussie Moran, who later won fame by wearing lace panties at Wimbledon, but who played for the service men in form-fitting shorts and pink sweater, was corny, but it went over big, and the girls, as Bill put it, "did much to make the scenery beautiful."

After the war, it was Bill Tilden who got professional tennis going again, rounding up Budge, Perry, Riggs, and other pros, and staging a tournament in December, 1945, at the Los Angeles Tennis Club, billed as the World Hardcourt Professional Championship. With Gable, Chaplin, Bogart, and other movie stars in the stands, it was a sellout. Besides running the tournament, the fifty-two-year-old Bill, after losing to Budge in the semifinals, beat Perry for third place, 4-7, 6-4, 7-5, after being down 2-5 in the third set. Bill also suggested the formation of a Professional Players Association, got himself named tournament director, and arranged a series of pro tournaments in various cities along the lines of those in pro golf. He also negotiated a five-year contract with the West Side Tennis Club as the site of an annual world professional grass court championship.

Unhappily for both Bill and the Players Association, it lost his invaluable services in January of 1947, when he pleaded guilty in Los Angeles to a charge of contributing to the delinquency of a fourteen-year-old boy. Bill Tilden's homosexual proclivities (it seems quite certain they did not extend to his tennis protégés, as has sometimes been assumed, his regard for them being paternal) appear to have been pretty much latent during his amateur years, but later they became increasingly less so. His homosexuality was no secret to a good many people in tennis circles, but his morals conviction and one-year prison sentence came as a shocking surprise to the general public. Two years later it would learn that he had been given another one-year sentence on a similar charge.

Bill Tilden knew humiliation and disgrace during his last years, but this did not affect his reputation as the greatest of tennis players. Early in 1950, shortly after he had finished serving his second sentence, he received 310 votes in an Associated Press poll as the outstanding player of the past half century, his closest rivals being Jack Kramer with 32 votes and Don Budge with 31. Grantland Rice, one of the sports writers who contributed to Bill's overwhelming margin, has written how he saw Bill for the last time in January of 1953, six months before Bill's death of coronary thrombosis. From the window of his fifth-floor room overlooking the tennis courts of the Beverly Wilshire Hotel in Beverly Hills, where Rice and his wife were vacationing, he could see Bill, "a gaunt, bespectacled figure in shorts," working out withFrank Feltrop, the hotel's teaching professional. Although Rice knew Bill well he did not go down to say hello to "the shell of a person who once was the complete headline," because he wanted instead to remember Bill Tilden—as surely he deserves to be remembered—not as a man who came to the end of his life under a tragic cloud, but as a great artist-athlete, a tennis immortal.

NOTES AND SOURCES

General

The two general sources I have drawn on most heavily for information about the period covered in this history are the relevant issues of *American Lawn Tennis* magazine (1907-1951) and the files of the New York *Times.* Other such sources consulted include Maurice Brady, *Lawn Tennis Encyclopedia* (London, 1969); Lamont Buchanan, *The Story of Tennis* (New York, 1951); Gianni Clerici, *The Ultimate Tennis Book* (Chicago, 1975); Parke Cummings, *American Tennis* (Boston, 1957); Allison Danzig, ed., *Sport's Golden Age* (New York, 1948); Allison Danzig and Peter Schwed, eds., *The Fireside Book of Tennis* (New York, 1972); Philip B. Hawk, *Off the Racket* (New York, 1937); Will Grimsley, *Tennis: Its History, People and Events* (Englewood Cliffs, New Jersey, 1971); Al Laney, *Covering the Court* (New York, 1968); Paul Metzler, *Tennis Styles and Stylists* (New York, 1970); *Official Encyclopedia of Tennis,* ed. by the Staff of the U.S.L.T.A. (New York, 1972); Edward C. Potter, Jr., *Kings of the Court* (New York, 1963); Maxwell Robertson, *The Encyclopedia of Tennis* (New York, 1974); Richard Schickel, *The World of Tennis* (New York, 1975); Eugene Scott, *Tennis: Game of Motion* (New York, 1973); *Spalding Tennis Annual* (New York, 1895-1931); Bill Talbert and Pete Axthelm, *Tennis Observed* (Barre, Massachusetts, 1967); *Wright and Ditson's Official Guide to Lawn Tennis* (New York, 1891-1935).

Prologue

Estimates vary considerably as to the number of Americans who were playing tennis by the late 1970's. An A. C. Nielsen study reported it to be in the neighborhood of 30 million, if those who played only occasionally were included. There is considerable discussion of the phenomenal growth of tennis during the decade of the seventies in Herbert Warren Wind, *Game, Set and Match* (New York, 1979), a collection of articles which originally appeared in *The New Yorker.* The growing popularity of the game during the second and third decades of the twentieth century is described in L. Graves, "The Rise of Tennis," *Century,* Vol. XC (August, 1915), 628-633; in "Tennis is the National Amateur Game," *Literary Digest,* Vol. LXIX (April 9), 1921, 58-61; and in John Tunis, "Tennis the Universal Sport," *Review of Reviews,* Vol. LXXI (October, 1927), 390-394.

Chapter One

Bill Tilden's autobiographical volumes are *Me-the Handicap* (London, 1929), *Aces, Places and Faults* (London, 1938), and *My Story* (New York, 1948). There are also numerous autobiographical references in *The Art of Lawn Tennis* (New York, 1921 and later editions), *Match Play and the Spin of the Ball* (New York, 1925); and in the many "Passing Shots" columns Tilden contributed to *American Lawn Tennis* magazine. The only full-length biography is Frank Deford, *Big Bill Tilden: the Triumphs and the Tragedy* (New York, 1975). There is a good account of the Philadelphia cricket clubs in Nathaniel Burt, *The Perennial Philadelphians* (Boston, 1963). Tilden's stroke equipment is analyzed in detail in J. Parmley Paret, *Mechanics of the Game* (New York, 1926).

Chapter Two

Al Laney's description of the young Suzanne Lenglen is in his *Covering the Court* (New York, 1968). Laney's memoir (subtitled "A Fifty-Year Love Affair with the Game of Tennis") has other references to Lenglen as well as to Tilden, Helen Wills and other great players he saw in action during the 1920's. Ted Tinling, who knew her well, reminisces about Lenglen and tennis on the Riviera in *Love and Faults* (New York, 1979). Claude Anet, *Suzanne Lenglen* (Paris, 1927) contains biographical details and accounts of her matches. Helen Jacobs, *Gallery of Champions* (New York, 1949) includes good profiles of Lenglen and Wills. For the history of Wimbledon, see G. W. Hillyard, *Forty Years of First-Class Lawn Tennis* (London, 1924); F. R. Burrow, *Last Eights at Wimbledon, 1877-1931* (London, 1932); Duncan Macaulay, *Behind the Scenes at Wimbledon* (New York, 1965); Lance Tingay, *100 Years of Wimbledon* (Enfield, England, 1977).

Chapter Three

The fullest account of the early years of Davis Cup competition is S. Wallis Merrihew, *The Quest of the Davis Cup* (New York, 1928). Dame Mabel Brookes writes about her husband's long and distinguished career as tennis champion and Australian tennis official in *Crowded Galleries* (London, 1956). Anthony Wilding recounts his experiences as world traveler and tennist in *On the Court and Off* (London, 1912). The references to Tilden's life style at the end of this chapter come from Al Laney's *Covering the Court* and George Lott's "Bill Tilden as I Knew Him for 33 Years," *Tennis,* Vol. VI (July, 1970), 5, 10-11 (August, 1970), 32-33.

Chapter Four

The boil that Tilden suffered from in his match with the Japanese Shimizu is referred to by Al Laney in *Covering the Court* and by Grantland Rice in his *The Tumult and the Shouting* (New York, 1954). Besides all the publicity given to Lenglen's visit to the United States in the New York *Times,* the great interest it engendered was reflected in other publications, a number of which were quoted or commented on in "A Temperamental Jeanne D'Arc of the Tennis Courts," *Literary Digest,* Vol. LXIX (August 27, 1921), 35-46. Suzanne gave her side of the story of her American visit in "My Tennis Adventures in America," *Living Age,* Vol. CCCXII (February 11, 1922), 351-354.

Chapter Five

For accounts of the building of the new Wimbledon see the works by Hillyard and Macaulay cited in the notes to Chapter Two.

Chapter Six

The Amateur Rule Committee report condemning Bill Tilden for his tennis writing was published in full in the New York *Times,* as was the exchange of letters between him and Julian Myrick. Tilden's position in the player-writer controversy was defended by S. Wallis Merrihew in "Amateur at Bay," *Atlantic Monthly,* Vol. XCCCIV (October, 1924), 497-502. That the controversy was pretty much resolved in Tilden's favor is indicated in "Decided That Champion Tennis-Players May Write About the Game," *Literary Digest,* Vol. LXXXIV (January 3, 1925), 55-59.

Chapter Seven

Autobiographical writings of Helen Wills are *Fifteen-Thirty* (New York, 1936); "My Life on the Courts," *Saturday Evening Post,* Vol. CCV (June 10, 1933), 3-5, (June 17, 1933), 24-25; Vol. CCVI (July 22, 1933), 28-30; and "Education of a Tennis Player," *Scribner's,* Vol. XCIX (May, 1936), 268-272, (June, 1936), 336-339. W. C. Fuller tells how he coached Helen Wills and Helen Jacobs in "Girls Are Made of Star Dust," *American Magazine,* Vol. CXX (August, 1935), 28-29, 118. For the building of the West Side stadium see Edward C. Potter, Jr., *The West Side Tennis Club Story* (New York, 1952) and Robert Minton, *Forest Hills: An Illustrated History* (Philadelphia, 1975). Richmond Barrett describes the Newport Casino during the years when it was still the site of the National Championships in *Good Old Summer Days* (New York, 1941). Mrs. Wightman's long and varied association with the game of tennis is portrayed by Herbert Warren Wind in "Run, Helen!", *The New Yorker,* Vol. XXVIII (August 30, 1952), 31-46; and in Melvin Maddocks,

"The Original Little Old Lady in Tennis Shoes," *Sports Illustrated,* Vol. 36 (April 10, 1972), 36-42.

Chapter Eight

Contemporary newspaper accounts of the Lenglen-Wills match and the events surrounding it include John Tunis, "Riviera Background," *Boston Globe,* February 14, 1926; A. Wallis Myers, "Lenglen-Wills Match at Cannes," London *Daily Telegraph,* February 18, 1926; Ferdinand Tuohy, "Two Queens," New York *Times,* February 18, 1926; and James Thurber, "Lenglen-Wills Match at Cannes," Chicago *Tribune* (Riviera edition), February 18, 1926 (all reprinted in Allison Danzig and Peter Schwed, eds., *The Fireside Book of Tennis*). The Thurber story is an unusual piece of sports journalism with Thurber, who was a great admirer of Henry James, depicting the encounter in the form of one of that novelist's international fictions, Wills being the young, naive Jamesian heroine and Lenglen the mature, worldly European woman who exploits and defeats her. One of the most memorable eyewitness accounts is that of Al Laney in *Covering the Court.* Helen Wills gives her recollections of the match—"the unique experience of all my tennis-playing days"—in *Fifteen-Thirty.*

Chapter Nine

The varied reactions of players and tennis officials to Lenglen's professional tour are discussed in "Suzanne and Mary K., 'Pro' Tennis Pioneers," *Literary Digest,* Vol. XC (September 25, 1926), 51-55. How playing regularly against Lenglen on their professional tour improved Mary K. Browne's game is described in "What I Learned from Suzanne," *Collier's* Vol. LXXIX (May 7, 1927), 14. Helen Jacobs tells how she was coached by Lenglen in her autobiography, *Beyond the Game* (Philadelphia, 1936).

Chapter Ten

For the reminiscences of the four French players upon the occasion of their induction into the Tennis Hall of Fame, see Bud Collins, "Four Cheers for the Musketeers," *World Tennis,* Vol. XXIV (October, 1976), 55-59. There are good profiles of the Musketeers and accounts of his matches against them in Tilden's *My Story.* Borotra's hyperactive career as business man and tennis player is described in John Tunis, "Borotra, Veteran Athlete and Manufacturer," *Saturday Evening Post,* Vol. CCIX (July 25, 1936), 23-25. Vincent Richards wrote in "Why Play Tennis?", *Outlook,* Vol. CXLI (October 7, 1925), 187-188, that for Lacoste "tennis is business" and that opposite Richards's own name in Lacoste's notebook on how to play his opponents was the entry: "One must drive deep to his backhand and come to the net for a volley." An interesting interview with Lacoste at the age of 74 is Alexander McNab, "Le Crocodile," *Tennis USA,* Vol. XXXI (October, 1978), 44-47.

Chapter Eleven

Tilden's *My Story* and Al Laney's *Covering the Court* are the chief sources for the discussion of Tilden's troubles with his knee and of the strategy which enabled Lacoste to defeat Tilden.

Chapter Twelve

Tilden confesses to his infatuation with the stage and comments on the plays in which he acted in *My Story.* Frank Deford's *Big Bill Tilden* also has considerable information about Tilden's stage career. For George Agutter and his long association with the West Side Tennis Club see the profile by Al Laney in *The Fireside Book of Tennis,* pp. 321-322. The articles on "shamateurism" referred to in this chapter are Vincent Richards, "Netting Results," *Saturday Evening Post,* Vol. CXCVIII (May 15, 1926), 10-11, (June 5, 1926), 30-31, (June 12, 1926), 18-19; George Lott, "Tennis Money: It Doesn't Pay to Be an Amateur,"

Collier's, Vol. CII (September 3, 1938), 22, 28-29; Jack Kramer, "I Was a Paid Amateur" (published in a 1955 *This Week* magazine Sunday newspaper supplement); Lew Hoad, with Will Grimsley, "I Was a Tennis Slave," *Saturday Evening Post,* Vol. CCXXX (September 14, 1957), 37-39. The persistence and determination of the French and how it finally paid off in their prolonged quest of the Davis Cup is recorded in René Lacoste, *Tennis* (London, 1928).

Chapter Thirteen

Bill Tilden's practice of throwing points is discussed by Don Budge in his *A Tennis Memoir* (New York, 1969). George Lott coined the phrase "tennis bum" in his article cited previously, "Tennis Money: It Doesn't Pay to Be an Amateur." Good accounts of the epic 1928 Davis Cup match between Lacoste and Tilden are to be found in Tilden's *My Story,* Al Laney's *Covering the Court,* and George Lott's "Tight Spots in Tennis," *Atlantic Monthly,* Vol. CLXII (August, 1938), 196-202.

Chapter Fourteen

John Tunis's discussion of the ways in which officials and players exploited tennis for their financial benefit is in his "Lawn Tennis Industry," *Harper's,* Vol. CLVI (February, 1928), 289-298. Other articles which echo Tunis's criticisms are Fred Hawthorne, "Commercialization of Tennis," *North American Review,* Vol. CCCXII (December, 1926), 614-621; and G. Trevor, "Needed: a Davis Cup Vacation," *Outlook,* Vol. CLV (August 27, 1930), 675-676. Paul Gallico in *Farewell to Sport* (New York, 1941) takes a somewhat jaundiced view of the state of tennis during the 1920's and 1930's, as he does of certain other sports, although in the main his strictures regarding the administration of the game appear to have been justified. Helen Wills' relative unpopularity as compared to Mrs. Mallory and other opponents is commented on in "Helen Wills as the Killer of the Courts," *Literary Digest,* Vol. CII (September 7, 1929), 56-61. Ted Tinling, who served as an assistant director of tournaments on the Riviera circuit in 1930, says in his *Love and Faults* that Tilden's loss to the Englishman E. C. Peters was due to "fish poisoning." Helen Jacobs tells how Tilden improved her strokes in *Beyond the Game*.

Epilogue

That Tilden was indefatigable in his professional tennis touring is emphasized in "Big Bill Tilden Rolls Along with Youth on a 25,000-mile Tour," *Newsweek*, Vol. XVII (January 13, 1941), 46, and in Don Budge's *A Tennis Memoir*. In his *Tennis is My Racket* (New York, 1949), Bobby Riggs pays tribute to Tilden for his hard work and effectiveness in promoting post-war professional tennis. Grantland Rice's description of his last view of Tilden comes from *The Tumult and the Shouting*.

INDEX